Laying Down the Law

Laying Down the Law

What You Need to Know About the Law, Lawyers, Lawsuits, and the Courts

By Michael J. Larin

Surrogate Press®

Published in the United States by
Surrogate Press®
an imprint of Faceted Press®
Surrogate Press, LLC
Park City, Utah
SurrogatePress.com

ISBN: 978-1-964245-29-4
Library of Congress Control Number: 2026904222

Book cover design by: Michael Larin
Interior design by: Katie Mullaly, Surrogate Press®

This is my first book. So, I had to think about a dedication, and whether it should be to a person or an idea. I opted for the latter.

This book is written and published during a time of great discord. I dedicate this book to the idea that we should solve our differences, if possible, with civility and compromise, just as it should be in legal disputes.

Here's hoping we all strive for peace, harmony, and mutual respect.

Table of Contents

Introduction

Baseball started to be popular before and during the Civil War, when soldiers played the game to pass the time. Baseball became a cultural phenomenon, reflecting American values like collaboration, fair play, and the pursuit of the American dream. Anyone, regardless of social class or background, could play. The newspaper, the New York Sunday Mercury, dubbed baseball America's "National Pastime" in 1856. Baseball is no longer the only American pastime; lawsuits now represent a cultural passion, too. Suing is culturally acceptable, provides monetary reward, and serves as a way to vanquish evil. And anyone, regardless of social class or background, can play.

More than sixty million lawsuits of all kinds are filed each year in the United States.[1] A reasonable estimate is that about eighteen percent of the U.S. population file suit annually. Lawsuits include business cases, injury or property damage cases, family law, probate, civil rights, and so on. Only about five percent of injury cases make it to trial, and insurance companies settle many more before suit is filed. Thus, the number of people who participate in the legal system is far greater than the sixty million actual suits.

The population of the United States is approximately 335 million at this time, and there are at least 33 million businesses, excluding foreign businesses, that could be involved in the court system. Of the roughly 368 million people and businesses available to file lawsuits, one in every six files suit every year. For every lawsuit filed, there is also at least one party sued.

When all participants in lawsuits are considered, including those who settle before filing suit, nearly a third of the country is in litigation every year. Staggering, right? The inescapable conclusion is that you are either in a lawsuit

---

1 https://www.consumershield.com/articles/how-many-court-cases-are-filed-each-year

or know someone who is. The fact is that if you are not aware of the prevalence of lawsuits in our society, you live under a rock. The proverbial American dream is to have a family, a home, a car, and maybe a pet. Now, we add a lawsuit to that cultural norm.

For all of you who are suing or being sued, or who might be, you rely on your lawyer to pilot you through the complicated, stressful, molasses-like process. For the few who try it on your own, best of luck. I have practiced law for forty-eight years, and to my observation, there are few publications, or even short blogs, providing guidance, and even fewer that give you a peek behind the curtain. Understanding how litigation works, so that you will be prepared to make the right decisions about your case, your money, and your rights, requires more than a list of procedures, a brief explanation of steps in the process, or a basic primer on a certain kind of law. You do need to understand the procedures, and this book will provide that, but it will also help you understand the legal background and environment of your case.

You also need to know how to deal with your lawyer, how your lawyer thinks and operates, how judges and juries make decisions, what the strategies and tactics are, what the economic realities are, how cases are settled, and how trials work. These are but a few of the areas on which this work is intended to coach you, to help you make important decisions as well as cope with the stresses of litigation. Once you memorize all this information (ha!), it is my goal to provide you with enough understanding of the law and its process so that you will recognize what is happening along the way and be your lawyer's informed partner on the journey.

The guidance in this book is not limited to non-lawyers. If you are a young lawyer, a law student (especially interns), or you are thinking of going to law school, this book is a roadmap. You will see how pleadings work, interactions with the court, motions, the discovery process, and what experts are for. In Part Two, I will play out a jury selection process for you and show you how the arguments the lawyers make track the facts.

I will put you behind the scenes, give you a sense of what goes through a lawyer's mind in certain situations, and explain legal thinking and legal procedures with enough practical depth that starting law school or your first job with a litigation firm won't seem completely bewildering. There's some stuff here they don't teach you in law school.

We will start with some basics, the role law plays in our society, how the courts are set up, what one goes through to become a lawyer, and what is studied in law school. You will get pointers on the fundamental topics that make up the law and lawsuits. I will show you how lawyers and their law firms function (including how lawyers charge for their services), and you will get some tips on how to find a lawyer best suited for your case. Then, we will get into the anatomy of a lawsuit, from filing through trial. The case we will litigate in Part Two will involve a serious injury and explore the thinking of the lawyers on both sides as they progress toward trial, analyzing the strategies, the difficulties, and the frustrations.

If you are unfamiliar with the legal process, a lawsuit can be highly stressful, and because a suit can last years, it can take up a sizable chunk of your life and your money, or your client's life and money. By the end of this book, you will be in a position to know how to deal with your lawyer, or how to deal with your client, what will be expected of you. Armed with this knowledge, you should be better able to navigate the voyage.

In short, I will lay out the process of a lawsuit for you, from the time the dispute arises through trial. Hence, Laying Down the Law!

Okay, counselors, let's begin.

PART ONE

A Practical Primer on the Law

Why We Have Laws – The Briefest History
of the Civilized World

CHAPTER ONE

"Court Martial" was a Star Trek episode in which Captain Kirk was court-martialed for his actions that led to the death of a crewman. The evidence against him came from a computer, not an eyewitness. His lawyer argued the captain was denied his rights: "Rights, sir, human rights! The Bible. The Code of Hammurabi and of Justinian. The Magna Carta. The Constitution of the United States. The Fundamental Declarations of the Martian Colonies. The Statutes of Alpha III. Gentlemen - these documents all speak of rights. Rights of the accused to a trial by his peers, to be represented by counsel. The rights of cross-examination. But most importantly, the right to be confronted by the witnesses against him - a right to which my client's been denied."

Ever heard of the Code of Hammurabi? I have, but have you ever heard of the laws of the Martian colonies or Alpha III? Me either. The Code of Hammurabi was written during the reign of Hammurabi, the sixth king of the First Dynasty of Babylon, sometime between 1755 and 1750 BC, to make sure the strong could not oppress the weak. The code covered social order, crime, and commerce, much like our laws today. It helps to understand where these laws came from by briefly considering how civilization developed.

To live in any civil society (even in outer space), we must have some rules to follow; otherwise, there would be chaos. At some point, bands of people tired of having their food pilfered and their caves and families attacked. As people started to live in communities, there had to be government. Governing means the establishment of rules and the means to enforce them.

Society operates on social, economic, and political levels too numerous to mention here, as it was in Babylon. In our government, laws initially stem from the United States Constitution. Whether federal, state, or local, we have bodies that make laws needed in addition to the rights-protecting edicts of the Constitution (such as Congress, state government, local government), bodies that enforce laws (police for criminal law or government agencies for civil law) and bodies that manage and interpret laws (the courts).

Today, our laws come in two forms. Written laws, known as statutes, such as the rules of the road incorporated into the Vehicle Code. We all know the government sets the maximum speed on any given roadway, or that you can't run a red light. Violations of these statutes of course are punishable. Unwritten laws, or the "common law," derive mostly from past case decisions addressing legal principles. One of the best examples of the common law is what negligence means. In short, negligence means carelessness. Texting while driving, which results in an accident, would be a negligent act because being careful, by paying attention to the road, would avoid the accident. (A more complete discussion of negligence is provided later.)

There are laws we all value, and we are glad they exist. No doubt, some laws may be unjust, may be ineffective for what they are intended to protect against, or may favor one class over another. There are political or legal mechanisms to enact, revoke, or modify laws. Whether the system works for you or frustrates you, these systems developed from ancient civilizations and evolved, as has our own system. I, for one, am glad we no longer burn people at the stake.

Our focus, of course, is on the court system branch of government. Let me now guide you through the court systems in our country, both state and federal. Let's see how the courts are set up.

Legal Systems – You Can't Tell the Courthouse Without a Scorecard

CHAPTER TWO

Generally How the Court Systems Are Tiered

"I am going to sue the pants off you! I will take this to the Supreme Court if I have to!" Well, hold your horses, pal. It's not that easy. A lawsuit has to be filed somewhere, and there are several different courts to choose from. The court you go to depends on the kind of case you have. You first have to get your case decided at the "trial" level court, and if either party wants to challenge the outcome, you can then appeal it. There are two more levels of the courts, a Court of Appeal, and a Supreme Court above that. Let's dig into this and break it all down.

Federal and state court systems generally have three levels: the trial court, the intermediate appellate court, and the highest-level appellate court. Each tier has a different general function within the system, which I describe for you below. After that, we'll examine more specifically how the federal and state systems operate, along with alternatives to going to court.

1. **Trial court:** Cases are initially filed in the trial court, which manages the litigation and ultimately conducts the trial. It is in the trial court where the evidence supporting the claim and the defense is set forth, with the trial court judge supervising the process and intervening between the parties as needed.

    When all the evidence is exchanged, the case goes to trial here, whether to a judge (called a "bench" trial) or to a jury trial. If both parties agree to the outcome at the trial level, then the case is done. However, if either party feels the outcome is unjust or mistaken, they can appeal the trial court result to the next tier, which, in most circumstances, is the intermediate appellate court.

2. **Intermediate appellate level:** The intermediate appellate courts rule on whether there were mistakes in the trial court or if some aspect of law needs to be expanded or rejected. For example, suppose a trial judge allows a plaintiff to testify at the trial that the defendant offered a lot of money to settle. To a jury, this might give the impression that the defendant agreed to fault in the case. In reality, the settlement offer might have been a practical choice because of the high expense of the case, even though the defendant denied responsibility. There are rules protecting and fostering attempts to settle because if an offer could be used against someone, the motivation to make an offer would be chilled, and therefore, there would be no settlements.

    The appellate court might then rule that allowing into evidence that the defendant was willing to settle the case was prejudicial because of the impression it might have on the jury, and order a re-trial. If either side still isn't happy with the outcome of the appeal in the intermediate appellate court, they may appeal the case to the highest level appellate court – in most states, the Supreme Court.

3. **Highest-level Appellate Court:** The highest court, most often called the "Supreme Court," rules on whether the lower court's decision, the trial court or the intermediate appellate court, was correct and generally has the choice to accept a case from the courts below it. The United States Supreme Court usually hears a case when it could have national significance, might resolve conflicting decisions in the lower federal courts, and/or could have precedential value affecting all similar cases. These cases will include important constitutional, social, or economic issues.

    A state supreme court, by contrast, also has discretion as to what state court disputes to take up, though usually it must accept death penalty cases. Similar to the U.S. Supreme Court, the general criteria for appeal to a state supreme court are whether review is necessary to secure uniformity of decision among the appellate courts or to settle an important question of law.

How The Federal System Is Tiered

The federal court system's three levels:

1. **Federal trial level:** The trial court in the federal system is called the United States District Court. The states and U.S. territories have at least one district court, but more populous states, like California or New York, have as many as four district courts. The number of judges is also affected by the population size of the state. The U.S. District Court also operates a separate unit for bankruptcies.

2. **Federal intermediate appellate level:** The intermediate federal appellate court is called the Court of Appeals. There are thirteen United States Courts of Appeals in the federal judicial system, called "circuits".[1] Unlike "judges" presiding in the trial court, appellate-level judges are called "justices," and this is true in both federal and state systems.

    An example of an issue that would be handled in the Court of Appeals would be what standard of conduct amounts to a violation of the constitutional right against unreasonable searches and seizures, a right embodied in the U.S. Constitution.

3. **Highest level federal appellate court:** The highest of all courts is the United States Supreme Court, located in Washington, D.C. The Supreme Court has discretion as to what cases it will hear, generally hearing cases of significant societal importance. For example, it came to the Supreme Court in 2000 to decide whether to allow a recount of Florida votes, which would affect who won the presidential election between George Bush and Al Gore.

All federal judges, from the district courts to the Supreme Court, are appointed. They are nominated by the executive branch of government but must be approved by the U.S. Senate. They are appointed for life, intending to insulate them from political and electoral concerns.

---

1 To find out what federal appellate circuit you are in, check out: https://www.uscourts.gov/sites/default/files/u.s._federal_courts_circuit_map_1.pdf

State Systems

The exact setup of state court systems may vary, but generally consists of three tiers: trial courts, intermediate appellate courts, and a supreme court.[2] In California, where I practice, the trial court is called the Superior Court. There is one superior court per county, though there are several branches of the county's superior court in the larger counties. The intermediate level appellate court is called the California Court of Appeal, and the highest level of appellate court is the California Supreme Court. Your state may use different names for the three tiers, but the organization is basically the same across the country and the pattern is similar to the federal system. Unlike federal judges and justices, state judges are typically elected and serve specific terms.

Exceptions and Alternatives to the Courts

States establish specialty courts for some kinds of cases. In addition, because cases can be expensive, systems have developed to offer equally binding but less expensive options. Let's take a look at examples of such situations.

Workers' Compensation - A Separate Court System

If you are injured on the job in California, you can file a workers' compensation claim. Workers' compensation claims are not handled in the court system, but rather by a state agency; in California, the agency is called the Workers' Compensation Appeals Board, or WCAB.

A workers' compensation claim is a request for financial benefits, medical costs, and disability payments. An example of financial costs would be a claim for lost earnings. Medical costs would include the cost of medical treatment, such as bills from medical providers, medicine, travel for treatment, and equipment. A disability amount compensates to the extent an injury temporarily or permanently prevents return to work.

Proving a workers' compensation claim requires proof of only two things: that you were working at the time of the injury and the extent of your injuries. There is no requirement that you prove someone did something wrong, like you

---

2 Not all states use the same terminology. For example, the State of New York calls its trial court the "Supreme Court," the intermediate level of appellate courts the "Appellate Divisions," and the ultimate court, the "Court of Appeals."

would in a lawsuit; this is called a "no-fault" system. Filing a workers' compensation claim does not limit you from suing the person who harmed you, except that you are not allowed to sue your employer directly in a civil suit rather pursue the claim through the WCAB no-fault system.[3]

The process begins with making a claim to the employer, which refers the matter to the workers' compensation insurer. If the insurer's (or employer's) decision is not accepted by the employee, the dispute is filed as a formal legal proceeding with the WCAB.

Arbitration - An Alternative to a Lawsuit

Many contracts today require arbitration, where the parties to the contract agree to forego suing each other in court if there's a disagreement and instead use arbitration. Arbitration is a private process for resolving disputes outside of court. If the arbitration clause in the contract says it's "binding", not only will there be no lawsuit, but there may be no right to appeal the outcome. Arbitration clauses appear in many everyday contracts, including credit card agreements, cell phone plans, and employment contracts, or your medical provider will not accept you as a patient without it, preventing even malpractice claims from going to court, to name a few. (Read the fine print.)

Arbitration involves a neutral third party, called an arbitrator, who, like a judge in court, hears evidence and argument from both sides and makes a decision. The contract also usually specifies what rules will be followed. Often, the agreement will specify the use of a particular arbitration company, which has its own rules that mirror, but simplify, court rules. If not, some statutes direct how the arbitration process must be conducted.

One Size Does Not Fit All (But It's Close)

As applied to a lot of information in this book, there are differences among states, as well as regions within states, and there are always exceptions to the rule. In different parts of the country, certain kinds of laws have developed to

---

3 About "no-fault," in most states you must prove your case, that is, you must show that someone is responsible for your damages. However, you may live in a state where some portion of the legal system is "no-fault." For example, New York State requires Personal Injury Protection insurance, a no-fault claim system. Lawsuits can be filed only if the claim qualifies as "Serious Injury," defined by statute.

address a dominant industry or historical roots. For example, Nevada law necessarily abounds with gaming laws. Texas has a lot of law addressing the oil industry. In Louisiana, the legal system developed from its French and Spanish origins before the Louisiana Purchase of 1803. After the Purchase, Louisiana's civil code remained influenced by the Napoleonic Code, although it substantially Americanized over time. The idea behind this book is to give you a road map for how civil disputes are resolved, even if they vary.

What Kinds of Cases Go to Which Courts

The United States has both federal and state court systems because the U.S. Constitution divides power between federal and state governments. Whether a case falls into a federal or state category is a determination of which system has "jurisdiction," that is, what court has the legal authority to decide a case over another court system.

Federal Court

Federal courts handle cases involving the U.S. Constitution and federal statutes. Examples of federal court cases include prosecution of federal criminal laws. Famous gangster Al Capone was sent to Alcatraz, not for his bootlegging, gambling, murder, or prostitution enterprises, but for federal tax evasion. Federal civil cases include matters like discrimination and violations of other civil rights, cases involving the federal government, social security, Native Americans, bankruptcy, etc.

State Court

State courts, on the other hand, handle most everything else you can think of, such as crimes set forth in state penal codes, and civil disputes arising from contract, accidents, property disputes, family law, etc.

When Federal and State Courts Collide

Federal courts also handle cases that ordinarily would be filed in state courts but when the parties in dispute are from different states or countries. This is called "diversity of citizenship".

For example, what happens when a California resident is hurt by someone from Nevada? An injury case does not involve a federal subject and so falls under state jurisdiction. (And of course the California person wants to avoid the expense of traveling to Nevada for the case.) If the Nevada party has a residence in California, does business there, or commits the wrong there, the Nevada party has submitted to California's jurisdiction and can be sued in California. But, while the California party must file the case in California, the Nevada resident can "remove" the case to federal court because the residencies are "diverse." The federal court, then, has "diversity" jurisdiction to handle the state subject.

Where Does Your Case Fall?

So how do you know if you have a federal or state case? If your case, for example, involves freedom of speech, freedom of religion, freedom of the press, due process under the law, or a federal statute, you file in federal court.

On the other hand, if your case involves an accident, a contract, or a state statute, you file in state court. If the sued party is from another state, that party has the option to take a state-filed case to federal court.

I move on now to show you what law students study, how they become lawyers, and how law firms operate.

The Study of Law and Admittance to Practice

CHAPTER THREE

Law School and What You Study

Why become a lawyer? A friend of mine, a Harvard Law School graduate, told me a joke. The top third of the Harvard law class gets the teaching positions. The middle third of the class gets the government jobs. The bottom third of the class makes all the money.

Like any profession, doctors, lawyers, engineers, architects, people want to get ahead in the world, earn a good living, learn a trade that only a limited number of people know how to do, have prestige, and maybe do some good in the world. To accomplish these aims as a lawyer, you have to be admitted to law school.

There are 198 accredited law schools in the United States. Admission standards vary, just like undergraduate institutions, but almost all law schools require you to take the main test developed for law school admission, the Law School Admissions Test (LSAT). The LSAT tests for reading comprehension, analytical reasoning, how well you think logically, how well you argue a point, and writing skills. Like all such things, there are bar preparation courses that coach you on how to take the test. With your LSAT results, together with your college grades and other criteria, you apply to your law schools of choice.

The typical course of study in law school takes three years if you go full-time. There are accredited night schools to accommodate people with full-time jobs or who have other reasons to take it slower, but that adds at least a year. Just as in college, there are required courses and, eventually, you can take courses in specialty areas that interest you.

The typical curriculum of required study includes civil procedure, criminal procedure, contracts, criminal law, torts, property, constitutional law, evidence, remedies, and legal research and writing classes. Later electives include subjects such as corporate law, environmental law, family law, wills and trusts, intellectual property law, and many others. Let's dive into these subjects, where I will describe what they cover and give some illustrations that show how they may apply to affect everyday life.

Civil Procedure

Simply put, civil procedure provides the rules of the road for lawsuits. In California, these rules are incorporated into the Code of Civil Procedure. The subject matter covers things like establishing jurisdiction (mentioned earlier), filing pleadings, how the court manages the case, how facts are obtained (known as "discovery"), pre-trial motions, trial procedures, and appeals. (Much of this will be illustrated later.)

Contracts

A contract (sometimes called an agreement) contains the terms of the relationship between parties that creates enforceable rights between them. For example, if you hire a service or buy a product, the seller offers to perform for a price and you accept the offer by agreeing to pay. You may agree with your neighbor not to build a wall above a certain height to avoid a legal dispute. Even marriage is a contract. Any agreement to do something, or to refrain from doing something, is a contract as long as each side gets a benefit out of it. That benefit is known as "consideration."

An insurance policy is a contract, too – the company promises to take care of you in case of an accident, and you agree to pay a premium for it. Employment is also a contract; the relationship between an employer and employee is governed by state law, but also may include a legally binding agreement that outlines the terms and conditions of the work, such as an actual written contract, or the terms may be contained in an employee handbook. A lease is a contract, containing not only the amount of rent and duration of the lease, but also rules of conduct to protect the property.

Criminal Law

Criminal law class, the study of crimes, deems what is considered harmful or threatening to society, and provides punishments for committing crimes. All the crimes you ever heard of have definitions, and certain conduct must occur for the crime to be committed. The definitions and penalties for committing crimes are contained in the Penal Code.

Here are some examples. What is the difference between burglary and robbery? Burglary is entering into a structure to commit a crime, like stealing. (A "break-in.") Robbery is the direct taking of money or property from a person through force, threat, or intimidation. (A "stickup.")

What is the difference between a misdemeanor and a felony? A felony is a crime that can be punished by death, state prison, or county jail. Lesser crimes are considered misdemeanors unless they are classified as infractions. Murder, of course, is a felony. Disturbing the peace, trespassing, certain levels of drug possession, and reckless driving are misdemeanors. A violation of much in the Vehicle Code is an infraction. Infractions rarely call for imprisonment, just fines or related requirements, like traffic school.

Criminal Procedure

Criminal procedure covers how criminal laws are administered, and how they affect our rights. Until the early 1960s, police often got away with treating suspected criminals any way they wanted to assure a conviction. But all that changed, starting in March of 1963, when Ernesto Arturo Miranda was a person of interest for the kidnapping and rape of an eighteen-year-old woman.

Mr. Miranda was not taken into custody at first, but voluntarily came to the police station for a lineup at the request of the police. After the lineup, the police placed him under arrest and interrogated him in a room cut off from the outside world for two hours. They told him he was positively identified in the lineup (which he wasn't), and subsequently, he signed a confession.

The case of Miranda v. Arizona was about why the right to self-incrimination for anyone arrested for a crime must be preserved. An arrestee, guilty or innocent, cannot be forced or tricked into a confession or it will be considered unjust. The U.S. Supreme Court decided the case in 1966 and the case decision discusses giving a prisoner the "third degree," that is, the use of force, psychological gamesmanship, even brutality, to extract a confession. (The phrase, "the third degree" comes from methods used in the Spanish Inquisition.)

As to the extraction of a false confession, the Supreme Court stated "It is not admissible to do a great right by doing a little wrong. It is not sufficient to do justice by obtaining a proper result by irregular or improper means." The end result was that the Supreme Court decided to ban intimidation tactics. To assure a person's rights, the court said the Fifth Amendment of the Constitution requires that law enforcement officials advise suspects of their right to remain silent and to obtain an attorney during interrogations while in police custody, now known as the "Miranda Warning."

Torts

Even if you have never heard of the word "tort", this is the area of law most people know.[1] A tort is a civil wrong that inflicts harm, whether it's to a person or an organization, and whether intentional or unintentional. Examples include things like punching someone in the nose (an intentional tort), committing negligence (unintended carelessness), defamation (ruining someone's reputation), damaging property, defective products that cause harm, etc.

Property Law

Property law involves the ownership and use of things, such as land, buildings, personal belongings, and investments, as well as intellectual property, like trademarks or copyrights. Ownership of property quite often comes into dispute, so let's take a look into some brief examples to further understand how property law works.

Land

Property Law covers land use, which includes the right to own and rent real estate.

Rights relating to property are guaranteed in the U.S. Constitution, specifically the 5th Amendment. You know that one, containing the right against self-incrimination, that is, "pleading the 5th". But the 5th Amendment preserves other rights as well, such as the rule against double jeopardy, the right to a grand jury for certain crimes, and no one shall "be deprived of life,

---

1 This is not to be confused with a torte, which can be criminally delicious.

liberty, or property, without due process of law; nor shall private property be taken for public use, without just compensation."

On the subject of taking property for public use, you can own property, but sometimes the government can take it from you if there is a public need. This is called "condemnation." An example would be that the government wants to build a freeway across your land. The government would have to pay you for it, but you might not be able to stop it.

If you rent property to others, or alternatively if your landlord does not provide a habitable apartment, you may need a landlord-tenant lawyer. Maybe you want to build on your land or make improvements to your house. If so, you may need a real estate lawyer.

Personal Property

In a case called Parker v British Airways Board, decided in 1982, a traveler in a London airport executive lounge found an expensive bracelet on the floor. As an honest guy, he turned it in to the airline to see if they could find the owner, but said if they could not find the owner, the bracelet should be returned to him. The axiom we all know is "finders keepers." The full phrase as the law would be applied is "finders keepers unless the true owner claims it."

The airline could not find the owner but sold the bracelet. The traveler was found to have a greater right to the lost bracelet than the airline did. We've all dreamt about this, right? You're on a hike in rough terrain; it's raining, so you find a small cave for shelter. You notice something in a corner that looks like plastic. You push away a layer of dirt to reveal a trash bag containing a briefcase. You open the briefcase, and it is filled with gold coins.

What would happen? Not all states have finders-keepers laws, but those laws may require you to make an effort to find the owner before it can be legally yours. I am not sure I'd report it. How about you? Just kidding - maybe.

Possibly the best treasure story ever written, in my opinion, is The Count of Monte Cristo, by Alexander Dumas, in which a young man wrongly accused of a crime escapes prison, finds lost treasure while on the run, and uses it to re-enter society as a wealthy aristocrat. He then gets great revenge against those who wronged him. If you never read the book or saw any of the movies about it, it's a very satisfying story because the bad guys really get their comeuppance.

Intellectual Property

Intellectual property is an idea, a creation of the mind, that has value; for example, inventions, stories, designs, blueprints, symbols, logos, and brand. Usually the owner copyrights or trademarks their intellectual property to prove not only that it's theirs, but also *when* they thought it up.

Copyrights (protecting authorship) and trademarks (protecting brands) can result in interesting cases. Try using ,Mickey Mouse in your own advertising and see what Disney, which owns the Mickey Mouse image, does about it.

And you may know the case that involved the famous 1970 George Harrison song, *My Sweet Lord.* It turns out the chords to that song and much of the melody were the same as an earlier famous song from 1963, *He's So Fine*, sung by the Chiffons and written by Ronnie Mack. The case found that Harrison had unwittingly (unintentionally) plagiarized *He's So Fine.*[2]

Constitutional Law

Constitutional law is the study of the United States Constitution and how it's applied and interpreted. It covers a wide range of topics, all stemming from its text and amendments. These include, among other things, the right to vote, freedom of speech, the right to privacy, how the government is organized and how powers among government institutions are separated, the right to due process, freedom of religion, freedom of the press, the right to assembly, the right to bear arms, and the organization of the courts. The rights in the Constitution came about because:

- American colonists were taxed by the British government without having representation in that government;
- Only one religion was tolerated in England;

---

2 I say you "may" know *My Sweet Lord* by former Beatle, George Harrison. I grew up a Beatles fan, but I am still amazed that some younger folks are out of touch with that music. There's a fun story that two young people are in line to go into a Paul McCartney concert, and one says to the other, "You know, Paul used to be in another band." Okay, I'm old. I know.

- Any random citizen could be arrested and imprisoned without knowing why and without the speedy chance to defend oneself;
- The military could simply take over anyone's home as barracks and kick out the owners;
- Speaking out against the government was prohibited; and
- The press was restricted from expressing opinion about the government.

As a result, the founders of the new United States of America made sure all these rights were set in stone – in the Constitution. The U.S. Constitution, of course, includes the right to be judged by your peers, from the Magna Carta; that is, trial by jury. (The Magna Carta, meaning the Great Paper or Great Charter, is discussed later.)

The idiom "set in stone," by the way, is believed to stem from the Ten Commandments, also a set of laws in its own way; that is, engraving rules into stone symbolizes permanence and immutability. There is also some indication that the phrase came into vogue in the 17th century, when people started using headstones to mark graves. (The stuff you find researching to write a book, huh?)

Evidence

Evidence consists of the facts, information, or physical artifacts used to support a case. Litigation, or a lawsuit, is the process we have to resolve disputes. In fact, the Latin root, *liti* means "quarrel." Resolving disputes, in Latin, is *litigium*, which also means "dispute." Resolving disputes must be accomplished based on reason and facts and the process must be carried out evenhandedly. Evidence of a dispute or crime must be *fairly presented* for the judge or jury to decide what happened from competing versions of a story. Hence, the phrase "justice is blind." We are all familiar with the image of blindfolded Lady Justice, holding scales to show justice is to be "weighed" fairly.

Lady Justice derives from the Greek goddess of justice, *Themis*, or the Roman goddess, *Justitia*. But why does she hold a sword? The sword represents the power of the law. The toga has meaning too, representing the philosophy of the law.

Interestingly, Lady Justice was not always depicted wearing a blindfold. The original idea of adding the blindfold was actually a cynical portrayal, supposedly showing that justice was not blind in the administration of justice during that era, but rather that the justice system in fact was blind to fairness. The meaning reversed over time.[3]

Evidence is required in the process to prove, or disprove, facts. Evidence class covers the rules about how to prove your case. Evidence can be oral or written, as in testimony or documents, or it can be photos and videos.

An important concept in evidence class is that evidence can be direct or circumstantial. For example, A statement that "I saw the defendant pull the trigger" is direct evidence, that is, it is an eyewitness account from someone with "personal knowledge". But a statement that "I heard a gunshot and when I ran into the room, the defendant was holding a gun while the victim lay dead on the floor," is not direct evidence, but rather, it is circumstantial evidence. The fact that the defendant was seen holding the gun while standing over the victim may be enough evidence to convict without actually seeing the trigger pulled. But the "circumstances" of circumstantial evidence matter. If the witness heard the gunshot from some distance and it took a few moments to get to the scene of the crime, another, closer person might have entered the room and picked up the gun, and is therefore not the shooter. But if the witness ran into the room fast enough and saw a hostile look on the defendant's face, maybe we have enough to convict.

Another oft-used example of circumstantial evidence is the story of a parent who comes into a kitchen and sees a cookie jar with the top off and crumbs on a child's face. "Honey, did you eat a cookie?" The child answers, "No." The parent did not see the child take out the cookie jar, open it, and eat the cookie, but the fact of the jar on the counter and the crumbs on the child's face are circumstantial evidence of the crime.

Direct and circumstantial evidence are both sufficient to prove a fact, in these examples, that the defendant committed the murder or that the child ate the cookie.

---

3   https://www.illinoiscourts.gov/News/1294/Illinois-Supreme-Court-history-Blindfolded-justice/news-detail/

The subject of evidence will be explored in more detail as we move along, but a widely known example of an evidentiary rule, studied carefully in law school, is the hearsay rule. Hearsay is when someone testifies to a fact using what someone else said rather than establishing that fact by getting the information from someone having direct knowledge or observation of what happened. Essentially, hearsay is a rumor. If someone testifies to hearsay, that's when you would hear the familiar "Objection," or "I object," which requires the judge to rule on whether that testimony is "admissible" to prove a fact, that is, whether the jury is allowed to consider that evidence in deciding the case.

Remedies

A remedy in the legal system refers to how the outcome of a case can be enforced. If you win a case, what damages can you obtain? What can the court require someone to do? And what are the means to enforce the judgment?

In either a tort or contract case, for example, you go to trial and the jury gives you an award of money. This is called "compensatory damages." Compensatory damages are intended to make the injured party whole again by addressing their financial, emotional, and physical losses. If someone loses a limb, money cannot restore the limb, but it can help make up for the physical pain, the emotional impact of the loss, the costs of medical treatment, and the inability to work.

If the wrong was intentional or so reckless that the conduct was "malicious", there also can be an award of "punitive damages." (Punitive damages apply to a tort, that is, harmful conduct; thus, it is not available in contract cases.) An example would be hurting someone in a bar fight. Certainly, the assailant could be arrested for the crime of assault and battery, but that person has committed an intentional tort and also could be sued for it in a civil case.

Punitive damages are intended to both punish and deter the assailant or others from similar behavior in the future. For example, O.J. Simpson was acquitted of the crime of murdering his wife and her friend. He was later sued in civil court by the families for the tort of wrongful death. The jury in that case decided he did it and awarded $8.5 million in compensatory damages and $25 million in punitive damages.

Conduct may be specifically unintentional but still allow for punitive damages. Driving under the influence, a person may not intend to hurt anyone, but if it happens, the law considers the conduct both a crime and conduct reckless enough to be malicious for the purpose of awarding punitive damages. The intent was not to harm, but rather to drive under the influence, and that is what is being punished.

Some cases do not necessarily result in a monetary award. For example, if your neighbor builds a perimeter wall and some or all of it ends up on your property, the court can issue an "injunction," which is an order forcing the neighbor to take down and relocate the wall. A person can also be "enjoined" from bothering you, usually known as a "restraining order."

There are many other kinds of remedies, and the court system provides these remedies for a lot of what goes on in life, and the means to enforce it.

Legal Research and Writing

Legal Research

Legal research is the process of locating and studying the law, that is, cases and statutes, applicable to a client's issue or litigation. The American legal system is based on English law. The cases decided by courts go back hundreds of years. Each case in each area of the law builds on itself as new fact patterns are tested in the courts. This is done by reviewing existing law and deciding whether to keep it as is, reject it, or change it, causing it the law to evolve.

Most cases simply apply the established law to the facts to determine the outcome. This process, of looking at cases decided in the past and applying them to current cases, is known as "stare decisis," meaning "to stand by things decided." The older cases that established the law are called "precedents."

How do we find and read the cases? Take a deep breath as we launch into this. The study of legal research means learning a kind of code. As an example, until we had computers, and maybe still in some libraries today, finding a book means understanding the Dewey Decimal System, which itself is a kind of code, that is, a system or procedure. We locate library books by deciding among ten numerically identified subjects the book falls into and then looking for subcategories within those subjects.

Finding case law requires understanding how cases are identified in a published set of books. (Nowadays, of course, the same identifying system is used electronically.) The books are chronologically numbered, and the case appears at a specific page within that volume. Seems simple, doesn't it? I wish. I will break this down for you, but it is technical. If you are a law student, a paralegal, or anyone just wanting to locate a case, read on. Some of you may wish to skip to the Legal Writing subsection that follows.

Cases are published in "reporters," a set of books. Several different reporter publications exist depending on the type of case or its location. There are also multiple versions of these publications. For example, U.S. Supreme Court cases are published in three different reporters, and they all have abbreviations: United States Reports (U.S.), which is the official reporter; Supreme Court Reporter ("S. Ct."), published by West Publishing; and United States Supreme Court Reports, Lawyers' Edition ("L. Ed."), published by a company called Lexis. Federal circuit court (appellate) opinions are published in the Federal Reporter ("F."). District court (trial level) opinions are published in a set called the Federal Supplement ("F. Supp."). When a set of reporters gets too long, the publisher starts a new set. Volumes in a later set are shown as the next numerical set in order, i.e., "F.2d.", or "F.Supp.3d.", etc.

State court reporters are similarly named. California Supreme Court opinions are published in three different reporters: California Reports (Cal., Cal. 2d, etc.), which is the official reporter; California Reporter (Cal. Rptr., Cal. Rptr. 2d, etc.), published by West; and Pacific Reporter (P., P.2d, etc.), which is a regional reporter published by West. State courts do not publish trial court level opinions.[4] Opinions of the California Court of Appeal are reported in California Appellate Reports or the Official Reports. are designated "Cal.App," "Cal.App 2d.", etc.

Over time, the individual cases fill up a given volume, and the next cases start a new volume. Eventually, the publications advance to a new edition, containing even more volumes. Finding the cases uses a numbering system that tracks from different reporters and by volume, and then by page, also showing the year it was decided. This is known as "Bluebook" style. For example, the Miranda case, in the U.S. Supreme Court, is cited as *Miranda v. Arizona*, 384 U.S. 436 (1966). Translated, the case is found in the United States Reports ("U.S."), volume 384, at page 436.

---

4 https://nyulaw.libguides.com/caselaw

In days past, law firms had to devote a substantial portion of their office space to stacks of these volumes or have access to a public law library. Today, most lawyers subscribe to electronic services, like Westlaw, Lexis/Nexis, Fastcase, and others. Regardless, the citation system is still used, but now you type it into a computer instead of walking the stacks, getting on ladders, and breathing dust. Many cases can just be Googled by typing in the name or the citation, but they do not have other assist features that the subscription services have, which summarize particular issues addressed in the case or prompt you to additional cases on the subject.

You also need to understand how statutes (meaning written laws) are constructed and researched. In this book, we will reference some California statutes. The statutes are divided and subdivided by topic and eventually broken down into sections, each of which are numbered. The code name abbreviation and section number are both included in a California code citation.

The § symbol means "section" and is placed before the actual section number of the statute. For example, the California Code of Civil Procedure (or CCP) covers how lawsuits are filed and litigated, including when depositions are to be taken. (Depositions, that is, live testimony in the pre-trial phase of litigation, is discussed in further detail in Chapter Ten.) CCP §2025.210 states:

Subject to Sections 2025.270 and 2025.610, an oral deposition may be taken as follows:

(a) The defendant may serve a deposition notice without leave of court at any time after that defendant has been served or has appeared in the action, whichever occurs first.

(b) The plaintiff may serve a deposition notice without leave of court on any date that is 20 days after the service of the summons on, or appearance by, any defendant. On motion with or without notice, the court, for good cause shown, may grant to a plaintiff leave to serve a deposition notice on an earlier date.[5]

---

5 "Leave" comes from Old English lēaf, meaning "permission" or "allowance." The practice of law uses many archaic terms from Old English. We'll come across another one later, the word "well", in Part Two, Chapter Seventeen, meaning the area between where the lawyers sit in the courtroom and where the judge sits.

So, if you want to tell someone where to find the rule about when a defendant can first schedule a deposition, you would say CCP §2025.210, subdivision (a).

Legal Writing

In legal writing class, law students are taught approaches to drafting legal documents, analytical opinions, and court briefs using certain standards and conventions. For example, there is a methodology, importantly used in taking the bar exam, called "IRAC", which stands for Issue, Rule, Analysis, and Conclusion. In one form or another, most case opinions are set out in this way.

Here is a simplified example that might be used in a brief to the court where an employer is sued because an employee got into an accident using a company-issued vehicle:

(I) In this case, the issue is whether the employer, the defendant corporation, is liable for the negligence of its employee, which occurred during a non-work-related activity.

(R) The rule applicable to this case is that an employer may be held liable for the negligence of an employee if the negligence was committed within the scope of the employee's employment, the law of "respondeat superior." However, the employer may not be held liable for the employee's negligence if the employee was at the time acting for their own purposes.

(A) The facts of this case were that the employee was using a company car, but only for a personal errand because the employee was stopping at a grocery store to bring food home for dinner. The employee was not performing any work-related duties at the time of the accident.

(C) Based on the above analysis, the employer should not be held liable because the employee was acting outside the scope of this employment at the time of the accident.

Though this example is very basic, it shows how the logic of the IRAC method of presentation, that is, what it's about, what law applies, what facts are to be applied to the law, and how issue should be decided.

Legal writing class also focuses on writing persuasively. This is a skill many lawyers must master over time, though some people just have a talent for it. Persuasion means the act of convincing someone to accept a belief, position, or course of action. Not trying to persuade might take the form of just presenting a position objectively, with no argument. A persuasive brief will present the facts and law in a way that supports a position.

For example, using the employee accident mentioned above, a less than persuasive presentation might say simply that the employee was on a grocery run and so not working at the time of the accident. A more persuasive approach might add more facts to show the personal errand at the time, like this: The employee is on duty Monday through Friday, and the accident occurred on a Saturday. The employee's wife was in the vehicle, which she would never be during working hours. The grocery run was from a weekend campsite the family had gone to, and thus was in a different city from where the employee's work would be performed. Therefore, your honor, there can be no doubt that the employee was not working in the course and scope of his employment at the time of the accident.

Corporate Law

Corporate law governs business entities; formation, operation, and dissolution. A business may be operated simply by a person, known as a sole proprietorship, or it may be registered with the state and become fictional entities, called corporations, partnerships, or similar things. (The Latin root for corporation is *corpus*, meaning "body.")

These entities may be public (like a city or school district), privately owned (by shareholders, partners, or members), or organizations (like a church). The theory behind allowing fictional organizations was to allow people to pool investors, enabling fundraising by selling shares. The company shields the owners and investors from personal liability, known as the "corporate veil." For the purpose of lawsuits, fictional business entities are considered "persons," meaning they can sue and be sued, and can own property.

Family Law

Family law covers family relationships, such as marriage, divorce, child custody and support, adoption, etc. Some courthouses have dedicated courtrooms for family law because it is a specialized area of the law, and because of the great volume of cases. The Los Angeles Superior Court has an entire division devoted to it.

The topics that often hit the news are celebrity breakups and pre-nuptial agreements. There are many notable such breakups, like Michael and Juanita Jordan, Tiger Woods and Elin Nordegren, and Steven Spielberg and Amy Irving.

What are pre-nups and why do pre-nups exist? Pre-nups is short for "pre-nuptial agreements." A pre-nup is a contract which provides for what happens if a marriage ends, instead of having it decided by statutory law (in California, divorce is governed by the Family Code). Paul McCartney had no pre-nup when he married Heather Mills, and it cost him $48 million when they divorced.

Perhaps you are old enough to remember Oscar-winning actor Lee Marvin, who starred in many films, including *The Dirty Dozen* (one of my personal favorites) and *Cat Ballou*. Mr. Marvin and Michelle Marvin were not married, but lived together for seven years. When they separated, Michelle claimed half the assets the couple acquired during that time, a claim usually made when a marriage ends.

In 1976, the California Supreme Court determined in the Marvin case that non-marital relationships were not governed by statutory law as were marriages, but if there was a contract between the parties, that contract would be enforced. Michelle was able to show an agreement with Lee about how they would split things up if the relationship ended. The recovery of a part of the assets of the relationship became known as "palimony."

Now that you know how to look up the case, check out *Marvin v. Marvin* (1976) 18 Cal.3d 660 – so, this was decided in the California Supreme Court, "Cal.", 3rd edition, at page 660. Or just put the name into your online search bar. Because of palimony, the use of pre-nuptial agreements developed as a protection for both sides.

Wills, Trusts and Probate

Practicing in this area is called estate planning and/or probate law.

A will is a legal document directing how a person's property is distributed at death. A trust is also a legally recognized document that may be used in place of a will. A trust sets up the power of a separate person or entity, known as a trustee, to own, hold, and manage assets apart from a person; the purpose of the trust is to manage tax obligations. Probate means the process of determining the validity of a will and carrying out its enforcement.

People die with wills; they die without wills. They leave their money to their cats. The study of wills and trusts includes their creation and administration, and estate planning strategies. Robin Williams, Prince, and Howard Hughes did not make wills, and their fortunes were fought over in court for years. This subject crosses into tax law as well.

The area of the law also includes legal issues arising from managing an incapacitated person's financial and medical decisions; depending on the situation, this is called either a guardianship or a conservatorship.

Death and taxes? This is the kind of law practice that never dies. The probate departments in the courthouse are always busy.

There are, of course, many other subjects of study in law school, as many as there are fields of focus in the law. A glance at the curriculum on any law school's website will give you an expanded picture of what is mentioned here.

Admittance To The Practice Of Law

I mentioned that lawsuits can be stressful. A lawyer's stress starts well before that. You can go to law school for three or four years, spend six figures in the process, struggle through all your final exams, but still, you cannot practice law. You must be licensed. To be licensed, you must pass (I hate even remembering this) the !B-A-R E-X-A-M! (Sound of thunder, sound of Beethoven's 5th.) There, I said it.

We could debate what event in life wins the award as most stressful. Stress is defined as physical, mental, or emotional strain or tension. We stress over death, divorce, serious illness, facing jail time, etc. Stress can be caused by worrying, and worrying relates to something that has yet to happen. While in law school, you look out over years anticipating the bar exam, and the anxiety over whether, after all that, the practice of law might be denied to you if you fail. There is the nerve-wracking run-up to taking the test. All this puts the bar exam right up there in the stress rankings.

The bar exam consists of six hours of multiple-choice questions, six thirty-minute essay questions, and three hours of performance tests. This is all done in two days. A third day is devoted to an ethics examination, a two-hour multiple-choice test. Piece of cake, right?

Why this torture? Why does the state require any kind of license? States issue licenses to regulate certain activities and professions, ensuring public safety and consumer protection by verifying that individuals meet minimum competency standards before engaging in those activities. In California, most occupations that require a license are contained in the Business and Professions Code. This code establishes the Department of Consumer Affairs, which presides over most licensing processes for a wide variety of professions.

The process of obtaining a license varies by profession. I am sure practitioners in other professions have a right to argue how tough it was to get their license, but in my opinion, those in the healing arts (i.e. medical practitioners) and lawyers have a particularly arduous path. Lawyers, whose job is to protect the interests of others in so many important aspects of life and business, are put to great task. It is a public imperative to be as sure as possible that the education and training of such professionals is strenuously tested and governed.

There's more. Once you have been admitted to practice, you are required to take a certain number of refresher courses. Periodically, you are required to report to the State Bar that you have completed the required amount of continuing education.

After law school, the bar exam, and with further educational maintenance, the practice of law is an exclusive club, but the public can be assured that most lawyers know and follow the rules and can be trusted to provide services professionally.

The Practice of Law and the Law Practice

CHAPTER FOUR

Advocacy and Zealotry – Being Your Client's Champion

The earliest known lawyers were in ancient Greece and Rome. In Greece, they could "plead" the case of friends but were not allowed to charge a fee. In Rome, lawyering was eventually legalized as a profession, but the fees charged were limited. (We have since fixed that.) The practice of law was abandoned in the Middle Ages, in areas replaced with "trial by ordeal." "Ordeals" could include having to pick up a hot iron bar or to take something from a boiling pot. If the accused healed quickly enough, God was said to favor them, and they were acquitted. There was also trial by combat to solve disputes, a form of dueling. People might be tied and thrown into a lake, and if they sank, they were innocent. (Innocence, it turned out, was not a life-preserving condition.)

The means of resolving disputes eventually evolved. The use of the word "court" in connection with the law comes from the fact that the king, or his designated person, such as a knight, would determine the outcome of civil disputes on the castle grounds, literally in the courtyard. Eventually, these judges would travel to different places to handle disputes locally, that is, traveling the "circuit," the term we still use today.

Later, King John of England enacted taxes to fund wars in France. The barons, whose assets were affected by the taxes and the wars, confronted the king, demanding certain rights. In 1215, these rights were enshrined in the Magna Carta, and the king signed it to avoid civil war. One key sentence in the Magna Carta was very important to the founders of our country: "No freeman shall be taken, imprisoned, disseised, outlawed, banished, or in any way destroyed, nor will We proceed against or prosecute him, except by the lawful judgment of his peers or by the law of the land."[1]

We talked earlier about the Fifth Amendment to the U.S. Constitution: "no person shall…be deprived of life, liberty, or property, without due process of law." This is the same concept found in the Magna Carta.

Litigators are modern-day combatants in dispute resolution, though done on behalf of someone else. This is called "advocacy." There is always an opponent, and therefore the setting, though it should be conducted respectfully, is fraught with tension caused by the need to win. Winning means more clients, losing means fewer clients. How many media advertising law firms tout their losses? Being ethical also means avoiding provocation, as can happen in sports, where winning and losing have monetary consequences, such as using cheap shots, trash talk, and cheating. It happens/

In the role of advocate, lawyers are required to represent their clients "zealously." Rule 1.5 of the American Bar Association's Model Rules of Professional Conduct, discussed further under the heading "Ethics", states:

> A lawyer should pursue a matter on behalf of a client despite opposition, obstruction or personal inconvenience to the lawyer, and take whatever lawful and ***ethical measures*** are required to vindicate a client's cause or endeavor. A lawyer must also act with commitment and dedication to the interests of the client and with ***zeal*** in advocacy upon the client's behalf. [The emphases are mine.]

What is "zeal?" Zeal, from Greek origins, means to act with passion and intensity, diligence, and determination. In history, the Zealots were political, even violent, foes of Roman rule in Judea shortly after the death of Christ. How does passionate and intense advocacy square with the other rules from the Model Rules, like prohibiting obstructive tactics and frivolous arguments (Rule 3.4), requiring decorum in the courtroom, and avoiding conduct meant to disrupt the proceedings? (Rule 3.5)[2] You might think, well, that's easy; we live in a modern world where we don't settle our disputes with our fists, something you

---

1 "Disseised" from old English means wrongfully deprived of possession, i.e., dispossessed.
2 Rules 3.1 and 3.2 of the California Rules of Professional Conduct also cover this, with similar rules in other states.

might say to a child sent home from school for playground fighting. Yet, boundaries may be crossed.

Overwhelmingly, lawyers deal with each other and the court courteously, though much is written on the subject of civility in the legal process. The reason for so much writing on this topic is the prevalence of those who go too far. Courts can impose financial penalties on lawyers, called "sanctions," for a variety of reasons, including uncivil conduct. Lawyers may try to intimidate, say, by belittling opposing counsel or acting aggressively or rudely on cross-examination of a witness. Lawyers may intentionally create hostility by falsely accusing opposing counsel of lying or misrepresenting facts to the court; this requires the other side to defend themselves, thereby distracting from the fact-finding and fact-producing intent of the process.

Lawyers also may "over-litigate" a case. In one case in 2021, a lawyer showed agitation in court, interrupted the judge, and made derogatory comments in a brief. The lawyer had won the case and was also entitled to an award of attorney's fees. The amount he claimed as fees was cut by two-thirds because he was uncivil toward his opponent, discourteous to the judge, and spent far more effort in litigating the case than the relatively small amount of damages the case was worth. (*Karton v. Ari Design & Construction, Inc.* (2021) 61 Cal.App.5th 734 – so, this is found in California Appellate Reports at volume 61, page 734.)

This happened again in 2023 in a case called <u>Snoek v. ExakTime Innovations, Inc.</u> (96 Cal.App.5th 908). In the Snoek case, it was shown that Snoek's lawyers engaged in an extensive, uncivil, and accusatory email campaign with opposing counsel, among other things they did. In addition, the lawyer engaged in disrespectful tones in open court. The court cut out of the attorney's fees claim the time billed for those communications.

The system works best if everyone approaches litigation as civil and reasonable advocates, respecting the system as a process for the resolution of civil disputes. George Washington, at age 13, studied the *Rules of Civility*, a French rulebook, and wrote many of them down, including, "Every Action done in Company ought to be with Some Sign of Respect to those that are Present." And "Use no Reproachfull Language against any one neither Curse nor Revile." (I admit I have struggled with the second one.)

In his farewell address, Washington said, "This government, the offspring of our own choice, uninfluenced and unawed, adopted upon full investigation and mature deliberation, completely free in its principles, in the distribution of its powers, uniting security with energy, and containing within itself a provision for its own amendment, has a just claim to your confidence and your support. Respect for its authority, compliance with its laws, acquiescence in its measures, are duties enjoined by the fundamental maxims of true liberty."

The court system is part of the government. George Washington said respect for the authority of that government is fundamental to freedom. We should keep it that way if we want it to work.

Ethics

I mentioned earlier that lawyers are taught and tested on ethics. In a law school ethics class, students learn about the rules governing lawyer conduct. These include, among other things, the attorney-client relationship, conflicts of interest, confidentiality, ethical decision-making in legal practice, and how to navigate potential ethical dilemmas they might face as lawyers. These concepts often stem from a published set of rules called the Model Rules of Professional Conduct established by the American Bar Association. (I'll call them the "Model Rules," going forward.) California's version is just called the Rules of Professional Conduct.

For example, lawyers do not just strive to protect your rights and interests; they also sometimes hold your money. Mishandling a client's money is a favorite target of the State Bar's disciplinary arm, resulting in suspension or revocation of a law license, or even criminal prosecution.

Rule 1.15 of the Rules of Professional Conduct requires attorneys who handle client funds or funds entrusted by others, including settlement checks, fees advanced for services not yet performed, or money to pay court fees, to hold those funds in one or more interest-bearing bank accounts labeled as a "Trust Account,", also called an IOLTA ("Interest on Lawyers' Trust Accounts").

There are well-known lawyers who lost everything because they succumbed to the temptation to use money for themselves that belonged to their clients. Porn actress Stormy Daniels sued the President over the well-publicized hush money scandal. Her lawyer was Michael Avenatti, who was seen frequently in the news on behalf of Daniels. Later, Mr. Avenatti was prosecuted and convicted of stealing a different client's money and was sentenced to fourteen years in federal prison.

Here's what he did. Among several allegations about mishandling clients' money, he represented a mentally ill man, Geoffrey Johnson, who was injured and became a paraplegic, meaning paralysis of the lower half of the body. Mr. Johnson was arrested and then attempted suicide twice while in custody, the second attempt resulting in a fall that produced the injury. There are rules in jails about protecting prisoners from themselves, and Mr. Avenatti sued for negligence and also alleged police brutality.

The case resulted in a $4 million settlement. The settlement money went into the firm's client trust account. Still, Mr. Avenatti did not tell Mr. Johnson about the settlement and instead used the money for himself, providing Mr. Johnson with small advances and lying about the status of the case. Wow.

Here's another wow, a more recent case in the news. Tom Girardi was a well-known Los Angeles lawyer. (And he was married to Erika Jane, of the Real Housewives of Beverly Hills.) Mr. Girardi had a reputation for achieving great results for his injured clients for many years. It turned out that he embezzled millions from his client trust account. He was disbarred and sentenced to prison. Great way to end an otherwise stellar career.

Lawyers must comply with many more rules of ethical conduct, most of which are contained in the Model Rules or the state equivalents. These rules cover the lawyer-client relationship, counseling, advocacy, dealing with people other than clients, responsibilities of lawyers in their firms, public service, communications about services, and maintaining the integrity of the profession. Here are some highlights from these rules, some you may know and some that are more obscure.

1. **Conflicts of interest.** A lawyer may not take a case against a former client, presumably because the lawyer has confidential information that could be used against the former client.

   - Your communications with your lawyer are sacrosanct. No one can find out what information you give your lawyer, not the opposing lawyer, not the judge, no one. You must be able to disclose fully and frankly everything to your lawyer, to give your lawyer the best chance to protect your rights.

- This gets us into the concept of "privilege." Privilege in the law refers to a special legal right that allows an individual to withhold certain information in court, such as the attorney-client privilege. There are other such privileges not to disclose, like a spouse cannot be forced to testify against their spouse, and what you say to your doctor is also private. There are several other such privileges, though some may not be immune from disclosure in a legal proceeding.

2. **Communications with others.** A lawyer may not communicate with someone who is represented by counsel.

3. **Advertising legal services.** In today's world, you can't turn on the television, the radio in your car, or travel any distance on a freeway without exposure to lawyer advertising. Lawyer advertising actually used to be a crime. Later, it was discouraged as unseemly to the profession. In 1977, the law firm of Bates & O'Steen advertised in a newspaper in Arizona. When the state bar sought to impose discipline, the firm sued, going all the way the U.S. Supreme Court. In *Bates v. State Bar of Arizona*, 433 U.S. 350 (1977), the court found that attorney advertising was protected speech under the First Amendment. Since then, it has been hard to get away from it.

All this confirms that the practice of law is heavily regulated. There are educational requirements, testing, and stringent rules to protect the integrity of the profession and the public.

The Law Practice

A law practice can be a sole proprietorship, a partnership, or a professional corporation. A professional corporation is specifically designed for businesses providing professional services that require a license, like legal or medical services.

Like any other business, a law practice has owners and employees, it may have a lease on office space or even own an office building, own or lease office equipment, and has expenses ranging from IT to telephone, to computers, copiers, and scanners, to office supplies, to snacks and coffee. Insurance is needed for the premises and equipment, malpractice, and employee benefits. The firm usually pays the annual license fees for its professional employees.

Lawyers may belong to many kinds of professional organizations that specialize in certain areas of the law, and it can be a distinction to author published articles for those organizations, to speak at the organization's meetings, or to just publish them on the firm's website in a blog-type format. A typical law firm website offers a description of the firm's specialties and biographies of the professionals, along with contact information.

The firm must be owned by licensed lawyers, and its professional staff is made up of the owners (sometimes they are shareholders if it is a professional corporation), partners (who may or may not have an ownership interest in the firm; if not, they may be called "non-equity partners"), or associates (a lawyer employee). A non-equity partner will be a lawyer who is more experienced and commands a higher fee than an associate. Typically, qualification for ownership or partnership in a law firm requires that the lawyer is not only an experienced and quality practitioner but also brings in business.

How a law firm functions, again, is like most other businesses. Nowadays, many employees work in a hybrid status, some coming into the office while others work from home. The workstation, like other businesses, consists of a computer usually with multiple screens, access to the internet (and internet-based research applications), and a telephone.

A typical day in a litigation office will include letter writing and brief writing, discovery preparation (discussed later), communicating by telephone or electronic means with clients, the court, other lawyers, experts providing case input, witnesses, and the typical other miscellany that other businesses have. The work might also include legal research and studying or preparing for discovery proceedings, court hearings, or a trial. (These kinds of tasks are discussed and illustrated for you later.)

At least as much as, or more, than other businesses, the workday is pressured by deadlines, some of which are known and planned for, and others that arise on a moment's notice. The workdays for many litigation lawyers cannot always be controlled; this is not a 9-5 business, it can feel like another Beatles song – *Eight Days a Week.*

Intellectual ability and learning acumen may enable you to get through law school and pass the bar exam, but that does not mean you are well-suited to be a litigator from a personality standpoint. Nor does it mean you know how to run a business, be a good boss, a good coworker, or a fair person. Being in charge, whether running the firm or simply having other lawyers and support staff working for or with you, can bring out over-exerted ego and reduced ability to empathize. To be sure, such personalities exist in all occupations and in life in general. Add winning and losing to the equation, and the result can be a tense environment.

For anyone reading this who is thinking about becoming a lawyer, I'm scaring you, right? Let me assure you that most lawyers are perfectly nice human beings who respect the people they work with and are well-intentioned, ethical practitioners who understand the importance and responsibility to protect the interests of their clients; they appreciate the efforts of their work staff, while also respecting the legal process. If you find yourself in a law practice, I hope this description will prepare you to develop coping strategies and to promise yourself to be as professional as possible, always looking to take the well-mannered, high road.

If you are a client or prospective client reading this, it is unlikely you will ever see the tension that can occur inside the firm or in your lawyer's daily activities, but it will help you to understand when your lawyer is, say, delayed getting back to you or has you communicate with staff instead of directly with them. Yet, client communication and client relationships are both especially important.

How to Pick Your Lawyer

CHAPTER FIVE

Finding and Vetting the Firm

Paul Simon said there are fifty ways to leave your lover, but there are also lots of ways to pick your lawyer. This book is focused on litigators, that is, lawyers who prepare and try lawsuits. But the first thing to consider is what kind of law covers your legal problem.

Law practices can be highly specialized, or they can cover multiple fields (a so-called general practice). Larger firms may have multiple specialized practice "departments".

Many states recognize and issue certifications for certain specialties. To qualify for certified specialties requires extra testing, education, and experience in those areas. In California, such special designations cover twenty-one different areas, including appellate law, bankruptcy law, criminal law, estate planning, trust & probate law, family law, and workers' compensation law, to name a few. Having a certification for the specialty is, naturally, a great addition to a lawyer's qualifications, but many lawyers choose not to obtain the certification, yet they are equally experienced and have terrific track records.

Let's start with the assumption that you have a legal problem, you need to find a lawyer, but you have had no involvement in a lawsuit before. If you have a tax problem, you do not want to go to a workers' compensation lawyer (unless that same lawyer also happens to practice in tax law). If you were in an accident, you want an accident lawyer (whose practice is handling and trying such cases), not an immigration lawyer or a securities lawyer. And lawyers must tell you if they are not qualified to handle it and decline to accept the case. (Model Rules 1.1 and 1.6, and similar in most states.) How can you be sure, then, that a certain lawyer is qualified for your matter? And how do you begin the process of searching?

Referrals

It helps if your mom, dad, or siblings are lawyers. (Representing family can be tricky, though, but it is done all the time.) But not everyone has a lawyer that close at hand. A good strategy is to get a referral from someone you trust, a family member, a coworker, a friend, someone in your church or synagogue, or a neighbor. Even then, the referral might not be to someone qualified to handle your matter. You go to a coworker and say, "Hey, wasn't your brother in court last year? Would you or he recommend his lawyer?" The coworker enthusiastically recommends his brother's lawyer, who got him off from a drunk driving charge. Yet, what if your case is not about drunk driving, but rather about making, say, a workers' compensation claim?

Advertisements

If your case falls into a category that lawyers advertise about, you certainly can call one of those firms, that is, a firm having a catchy radio slogan or even a jingle, a two-story billboard you pass every day on the way to work, or a commercial you see at midnight. To my observation, accident law firms clearly dominate such advertising. Undoubtedly, advertisers make sure you know what kind of work they do, and you can safely assume they have expertise in that field. They will let you know, too; either in the ad or on their website. They will list their successes, and for accident firms, they tell you amounts they've won. More to come later about the accident biz.

The Internet

Surfing the internet also works. The result is much the same as advertisements, but at least websites have more information, even though specially created to show their best to you, like all businesses. Using social media could certainly get you a name, but you still need to be cautious about whether there is a match to your kind of case.

Referral Agencies

There are also referral agencies. Be careful, though. These agencies are set up to refer you to specialists, but those specialists may have paid to be included on the roster. The California State Bar has a referral list, but the list is not made up of lawyers; but commercial referral agencies. The heading on the referral page says "Certified Lawyer Referral Services Directory"; this is not for certified lawyers, but for certified referral services. Yet, there are referral agencies that are highly specialized in their rosters, say, just for AIDS issues or crime victims. Even then, you really don't know how their lists were compiled.

If you belong to a union, chances are there are referral lists (or the union leaders know someone). Those lists likely show firms that concentrate on issues most affecting your trade.

A reliable search method is to ask a lawyer for a referral to another lawyer. For example, you may know a lawyer who does workers' compensation law, but that lawyer probably knows who the good accident lawyers are, since the fields are similar, and interact since they both involve bodily injury.

Checklist for Picking a Lawyer

The key to picking a lawyer is to get a name in any of the ways mentioned here (or however the name comes to you), but then take steps to research their qualifications and make sure you understand how the firm will handle your case, how you get information about your case, and how you pay for the legal services. Here is a brief checklist of information you'd want to know, and what I think you are entitled to know:

1. Do an online search for the lawyer's name, possibly finding something about their successes or failures.

2. Look up the lawyer by name on your state bar's website. This website may give you information about how long the lawyer has been in practice and may show if they have ever been disciplined for unethical conduct. (In California, Google "California Bar Member Search" (or "California Attorney Search State Bar"), which will bring you to the California State Bar website. You enter the name in the attorney search window and hit the "search" button. The attorney's name will come up, providing his or her firm's name, state bar number, and contact information. Scrolling down, any disciplinary action will show up.) If disciplinary action appears, consider this an important red flag.

3. Look at the firm's website. Check the bios and the areas of practice. Just like applying for a job, it helps to learn a bit about the company before the interview.

4. Look for experience in the field where your legal matter falls. And hey, listen, you might not know what area you fit into. For example, do you need a workers' compensation lawyer or a bodily injury lawyer? You might need both. You might need both a probate lawyer and a tax lawyer. So, that becomes part of the discussion. Here's how it might go: "Ms. Lawyer, I was referred to you, and I would like to tell you about my problem and see if this is something that is covered by your practice." The lawyer should ask you about the problem you need help with anyway, handling the meeting as a "client interview.". Remember, the lawyer is ethically bound to tell you if he or she is not qualified for your case.

5. In a multi-lawyer firm, you want to know who in the firm will be handling your case. Understand that it is often the practice that someone other than a partner will work on the case with the partner (hopefully) overseeing it at least up to the point where the case is getting ready for trial. The person you will deal with may be a junior partner, an associate, or even a paralegal (a non-lawyer trained in legal concepts who can perform basic procedural tasks on behalf of the lawyer).

6. 6. (a) Importantly, you want to know who will take your case to trial if it gets that far. If you have a small case, possibly the partner will have an associate handle it. However, you have the right to know this and to take your case elsewhere if you are not satisfied that the lawyer in the firm trying the case is up to the task.

    (b) Regardless of who in the firm does try the case, what is his or her experience level? Is this a person who is regularly in trial, in trial once every few years, or hardly ever? The most experienced lawyers often belong to certain trade organizations that require a certain level of trial experience to belong. Notably, there is the American Board of Trial

Advocates (ABOTA) and many others.[1] You might ask: "Mr. Lawyer, do you or anyone else in your firm belong to ABOTA? What other organizations do you belong to?"

(c) Another reality here is that many accident firms do not try the case with their own personnel. They are set up to bring the case in, invest in it, and are qualified to litigate it up to the point of trying to get it settled. If it gets close to trial, they may "associate in" another firm with a heavy-hitter trial lawyer. Your retainer agreement with the firm will allow your lawyer to do that. This practice is not a bad thing; you don't pay any more for that because the two firms will split the fee.

7. Be sure to understand all aspects of your case. Don't let your lawyer assume you know how it all works. You can ask questions like: "Mr. Lawyer, how will the case be handled? What do you intend to do to prepare the case for settlement or trial? What will my involvement be? How will we communicate and how often, and will you be providing me with status updates?"

8. Ask what the fees – and costs – of the case will be. Fees and costs are not the same thing. For example, in addition to the lawyer's fees, there are also expenses to file documents in court and to conduct the lawsuit (like court reporter fees), all of which the client is typically responsible for. Ask: "How will I be invoiced and how frequently? How will the charges be detailed for my review?"

So far, we have come at this largely from the perspective that the client approaches the lawyer with a claim against someone, and that claim might require a lawsuit. The person suing is called the "plaintiff." (The word "plaintiff" comes from Latin and, later, from Anglo/French, meaning lament or blameworthiness, and it shares the same linguistic origin as 'complain' and 'complaint.'")

Suppose you are the person who may have misunderstood your property boundaries and put your new block wall in a place that your neighbor thinks is on his property. He sues you for an injunction to move the wall. You are now the "defendant." You need a lawyer to defend you, and you have to go through

---

1 https://plaintiffparity.com/articles/trial-lawyers-associations/

the same search and vetting process. The tips I have given you on how to find and select a lawyer work in both directions.

Sometimes the Lawyer Comes with the Case

Sometimes your lawyer is selected for you, which is common in cases such as class action suits and mass torts.

Class Actions

A class action is where one person (the representative plaintiff) files a lawsuit on behalf of a larger group of people who have all experienced a similar injury or harm, allowing them to collectively seek compensation from the same defendant. The criteria for a class action include, among others, that the affected group is too large for each claimant to effectively sue individually, the members of the class all have the same type of claim, and they all have similar damages.

If you own any shares of stock, you have probably received form letters and postcards telling you a company in which you own shares has been sued in a class action lawsuit for some violation of law or contract you never heard of. You are told that if you opt in to the class, you will be one of many plaintiffs and may be entitled to some compensation. Sometimes, the case has already gotten to the settlement stage, and all you have to do is respond to the letters and wait for the outcome. The people reaching out to you typically are the lawyers who are suing the company. If you decide to join the existing suit, that is, "opt in," they will be your lawyers. But who picked those people? Sometimes, a client hires them, but sometimes, they pick themselves.

Here is how it works. Some firms specialize in class action suits. A person might approach the firm with a case that the firm recognizes as one meeting all the criteria for a class action. An example is Anderson v. Pacific Gas & Electric Co., involving residents of a town suing for improper dumping of wastewater – this was the famous "Erin Brockovich" suit. You also may not have realized that Roe v. Wade was a class action, that is, many women suing over that constitutional issue.

It is also common that a class action firm will keep abreast of various companies on diverse topics affecting large groups of people or simply monitor the news for such controversies. When they find a basis for suit, they might seek out a single member of the class and invite that person to be the representative plaintiff.

Related to the idea that lawyers might initiate suit over a controversy that affects a large group of people or a large swath of society, it does not have to result in a class action. There are situations where the controversy is initiated, say, by activists, and that might turn into a class action or simply an action that affects a large group of people. One of the most renowned cases in American history was The State of Tennessee v. John Thomas Scopes. In 1925, Tennessee made it unlawful to deny the divine creation of man, banning the teaching of Darwin's theory of evolution. J. T. Scopes was a biology teacher who taught evolution in his classroom and was then prosecuted under the new law; this became known as the "Scopes Monkey Trial."

Mr. Scopes' violation of the law was set up by the American Civil Liberties Union (ACLU), intending to put the law to the test. The Scopes case was not a class action, though it addressed an important constitutional issue that affected an entire state. The ACLU, and its lawyer, Clarence Darrow, initiated things.

The Scopes Monkey Trial also led to one of the best plays of all time and a memorable movie (my opinion, of course), *Inherit the Wind*, starring Spencer Tracy as Clarence Darrow. Law buffs still study Darrow, controversial for other reasons in his time, but he was famous for his rhetoric in the courtroom.

Mass Torts

Mass tort cases are related to class actions. A mass tort is a civil action where numerous plaintiffs sue one or more defendants for injuries caused by the same or similar act or event, such as a plane crash (where all the passengers have the same cause for their claim) or an explosion in a factory injuring people nearby. The distinction is that with class actions, a single suit is filed by a representative claimant on behalf of everyone similarly situated, while a mass tort event will result in individual suits by all affected by the event.

As a practical matter, those many individual suits may be consolidated to the same judge because each claimant has a similar right or claim to be adjudicated, which affords a consistent outcome. In mass tort cases, you can hire your own lawyer, but it often happens that you end up with a lawyer who is already up to speed with other, similarly affected clients.

Insurance Defense

Here is a little insurance lesson. A fact little-known unless you're an insurance specialist is that you get two benefits from your "liability" insurance policy: (1) coverage for the loss, and (2) a lawyer, for free. By "liability," I am not talking about damage that happens to you, like fire, wind, or water damage to your house; this is called "first party" property coverage, that is, you are the first party and the insurance company is the second party; getting your property repaired is directly between you and the insurer. A liability claim, on the other hand, is when someone else makes a claim against you for negligence, and you have to defend yourself. That claimant is the "third-party", having no relationship to your insurance company.

Your homeowner's policy, or your renter's policy, will have both first-party (property damage to you) and third-party coverages (liability protection), and more. Your auto policy provides the same two protections; the insurer will pay for damage to your car (a first-party claim) and will pay for damage you cause with your car (a claim from a third party).

If you have a business, you will have a separate "commercial liability" policy. In a professional practice, you will have a policy covering your liability for malpractice, known as an "errors and omissions" policy. The liability coverage in your homeowner policy, your commercial liability policy (for your business), or your malpractice policy would be triggered by a claim made by a third person. The key term for third-party coverage is the use of the word "liability."

The first benefit under a "liability" policy is that when a claim or suit is made against you, you submit it to your insurance company (either directly or, often, through your insurance agent or broker). The liability insurance policy pays the amount you owe to the claimant if you are at fault, but what they pay is limited to the amount of insurance you purchased.[2] (If you owe more than the amount of insurance you have, well, that discussion is for an entirely different book, though your lawyer must explain it to you if that situation comes to pass.)

The second benefit of the "liability" insurance policy is that while the insurance company will pay a loss you caused, **they also provide you with a lawyer**

---

2 As mentioned earlier, in a no-fault state like New York, this discussion would apply to serious injury claims, not those falling into no-fault insurance policies.

– at the insurer's expense. In the industry, these lawyers are usually referred to as "insurance defense counsel" or just "defense counsel."

This is what I did for forty-eight years. Here is how it works. The insurance companies typically have a panel of approved law firms that specialize in the types of claims covered by the insurance policies they have issued. The law firms approved for the panel are selected by the insurance company based on experience and qualifications and will negotiate a specific hourly rate for all cases falling into certain categories. When a case is reported to the insurance company, a lawyer will be assigned to you from the panel. Some insurance companies employ their own lawyers to represent their insureds, sometimes called "house counsel" or "staff counsel."

Why don't you get to pick? Well, an insurance policy is a contract. The contract dictates that the insurance company controls the defense. You bought insurance under that contract, and that contract's terms say that if you want us to cover you, you must use our lawyers. There is an important reason for this.

Insurers are in the business of handling lawsuits. Sure, they may try to settle a claim before it gets to suit, and most claims are settled pre-suit. But those claims that can't be settled end up in suits by the thousands. Lawyers don't work cheap, and think of the cost of thousands of lawyers. Plus, since liability insurance policies require insurers to provide you with a lawyer at their expense, they get to use the lawyers they deem qualified, with whom they have negotiated rates, and they impose reporting requirements on them to track whether to settle as well as to monitor costs. In this situation, the insurer protects both your rights and its own bottom line.[3]

You may be surprised at the number of things an insurance policy covers; it is not just typical accidents, like auto collisions or slip and fall accidents. Accident cases often intersect with areas of law that are independent of the claims themselves, yet defense counsel must deal with such issues as part of

---

3 Insurer-appointed lawyers still have the ethical obligation of loyalty and zealous advocacy to their client, the insured. But the insurer also has, by contract, the contractual right to settle a case without the insured's consent under an typical liability (non-malpractice) policy – it's their money. Therefore, the insurer is entitled to all necessary information about the case. There are exceptions to this, but again, that kind of detail is not the intended scope of this book. Perhaps this is a good moment to add that almost everything in this publication is subject to exceptions, and what are stated here, in large part, are general rules. The point throughout is to educate you on how and why all this works.

protecting the client's interests. For example, a party to a case may file for bankruptcy. Defense counsel is unlikely to specialize in bankruptcy but must understand enough about it to know how the bankruptcy will affect the case, and might even have to file something in the bankruptcy court.

Something else that happens often is that the claimant may have an accident on the job and so files a workers' compensation case against the employer, but also sues someone else who had a hand in causing the accident. It is necessary to understand how the workers' compensation system works, and that doctors in the workers' compensation case may have to give opinions that are only applicable to that case, such as a disability rating, which is not relevant to the liability case.

Liability claims also require the lawyer to know or learn about an amazing variety of subjects to properly handle a case. I tell anyone who asks, especially students who might have an interest in becoming a lawyer, that *you will use and rely on literally every subject matter you ever studied in school.*

Someone injured in an accident will claim bodily injury. Bodily injuries include everything you can think of, whiplash (a so-called "soft tissue" injury), fractures, spinal injury, loss of limbs, illness (including cancer), para- and quadriplegia, loss of sight or hearing, burn injuries, and death, to name a few. Bodily injury claims also will include emotional injuries, like depression or post-traumatic stress disorder. Your lawyer must understand these conditions in determining whether the injury occurred, whether it was caused by the accident, and if so, the severity of the injury.

An auto accident requires your lawyer to understand how to reconstruct what happened, using geometry, physics, chemistry, and the like. If your case involves damage to a building, your lawyer must understand how buildings are designed (engineering/architecture) and built (all kinds of construction trades), and even surveying. If your case involves a defective product, your lawyer must understand how the product is designed and manufactured.

Some liability claims do not involve bodily injury, like damage to reputation, that is, defamation. Defamation breaks down into two categories: libel (written defamation) and slander (oral defamation). Libel might occur by making disparaging and untrue comments about a competitor in an online ad. Slander occurred in a recent case in the news, Jones v. Sandy Hook Families, where conspiracy theorist Alex Jones falsely claimed on television that the Sandy Hook shootings never happened, and the grieving parents were mere actors. He lost.

Sometimes, a defamatory statement is protected as free speech. In a famous case studied in law school, New York Times Co. v. Sullivan, a police commissioner sued for libelous statements about him in the newspaper, but it was found that criticism of public figures was a fundamental constitutional right, and so even something false or inaccurate about the public figure was deemed not to be defamation. There are limitations even to that; the police commissioner could have won the case if he were able to show what was published about him was *known* to be false.

Suffice it to say, in my opinion, lawyers working on either side of liability cases arguably have the widest range of subject matter, requiring an ability to learn about many aspects of how the world goes around, and must have the ability to synthesize that knowledge in ways that best help to advance their client's case.

Guardianship and Conservatorship

There are situations where a person is incompetent to select their own lawyer. "Competency" in the law does not have the everyday meaning we think of, like whether you are capable of, or "competent at," doing your job. Rather, competency in the law means that the law deems you sufficiently mentally able, or you have the capacity, to understand your rights and responsibilities to allow you to legally bind yourself into transactions, like contracts or purchases.

As a matter of law, minors (under the age of eighteen in California), are deemed (automatically) incompetent. (California Family Code, §6500) Minors cannot enter into contracts without parental consent, hold certain kinds of jobs, purchase alcohol or tobacco, etc. If a minor has a claim, it must be brought by a representative, that is, a parent or guardian. (Part Two of this book is a story about an injury to a minor. In that case, his father is appointed by the court to serve as his "guardian ad litem" (In Latin, "ad litem" translates as "for the lawsuit."

Other than minors, there are people who are, or become, incapacitated, mentally or physically, to the point that they are incompetent to care for themselves and thus require protection or representation. Guardianship and conservatorship are related situations. Guardianship focuses on the personal care and well-being of a minor or incapacitated adult, while conservatorship focuses on managing the financial affairs of an incapacitated person.

A guardianship might occur, for example, where both of a child's parents die. Wills usually name who the guardian should be. The guardian makes all personal decisions for the minor until adulthood, just as a parent would do.

Conservatorship, on the other hand, applies to manage the affairs of an incompetent adult. Because it is a situation involving adults, those adults have rights. Therefore, when someone becomes mentally disabled, a court hearing to appoint a conservator is required. The result of that hearing, if the conservatorship is approved, is one where the court may remove those rights from the person. As such, it is an adversary proceeding and the disabled person must be separately represented by counsel to fight to keep those rights if appropriate to do so. Yet, in keeping with the theme of this chapter, counsel is selected for that person.

The Lawyer-Client Relationship

CHAPTER SIX

During my years of practice, I made it a point to keep my clients updated, and did so as frequently as my hectic schedule would allow. I always picked up the phone when a client called, regardless of whether it was an interruption of another important activity. I gave them my cell phone number and encouraged them to use it. I responded to emails with immediacy if possible. I did this even if I had people in my office, or maybe I was working on a brief due in court on a close deadline, or I may have been running through an airport. Regardless, I always took the call or got back to clients as soon as I could. There are three reasons for this.

First, I have always taken to heart that I am my client's representative, counselor, advocate, and protector. Whether the client is the plaintiff or the defendant, the client often will be a stranger to the process, baffled by the unfamiliar, lengthy ordeal, and nervous about the outcome. Communicating creates a relationship, even if it lasts only as long as the case, which enables the client to understand better what is going on, eases the tension, and tunes them in to think about information helpful to the case that maybe they had not initially realized was important.

Second, related to the above, that relationship gets the client involved and contributing to the progress of the case. I mentioned the "client interview" earlier. Whether the attorney-client relationship starts with a call from a client or an assignment from an insurer, that first contact is particularly important and needs to be done as soon as possible. In addition to basic information needed for decisions about deadlines (explained later), you need to hear the story of what happened.

When people give their version of the story, they want to do it in their own words, but they can be invested, sometimes emotionally, in what they say.

Believe me this is true, it is often the case that they have no clue what is important and what isn't. Yet, a lawyer must listen to the whole thing. This provides valuable information.

For example, your client may be much too talkative, maybe expressing things, shall we say, colorfully. Knowing this, you can coach them out of that if you think their form of expression may not be well-received in the form of testimony. That said, there are people whose personalities are such that you just have to live with whatever comes out of their mouths despite your best efforts.

The lawyer should ask in the interview who the witnesses are and what did they say. When did things occur? Are there photographs or videos of what happened? The client will answer your questions, often leaving out details they do not realize could be crucial. That's why the relationship matters, because these things come out eventually, often after several conversations during the evolution of the case. Therefore, it is important to include the client in the lawyer's thinking and to solicit their input, particularly so when the client is a technical specialist, say, a construction contractor, who can teach you about how their business, products, and operations. But as a client, remember, be sure not to discuss the lawyer's thinking with anyone, even family, if there is a risk the information will get out.

Third, a lawyer is in a service business. It is good business to communicate, to be available, and to be responsive. People appreciate it when they feel their interests are being served. They feel their interests are being served when their questions are answered, and they are included in the plan of action. When they feel that way, they become invested in the process, which can only help the case. They become your partners in the endeavor that takes up those couple of years to resolve, and that is how it should be.

So, if you are a client, initiate the relationship, provide details, and understand the case as best as you can with input from your lawyer; in that way, you can contribute helpful information. If you are a lawyer, cultivate the relationship and share updates. As stated, be wary of the fact that some people do not understand the seriousness of the attorney-client privilege and will blab your strategies to anyone who will listen. But after you give that caution, don't be afraid to explain the strategies and talk about why some moves succeeded while some did not. If both sides of the relationship follow this course, it will advance the objectives of the case and increase the chances of success.

Fee Structures – You Charged Me for What?

CHAPTER SEVEN

Law firms are for-profit organizations. Oh, you already knew that. There are three basic kinds of fee structures, with variations: contingency fees, hourly fees, and flat fees.

The lawyer-client relationship is contractual; the lawyer agrees to provide legal services, and the client agrees to pay for those services. The contract is called a "lawyer retainer agreement," or just "retainer agreement." Not all states require such a written contract, but it is highly advisable and best practice to eliminate any misunderstanding as to what the services will consist of and the terms and timing of payment. In California, if the fee is at least $1,000, there must be a written retainer agreement.

The retainer agreement should contain at least the following terms:

1. The nature of the fee (contingent, hourly, or flat) and clearly identify the percentage or amount, when and how payment is due, and what the charges will cover.

2. What services will be provided, such as handling your claim arising from the automobile accident of such and such a date against the specific defendant.

3. What services will not be included, such as pursuing an appeal for the same fee amount, representation on any other matter, or providing tax advice, etc.

4. A cooperation provision.

5. When and how the client or the lawyer can withdraw from the agreement; and

6. How any disputes about the agreement will be handled.

Contingency Fees and an Illustration of How They Work

No win, no fee, no cost. People from all walks of life need access to the legal system. Hourly rates vary by region, type of law, and demand for any particular lawyer's expertise. Say a lawyer's standard hourly fee is $500/hr. The case will last a year or more, will be actively contested, and multiple lawyers within the firm will participate. The estimated cost of the case might be over a million dollars, plus hundreds of thousands of dollars in other costs. Can you afford that?

Now, think about an accident that could happen to someone who clearly could not afford to pay an hourly fee. Let's say the injured party is a construction laborer, earning $30/hr, or about $52,000/yr. This laborer is on his way home, and his Toyota Camry is pushed off the road by a truck as part of a multi-vehicle pileup in the fog. His car crashes into the guardrail of the freeway and explodes, causing him severe burns. Can our laborer afford to pay an hourly fee to recover compensation for his injuries? Obviously not. What a contingency fee does is even the playing field; that is, it provides fair access to justice, not limiting it just to those who can pay.

Contingency arrangements can vary, but the basic setup is that the lawyer pays for everything: the lawyers and paralegals employed to work on the case, fees to file papers in court, expert witnesses to help prove the case, and other outside vendors necessary in the litigation process. The lawyer is investing in the case.

If the case is lost, the lawyer loses his or her investment, but the client pays nothing. If the case is settled or a judgment is obtained, the client now has to pay the lawyer's fee, calculated as a percentage of the amount received, and you have to pay the lawyer back for the costs incurred for you. You will receive a written calculation of how the money will be distributed. Let's show how this would look if our laborer client settles for $4 million:

Settlement: $4 million

Fees at 40%: ($1.6 million)

Experts: ($250,000) (including three doctors, two engineers, and an accountant)

Reimbursement to medical providers: ($160,000)

Court and litigation vendor Costs: ($80,000)

Net to Client: $1,910,000

Did the client (the plaintiff) get enough? Be careful, this is a trick question. Proving a liability injury case requires a showing of two factors: (1) that the defendant is at fault and (2) the damages. The damages include the amount that will compensate the plaintiff for his medical costs (past and future), lost earnings (past and future), and pain and suffering (the amount attributed to enduring the pain, inconvenience, disfigurement, and change of life circumstances caused by the injury). To know if the above settlement was a good deal, we have to know more about the case. The following set of hypothetical facts will illustrate how a contingent fee structure works. And you will at the same time learn a little about how a negligence case is evaluated.

We'll start with factor (2), the damages, or the value of the injury. How severely burned was the client? Assume he had the awful pain that can be caused by a burn injury, had to undergo graft surgery on his forearm, and will have a nasty scar for the rest of his life, but the pain subsided, and he can go back to work relatively quickly. In today's verdict climate, $4 million may be considered a very good settlement.

Now, let's change the assumption and say he was burned over seventy percent of his body, nearly died, will never work again, and will require frequent medical care for the rest of his life. It is likely a jury, again in today's dollars, would award many millions more. So, why did he and his lawyer agree to take only $4 million?

Let's go back to factor (1). Who was at fault? Finding fault breaks down into whether the defendant has an obligation (a duty) to be careful as to the plaintiff, that the defendant was not careful, and that the defendant's lack of care resulted in (caused) the injury.

Scenario 1: Let's assume the police report described the accident like this:

Toyota with injured driver: Toyota found at rest on the right shoulder with obvious collision and burn damage. The injured driver had been removed by fire personnel before my arrival and taken to the hospital. On interview with the injured driver at the hospital, he was medicated for pain but related that he was driving in the number 4 (right) lane at approximately 55 mph, below the 65 mph speed limit due to foggy conditions, when a big rig truck in the number 3 lane, immediately to his left, suddenly swerved into his lane and collided with his vehicle.

Truck driver: Peterbilt truck pulling a five-axle trailer found parked on the right shoulder north of the Toyota, with light damage to the right side of the trailer just above the rear wheels. Truck driver related that he was traveling in the number 3 lane at approximately 55 mph due to foggy conditions when a light-colored pickup truck ahead of him suddenly braked, causing him to have to veer to the right to avoid a collision. He did not feel the impact with the Toyota, but heard a horn honking to his right and saw the Toyota hit the guardrail out of his right mirror. The truck driver did not have any further identifying information for the pickup ahead of him, which continued on after the accident.

Conclusion: Truck driver is at fault for following too closely for the weather conditions, despite driving under the 65-mph speed limit. [Vehicle Code §22350.]

Assuming these facts are verifiable in court, the plaintiff (the laborer driving the Toyota) is essentially free of fault. Traffic was not particularly congested if it was moving at 55 mph, though slowed due to poor visibility, so there was the opportunity to maintain more distance from the pickup ahead of the big rig, especially under those conditions. Therefore, the truck driver bears some or all of the fault for lack of caution to leave enough space. Based on this allocation of fault, if the laborer was severely burned as in the second outcome described above, the $4 million does not seem enough.

Scenario 2: What if the police report said this instead? (I have underlined the change to the truck driver's story, added another witness's version of the accident, and further investigation by the officer based on the witness's statement.)

Toyota with injured driver: Toyota found at rest on the right shoulder with obvious collision and burn damage. The injured driver had been removed by fire personnel before our arrival and taken to the hospital. On interview with the Toyota driver at the hospital, he was medicated for pain but related that he was driving in the number 4 (right) lane at approximately 55 mph, below the speed limit due to foggy conditions, when a big rig truck in the number 3 lane, immediately to his left, suddenly swerved into his lane and collided with his vehicle.

Truck driver: Peterbilt truck pulling a 5-axle trailer found parked on the right shoulder north of the Toyota, with light damage to the right side of the trailer just above the rear wheels. The truck driver related that he was traveling in the number 3 lane at approximately 55 mph due to foggy conditions when a light-colored pickup truck ahead of him suddenly braked, causing him to have to veer to the right to avoid a collision. <u>Before he had to swerve, there was no traffic to his right. He had noted a small car that was tailgating him for a couple of miles, causing him concern because of the fog.</u> He did not feel the impact with the Toyota, but heard a horn honking to his right and saw the Toyota hit the guardrail out of his right mirror. The truck driver did not have any further identifying information for the car ahead of him, which continued on after the accident.

Witness (Honda): Related that she was traveling in the same direction as the accident vehicles in the number 2 lane (third from the right shoulder) and to the left of the truck and Toyota. She was slightly behind the truck to her right. Just before the accident, she noted the Toyota closely following the truck in the number 3 lane which she remembered because it seemed too close considering the weather conditions. She did not see what caused the truck to veer to the right nor did she see the truck hit the Toyota, rather it appeared to her that the Toyota steered to the right to avoid the truck stopping in front of him, then careen into the guardrail on the right. Because she proceeded forward, she was past seeing the explosion but heard the pop. She pulled over as soon as she could.

Subsequent Investigation: I contacted the department's special accident investigator and asked her to check the event data recorder (EDR) in the Toyota.[1] I was told the data shows steering input occurred at about the time of the accident consistent with the statement provided by the witness. I then located the Toyota at the impound lot and found the injured driver's cell phone. I returned to the hospital and asked the injured driver to unlock

---

1   An event data recorder (EDR) or electronic control module (ECM), is not unlike the black boxes found in airplanes. It is a device that records information about the vehicle before, during, and after a crash. Depending on how old your car is, you probably have one.

the phone. At that time, I noted a text exchange at about the time of the accident, and the last entry was by the driver, but only partially typed.

Conclusion: Truck driver is at fault for following too closely for the weather conditions, despite driving under the 65-mph speed limit. [Vehicle Code 22350.] Toyota driver is at fault for following too closely for the weather conditions, despite driving under the 65-mph speed limit. [Vehicle Code 22350.] Toyota driver is also at fault for texting and driving. [Vehicle Code 23123.5.]

If the case had gone to trial on Scenario 2, the result would probably be that both the plaintiff and the truck driver would be found at fault in some percentage. Considering that the plaintiff might be found substantially at fault for texting and driving, and that his statement about which lane he was in was incorrect (or maybe even false), his damage award would be substantially reduced. Therefore, it might be reasonable to accept $4 million even for a claim with injuries that might otherwise have gotten three or four times that amount.

There is yet another reason the plaintiff would accept an amount that does not fully compensate him, even if the plaintiff is fault-free. If the case had gone to trial, a jury might have awarded, say, $15 million for the severe injuries. During the litigation, though, it might come out that the truck driver (the defendant) has his own independent business; he is not an employee of a giant company. He has insurance, but the limit of that insurance is – wait for it - $4 million. The truck driver has only a small-sized business and lives in a modest neighborhood. His earnings are barely enough to support his family, and he has no savings. Even though the law would allow the plaintiff to go after his assets beyond his insurance, there would be no point to it. Frankly, this is something that happens every day.

How is the plaintiff affected under these scenarios? Let's summarize. If he did recover from injuries that healed and were not life-changing, he got a good deal; maybe he was even over-compensated. He had to take less, though, if his actions contributed to the accident. Or, maybe he was forced to be under-compensated if there was insufficient insurance.

Keep in mind, there are plenty of people out there who have much less insurance, like $15,000, or maybe have no insurance at all. The ability to collect also affects whether the lawyer will accept the case, given how much would have to be put into it, as does the lawyer's opinion about whether the prospective client was so at fault that the case could be lost.

There is one more point to make on the topic of how contingent fees work. Let's assume the value of the plaintiff's case is exactly $4 million, all factors considered. But the plaintiff will get less than half that after his lawyer is paid and all other costs are reimbursed. This is the price to be paid to have the attorney advance all the costs and labor and to accept the risk of losing it all if the case is lost. Without the contingent fee, however, the client could be shut out of the system, unable to pursue his claim. A trade-off, but it ensures the ability to pursue a claim.

Hourly Fees and an Illustration of How They Work

An hourly fee is what you pay your lawyer, win or lose. We are now talking about almost all kinds of litigation practice other than plaintiff cases taken on contingency. The concept is the same as other services, where you are charged for time spent on specific tasks and for costs associated with the work.

Let's say client Joe Schmoe is accused of building a block wall that supposedly encroached on his neighbor's property, and he sues to force it to be taken down and relocated. The original cost of the wall was $40,000 in engineering plans, contractor fees, material costs, and permit fees.

Joe realizes that rectifying the problem is more complicated than the original construction, because of demolition and relocation, and will cost another $50,000 in labor, engineering, and permit costs. Joe has a surveyor examine the situation and is told the neighbor is wrong, Joe has not built the wall in the wrong place.

Joe does his due diligence in finding a land use lawyer, Anne Dewey, using the recommendations in Chapter Five about how to find and vet a lawyer, and he is at the initial interview meeting with Ms. Dewey. "Anne, my surveyor says the case against me is defensible. If you agree and will accept the case, how much do you think it will cost, how much do you charge, and please explain how your invoices will be presented."

Ms. Dewey reviews the survey and preliminarily agrees that Joe may have a good defense, subject to other facts and information that could come out during the litigation. She makes clear she cannot guarantee an outcome because Joe's survey could be flawed, or even the historical city records about the location of the property line could be incorrect, noting the municipal records are eighty years old.

She tells Joe she can respond to the suit, which will cost a few hours of time and a $435 filing fee. She will have to hire either Joe's surveyor or someone else she selects as a more experienced expert on the subject to testify. She also tells you the work needed on the case will take at least six months, and possibly require about fifty attorney hours, though it could be much more if the plaintiff's side is aggressive in their litigation activity.

She says her fees are $500/hr. But her junior associate, Rob Berry, will conduct most of the work at $300/hr. The minimum time for any task will be one tenth of an hour, or six minutes (the time entry will appear as ".1". (Think about what this means. One quick call to the associate, lasting maybe three minutes, costs $30.)

Ms. Dewey estimates the minimum cost of the case at $20,000 with fees, filing fees, litigation costs, and the cost of the expert. Since the firm has no track record with Joe, she will require a $10,000 advance retainer, which will be held in her client trust account, to be taken out only with Joe's approval of her monthly invoice. When that amount is spent, Joe will have to replenish it.

Now, what does Joe do? If the case is lost, Joe will be out $20,000 in attorney's fees and costs and still have to pay $50,000 to relocate the wall. Plus, the original $40,000 construction cost will have been wasted. And the court might make Joe pay the plaintiff's court costs, too. But Joe is certain he did the work correctly. Should he invest in the case or agree to move the wall to avoid litigation?

Joe asks Ms. Dewey if there is any other way to deal with the problem. She says he might be able to settle the case by offering to buy the six-inch strip of land along the border of the two properties where the wall now stands for, say, $25,000. Hmm, maybe. What if the plaintiff refuses or asks for a lot more? But then, doesn't the plaintiff also have to consider how much it will cost him to sue? Maybe a settlement is the best choice and should be attempted.

With this illustration, you see a quite common dilemma. No lawyer in his or her right mind will guarantee a result. There are too many variables. The client's case will be lost, though seemingly solid at the start, if the surveyor turns out to be wrong. Even if Joe's defense is good, the lawyer on the other side might be one who likes to run up the fees, costing Joe anyway.

Though it will not be part of the illustrative story in Part Two of the book, there are some ways lawyers can use the pre-trial activity process to increase the cost of the case, often as a tactic. And the judge to whom the case is assigned may be one who is known to have a very congested calendar, which will lengthen the case, and the judge may have a reputation for requiring many status conferences, which will mean going to court (and charging the client for it) over and over.

With procedures and tactics that require time and resources, and since the outcome of a case is so often uncertain, the client faces an unpleasant and costly reality: when someone chooses to sue you, they can cause you loss even if you are in the right. The choice to sue may be a strategy to force your hand.

Maybe the plaintiff in our block wall case wanted to break his neighbor's resistance to moving the wall, or maybe he was just hoping to fleece the neighbor in a settlement. Maybe the plaintiff happens to be a lawyer and will not incur any fees by handling it himself. It happens. The defendant here always has the choice to proceed on principle, that is, go to trial and win the case, and collect costs from the plaintiff, but, in our hypothetical wall case, not before paying his lawyer $20,000.[2] Even so, after that win, the wall would have a net cost of $60,000 (the original $40,000 construction cost and the $20,000 in attorney's fees) to ward off the lawsuit. And the client would still have the headache of the suit to boot.

Let's pretend the case goes forward. A month has gone by. Joe receives an invoice from the firm. This invoice would be sent to you asking for payment, or, in the alternative, to approve the charges and authorize the money to be taken from the $10,000 retainer held in the client trust account. Remember, the money in the client trust account is the client's money, not the lawyer's, and cannot be taken into the firm's general account until the client approves it.

This is what it looks like:

---

2 Once again, we come upon an issue for another book. Why not win the case and collect attorney's fees? Attorney's fees are not recoverable unless provided for in a contract in dispute or if allowed by statute. Neither applies in our block wall case. So the plaintiff is free to play the fleecing strategy, if that is the plan.

<u>DEWEY CHEATEM & HOWE, APC</u>

Invoice 1234 - 1/31/25

Case Name: Mean Neighbor v. Homeowner Client

DATE	PROVIDER	DESCRIPTION	HOURS	RATE	TOTAL
1/2/25	AD	Initial client meeting.	1.2	$500	$600.00
1/6/25	RB	Review client's survey report	.3	$300	$160.00
1/6/25	AD	Telephone conference with plaintiff's counsel to discuss possible settlement.	.2	$500	$100.00
1/7/25	AD	Receive call from plaintiff's counsel rejecting settlement.	.1	$500	$50.00
1/7/25	RB	Prepare, file, and serve answer to complaint.	1.0	$300	$300.00
1/7/25	RB	Telephone conference with expert, Forensic Survey, Inc. to retain and arrange for property inspection. (Sent client materials for review.)	.2	$300	$60.00
1/7/25	RB	Prepare discovery to plaintiff, including interrogatories and seeking documents.	1	$300	$300.00
1/23/25	RB	Receive served discovery requests from plaintiff's counsel and draft responses. (Task included responding to 47 interrogatories and 6 document requests.)	3.6	$300	$1080.00
1/27/25	RB	Attend property inspection with expert FSI.	2.2	$300	$660.00
1/27/25	RB	Travel to and from property inspection event. (Billed at ½ rate.)	.5	$150	$75.00
		TOTAL MONTHLY FEES	7.8		$3385.00
1/29/25	Costs	Forensic Survey Inc. Invoice 203			$2500.00
		PAY THIS TOTAL			**$5,885.00**

Adds up fast, doesn't it? In one month, the client is charged more than half the $10,000 retainer amount, and the case is just getting started. Do the charges look legit to you? How would you know?

Some tasks should seem intuitive. For example, the lawyer does have to read the material provided, whether from the client, the opponent, or the expert. "Discovery", discussed later, is the process each side uses to find out the facts of the dispute; in fact, putting off discovery could be considered poor lawyering. The lawyer has to talk to people on the phone, and sure, Anne and the dastardly opposing counsel may have spent part of the call chit-chatting about the weather, but the lawyer is entitled to charge for the reasonable time spent on the client's business. (Maybe the need to chat up opposing counsel was tactical to keep him off guard before springing the settlement idea on him.) He then checks with his client overnight; they decide the number is too little and it is too soon to consider a counteroffer. This results in a second call to reject the offer.

What about the travel time entry? The retainer agreement would likely mention that travel time is billable, but at a lower rate; the lawyer is spending time working for the client while going to and coming from the property inspection that he would otherwise spend working on someone else's case. But he might make a couple of business calls from the car, hence the lower rate to accommodate that possibility.

Why did it take more than three and a half hours to work on the discovery? Notice the time entry informs Joe that quite a few items had to be addressed. Never having done it himself, he has little basis to understand why it can't be done faster or why it takes as long as it takes. But if Joe looks into it, he might find that the forty-eight questions (interrogatories) were complicated, and Rob Berry had to look up a lot of things. On the other hand, he might find the forty-eight questions sought elementary information that a paralegal or secretary could have answered off the top of their heads in a half hour while Rob surfed the internet for a new set of golf clubs.

Billing is a kind of honor system, and by and large, lawyers are straight people. However, overbilling happens, which is why a client must pay attention to the invoices and ask questions if needed. You do have the right to inquire and have the charges explained to you. Later, in the discussion about how insurance companies deal with overcharging, you will see there can be distinct tension about billing.

And by the way, the great writer of legal fiction, John Grisham, centered one of his most famous stories, The Firm, around improper billing. If you haven't read the book or seen the film starring Tom Cruise, the law firm's biggest client was the mob, and their billings were heavily exaggerated. By putting the invoices into the U.S. mail, the fraudulent billing became a federal crime.[3]

Billing for Insurance Defense Services

The basic method of hourly fee billing is the same regardless of the size of the client or whether the client is an individual or an organization. The invoice looks about the same as the one from our block wall case, showing the date the work was done, who did it, a description of the work task, and a calculation of the charge, with all entries summed up at the bottom. Expenses are always "below the line," that is, they follow the time entry total.

Organizations frequently involved in lawsuits incur huge legal costs. Like any business, or anyone for that matter, the goal is to maximize income and minimize expenses. The more legal services are needed, the more impact on the bottom line. Curbing legal costs can be an important factor to consider on financial agendas.

I mentioned earlier that insurers are in the business of handling lawsuits. Though most claims are settled by insurers before they become lawsuits, even the small percentage that do become lawsuits total in the many thousands and are always pending in any insurer's claims department, hundreds assigned per claims person. Consequently, much of the insurance industry is particularly aggressive in strategizing to hold down legal costs for liability claims.

Once a law firm is approved to be on an insurer's approved defense counsel list, that is, "on panel," there will be a retainer agreement dictated by the insurer. The retainer agreement requires the firm to comply with a published set of "guidelines" for handling cases. This is a misnomer. They are not guidelines, they are contract terms – if you do not comply, you do not get paid.

---

3 Check the top of the invoice showing the name of Anne Dewey's law firm is Dewey, Cheatem & Howe. This comical law firm name was a gag used by the Three Stooges in a publicity photo, sometime before the mid-1950s. You should also know that Anne Dewey is married to Burnham N. Runne, also a lawyer, with the divorce firm of Ditcher, Quick & Hyde.

Here are some examples of the restrictions:

1. Only certain lawyers within the firm are permitted to work on the case, maybe a certain partner and the usual team associated with that partner's cases. If someone else does something, even out of necessity, the insurer will refuse to pay for that time. In actual practice, it is nearly impossible to comply with this rule consistently.

2. Permission is needed from the insurance claims person to conduct legal research. Research? That is the lifeblood of practicing law. The presumption seems to be that all the law needed to understand a case, provide advice about it, and include in legal briefs to be filed in court, is already in the lawyer's head, including the precise legal citations. In actual practice, this requirement affects literally everything the lawyer does. And you have to remember to reach out for permission or you do not get paid.

3. Permission is needed to hire experts. Experts include doctors, engineers, and other professionals. In a bodily injury case, you have the right to have the plaintiff examined by a doctor. You may need a surveyor, like in Joe's block wall case. You may need a specialty engineer to analyze how an auto accident happened, like reconstructing how close the big rig was to the car in front, as in our foggy pile-up case, or even someone to analyze data from the plaintiff's cell phone, like the police officer did in that case.

4. Experts tend to charge a lot. The insurer understandably reserves the right to approve your experts and their charges, possibly vetoing some or asking for a delay in hiring them so the case can possibly be settled before the expense is incurred. This can be tricky, though, because the insurer may be interfering with the lawyer's professional judgment on who the best expert might be for any particular case and thus force the use of someone who may not be as effective on behalf of the client.

5. Travel is to be charged at half rate and only if pre-approved. It is fair for the insurer, who has to pay for your time, to control the cost of

out-of-town travel, like airfare, hotel, taxi, and meals. But what about going to the courthouse or to local meetings outside the office?

- In some smaller municipal areas, all the law offices might be practically across the street from each other and the courthouse. If you practice in New York City, with its excellent municipal transport system, you might be able to hop on a subway and avoid the heavy traffic. On the other hand, in a city like Los Angeles, the circumstances are quite different. The city is so spread out that public transportation is not always useful.

- In Los Angeles, there are thirty-six courthouses. The City of Los Angeles is forty-four miles from north to south and twenty-nine miles from east to west. Los Angeles County stretches as far as one hundred miles, depending on direction. As everyone knows, people in Los Angeles are dependent on their cars. Adding in constant traffic delays, it can take a long time to get anywhere, even for short distances. Yet, under insurance billing rules, one size fits all sizes or municipalities. The lawyers have to eat that time, which effectively reduces the billable rate.

6. No billing for intra-office conferences. The aim here is that the insurer does not want to pay to train a young lawyer. Yet, practicing law can be a collaborative process, where an effective strategy comes about simply by talking it over with your colleagues. This is an arbitrary rule, but it's in the contract.

7. Some insurers will not accept an invoice earlier than ninety days. This means it takes longer to get paid, and the expenses the firm incurs are out of pocket that much longer. This, again, impacts the law firm's profitability. Any accountant will tell you that lagging collections matter in any business.

8. Insurers will not pay for "block billing." Block billing is listing multiple tasks in one time entry. Adding all the tasks together, the time entry might be completely fair, but the insurer wants to see how

long any individual task takes and what it costs. This is fair if not taken to the extreme.

9. Insurers will not pay for, or at least question, vague billing descriptions. It is fair to ask for an understandable task description, but objecting to a charge on this ground can be abused. It is clear to say, for example, "Telephone call with opposing counsel to discuss settlement"; you have said what is was about. It is inadequate to say, "Telephone call with opposing counsel." You really may have had the call and discussed something legitimate, but the client wants to know what's going on.

10. The most difficult, and frankly insulting, objection to a task entry is to question the amount of time the task took. Did the call take six minutes or less? Ten minutes? A half hour? Should it have taken less time? Did writing a motion take five hours? Ten hours? Should it have taken less time? Some lawyers are more efficient than others. Some motions are everyday stuff that require minor changes to an existing template. Other motions must be drafted from scratch and can take days. A lot depends on the nature of the issue. I could have a photographic memory of the law, and my administrative assistant and I might have the fastest keyboard skills imaginable. Yet, there are motions that simply take hours and hours. Then, the insurance company cuts the time in half, providing no substantive reason other than, "Task took more time than necessary." To get paid for the actual time then requires more unbillable time to explain the work and argue about it.

There are many other kinds of rules and limitations in the so-called billing guidelines. The time cuts may be challenged, but the system is rigged because the onus is on the lawyer to justify the time, not on the insurer, who provides no reason for the cuts in the first place, and the insurer remains the sole judge of your further explanation. Frustrating.

The bottom line here is that hourly billing is the dominant way legal services are charged. Not everyone has the economic power of a large organization like an insurance company, but you are entitled to clear and fair billing before you approve and pay for hourly legal services, or for hourly-billed services in any industry, for that matter.

Flat Fees

Lawyers often charge flat fees for predictable, straightforward legal services like drafting wills, handling uncontested divorces, or basic real estate transactions, providing clients with a fixed price upfront. Other examples include business formation, certain kinds of standard contracts, copyright registrations, and personal bankruptcy filings. In these situations, you get a bill with a single number showing that your will was prepared, or your corporation has been set up. (Don't let this short description leave you with the impression that flat fee legal services are not widely used or do not require expertise. It is just that the nature of the work is more predictable in terms of the time required and results provided.)

Essential Legalese

CHAPTER EIGHT

In Part Two, you are going to hear the tragic story of an unfortunate accident. We will construct the case from scratch, hire the lawyers, file the suit, conduct the discovery, file motions, try to settle it, and take it to trial. We will start with what happened, move through the stages and major events of the litigation, with interspersed explanation, returning to the story as we go along.

An important note here. Part Two's accident involves a severe injury, and the victim is a child. I needed the narrative to involve a big case, one with a very high possible verdict. The lawsuit has to show you some of the intensity, illustrate the sympathy factor that always exists in a catastrophic case, how the clients cope, and how the lawyers must carefully consider the potential outcome and develop appropriate strategies. The story will illustrate some of the complications, such as motions in court and the analysis involved in trying to settle the case.

Some of you may find reading about the injury sequence to be difficult. Maybe some of you know someone who has suffered a terrible injury. Trust me, though, it will be okay in the end, but you have to follow along to understand the medical issues, how the injury is explained in the arguments at trial, and wait to see what happens while the jury is out and the parties are anticipating the verdict.

Before going down that path, and in order to fully appreciate what is going on, it is important for you to understand the lingo. The practice of law, like many other professions, has its own technical terminology. Medical practice, for example, is largely based on the Greek language (with Latin as well).[1]

---

1 They really get Greek and Latin on you when naming medicines. How about "semaglutide" or "empagliflozin"? Maybe that's why they came up with Ozempic and Jardiance instead. Or how about the medical condition called "myocardial infarction?" Don't have a heart attack trying to figure it out.

Legal terms derive substantially from Latin roots, prefixes, and suffixes. I already gave you some word and phrase meanings, often showing you the Latin derivation. It will help you to liberally check the glossary of frequently used words and phrases at the end of the book. The glossary of key terms is my own creation. Many of the definitions are adapted from the Legal Terms Glossary of the Department of Justice, Offices of the United States Attorneys, with my added spin. I provide examples for some terms to help you get the concept. The definitions, by necessity, use other terms that also must be understood; I have put those other terms, in the glossary definitions, in italics to prompt you to find them as well for full context.

As the story progresses, I also provide some definitions in the text. Again, if you find yourself losing the thread of what's happening because of legal terminology, head to the glossary as needed. (There are also legal dictionaries available online. Just do an internet search for "legal dictionary.")

Before we move on to an explanation of how lawsuits are carried out, it will also help you to see what some legal documents look like and how they are formatted. The documents, in their own way, are part of the lingo. Some key terms explaining the documents may send you to the glossary; they are *italicized*. Below is an example of what a *complaint* looks like. The *complaint* example below is the lawsuit filed because of the accident that is the subject of Part Two of this book. That lawsuit is called Smithson v. Family Swim Club and Got You Covered Technologies.

The area below the court's name is called the "caption." The left side of the caption shows the names and roles of the parties and who is suing whom. On the right is the case number in the court record, the name and courtroom of the judge, the identity of the *pleading* (this particular *pleading* is a *complaint*), and the *causes of action* (the legal theories the lawsuit is based on). Notice also that the court stamp shows the case has been *filed*. The stamp usually appears at the top of the page or in the open space to the right of the address lines. Notice the lines are numbered in the left margin. This is so that any sentence or other entry can be found easily. For example, the name of the plaintiffs' lawyer, Anne Dewey, can be found at page one, line one. (Yes, she's back from her block wall case she handled for Joe Schmo.)

1 ANNE I. DEWEY, ESQ. STATE BAR 412345
Anne@deweycheatem.com
2 ISSA ROBERT BERRY, ESQ. STATE BAR #554321
Rob@deweycheatem.com
3 DEWEY CHEATEM & HOWE, APC
4 2000 Fault Line Street, 36th Floor
Los Angeles, California 90014
5 Telephone No. (213) 555-4321
Facsimile No. (213) 555-4329
6

7

8 Attorneys for Plaintiffs, PAUL SMITHSON; PATTY SMITHSON; and PETER SMITHSON, a
9 minor, by and through his Guardian ad Litem PAUL SMITHSON

10 **SUPERIOR COURT OF THE STATE OF CALIFORNIA**

11 **FOR THE COUNTY OF LOS ANGELES**

12

PAUL SMITHSON; PATTY SMITHSON; and PETER SMITHSON, a minor, by and through his Guardian ad Litem PAUL SMITHSON.	CASE NO. 21STCV887766
	Assigned to Hon. Lourdes O. Veryou, Dept. 2
Plaintiffs,	**COMPLAINT FOR:**
vs.	1. **NEGLIGENCE**
	2. **NEGLIGENT INFLICTION OF EMOTIONAL DISTRESS**
FAMILY SWIM CLUB, LLC. A California limited liability company: GOT YOU COVERED TECHNOLOGIES, INC., a New Jersey corporation, DOES 1 to 50, inclusive,	3. **PREMISES LIABILITY**
	4. **PRODUCT LIABILITY**
Defendants.	Complaint filed: March 12, 2024
	Trial Date: Unassigned

13
14
15
16
17
18
19
20
21
22

23　　　Plaintiffs, for each cause of action against Defendants, FAMILY SWIM CLUB, LLC. A

24 California limited liability company: GOT YOU COVERED TECHNOLOGIES, INC., a New

25 Jersey corporation and demanding a trial by jury, complain and allege upon information and belief

26 as follows:

27

28

Once the case starts, the discovery process will begin, often with each side sending a set of *interrogatories* to the other side along with a *request for production* of documents relevant to the case. Below is a sample of the first page of a set of *interrogatories* sent by the *plaintiffs* to one of the *defendants*, Family Swim Club, LLC:

1 ANNE I. DEWEY, ESQ. STATE BAR 412345
Anne@deweycheatem.com
2 ISSA ROBERT BERRY, ESQ. STATE BAR #554321
Rob@deweycheatem.com
3 DEWEY CHEATEM & HOWE, APC
4 2000 Fault Line Street, 36th Floor
Los Angeles, California 90014
5 Telephone No. (213) 555-4321
Facsimile No. (213) 555-4329
6

7

8 Attorneys for Plaintiffs, PAUL SMITHSON; PATTY SMITHSON; and PETER SMITHSON, a
minor, by and through his Guardian ad Litem JEROME SMITHSON
9

SUPERIOR COURT OF THE STATE OF CALIFORNIA

FOR THE COUNTY OF LOS ANGELES

PAUL SMITHSON; PATTY SMITHSON; and PETER SMITHSON, a minor, by and through his Guardian ad Litem PAUL SMITHSON. Plaintiffs, vs. FAMILY SWIM CLUB, LLC. A California limited liability company; GOT YOU COVERED TECHNOLOGIES, INC., a New Jersey corporation, DOES 1 to 50, inclusive, Defendants.	CASE NO. 21STCV887766 *Assigned to Hon. Lourdes O. Veryou, Dept. 2* **PLAINTIFFS INTERROGATORIES TO DEFENDANT SWIM CLUB. LLC. SET ONE** Complaint filed: March 12, 2024 Trial Date: Unassigned

PROPOUNDING PARTY: Plaintiffs

RESPONDING PARTY: Defendant FAMILY SWIM CLUB, LLC

SET NO.: ONE

TO DEFENDANT FAMILY SWIM CLUB, LLC, ITS ATTORNEYS OF RECORD:

The interrogatories (questions) are usually preceded by definitions that the responding party must adopt to prevent the responding party from playing games to avoid providing the requested information. For example, for a question that asks, "Identify all witnesses to the accident you have interviewed," the definition of "Identify" will require a name, address, and other contact information. The definition of "you" will include the party, his or her lawyer, and anyone else acting on behalf of the party – that way, the party cannot say "I don't know" if the information is being held by someone else on behalf of the party.

Here is a short set of interrogatories by the defendant to the plaintiffs, complete with the questions:

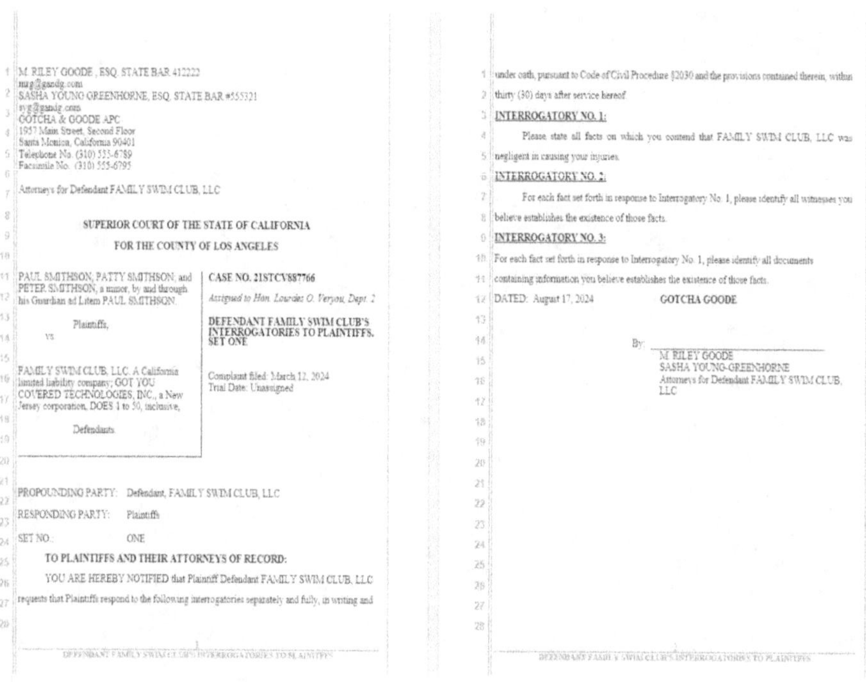

Responses are due within 30 days, which is stated in the document and is set by statute. If more time is needed, the parties can agree to it. If there is no response, if the responses do not properly answer the questions, or if they have unmerited objections, a motion may be required asking the judge to compel proper responses.

There is one more document type that will be helpful to see as we move along, as just mentioned: a "motion." A motion is a formal, written or oral request made by a party asking a judge to make a specific ruling, order, or decision in a case. Motions can address a wide range of legal or procedural issues, such as requesting a case be dismissed, asking for evidence to be excluded, or asking for a temporary order to be issued. The filing party, or movant, submits the motion, provides supporting legal arguments, and must "serve" (deliver) a copy to the opposing party, who then has the opportunity to file a written opposition (with reasons why the party should not have to comply) before the judge makes a final decision.

The example below is a "motion for summary judgment," which needs explanation. When you go to trial, you get a verdict, which then becomes a "judgment." If there can be no dispute about the facts, a party can file a motion asking the judge to decide the case before trial, a summary judgment. (As used here, the word "summary" does not have the usual meaning of a recap of some kind. Rather, as used here, it is an adjective meaning direct, prompt, or without further proceedings.)

A summary judgment motion is an evidentiary procedure, which means the motion must be supported with admissible evidence, usually in the form of declarations under oath. The other side opposes with its own argument and admissible evidence. If there is a dispute or discrepancy on a fact that could determine the outcome, the court must deny the motion and have the jury decide it at a later trial. If there is no factual dispute, if the opposing evidence is for some reason inadmissible, or if the opposing facts or law are inapplicable, the judge can award judgment to the moving party, thus eliminating the need for a trial.

A summary judgment motion procedure in most courts requires a package of related documents. These documents include, among others, a "memorandum of points and authorities" (which contains the argument and supporting law), the evidentiary documents (such as the declarations/affidavits and their documentary exhibits that establish the admissible facts), and a separate statement (which is a matrix listing facts showing what declarations or exhibits supports the existence of each fact).

A party also may move for summary resolution on a particular issue or individual cause of action, called a "motion for summary adjudication of issues." The sample document below is the notice to all parties that a summary judgment motion has been filed and when it will be heard.

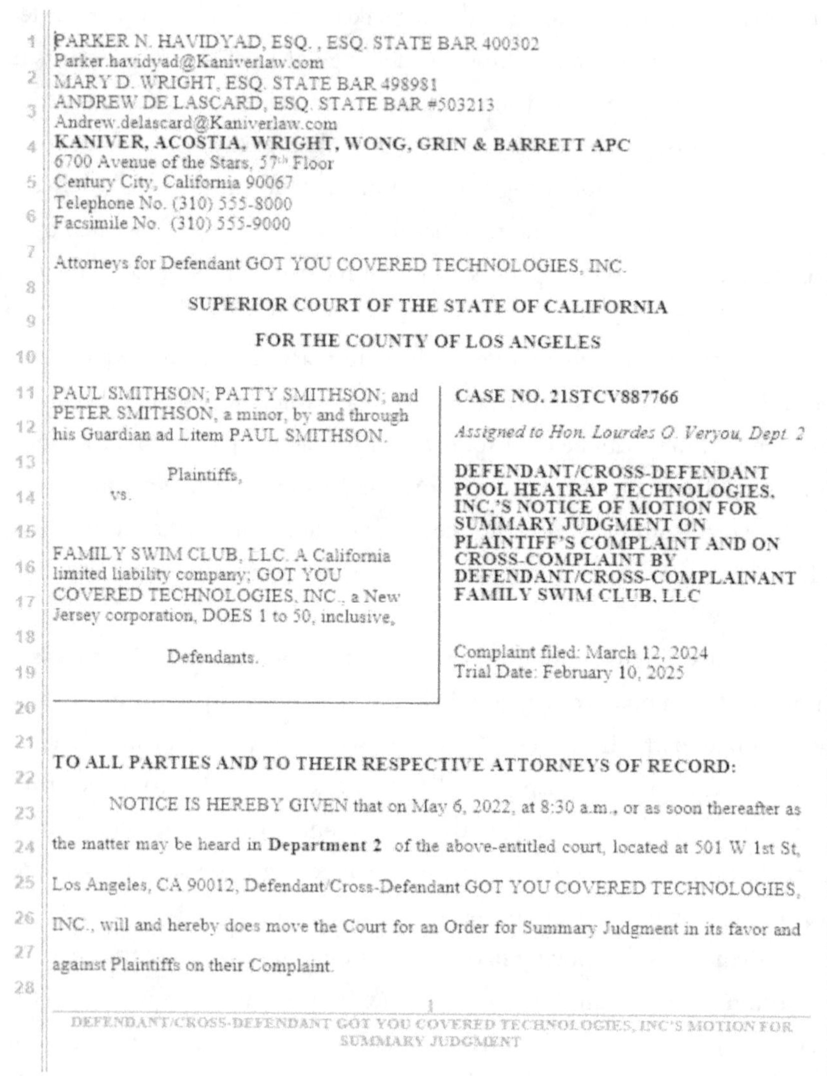

PARKER N. HAVIDYAD, ESQ., ESQ. STATE BAR 400302
Parker.havidyad@Kaniverlaw.com
MARY D. WRIGHT, ESQ. STATE BAR 498981
ANDREW DE LASCARD, ESQ. STATE BAR #503213
Andrew.delascard@Kaniverlaw.com
KANIVER, ACOSTIA, WRIGHT, WONG, GRIN & BARRETT APC
6700 Avenue of the Stars, 57th Floor
Century City, California 90067
Telephone No. (310) 555-8000
Facsimile No. (310) 555-9000

Attorneys for Defendant GOT YOU COVERED TECHNOLOGIES, INC.

SUPERIOR COURT OF THE STATE OF CALIFORNIA

FOR THE COUNTY OF LOS ANGELES

PAUL SMITHSON; PATTY SMITHSON; and PETER SMITHSON, a minor, by and through his Guardian ad Litem PAUL SMITHSON.	CASE NO. 21STCV887766
	Assigned to Hon. Lourdes O. Veryou, Dept. 2
Plaintiffs,	
vs.	**DEFENDANT/CROSS-DEFENDANT POOL HEATRAP TECHNOLOGIES, INC.'S NOTICE OF MOTION FOR SUMMARY JUDGMENT ON PLAINTIFF'S COMPLAINT AND ON CROSS-COMPLAINT BY DEFENDANT/CROSS-COMPLAINANT FAMILY SWIM CLUB, LLC**
FAMILY SWIM CLUB, LLC. A California limited liability company; GOT YOU COVERED TECHNOLOGIES, INC., a New Jersey corporation, DOES 1 to 50, inclusive,	
Defendants.	Complaint filed: March 12, 2024 Trial Date: February 10, 2025

TO ALL PARTIES AND TO THEIR RESPECTIVE ATTORNEYS OF RECORD:

NOTICE IS HEREBY GIVEN that on May 6, 2022, at 8:30 a.m., or as soon thereafter as the matter may be heard in **Department 2** of the above-entitled court, located at 501 W 1st St, Los Angeles, CA 90012, Defendant/Cross-Defendant GOT YOU COVERED TECHNOLOGIES, INC., will and hereby does move the Court for an Order for Summary Judgment in its favor and against Plaintiffs on their Complaint.

DEFENDANT/CROSS-DEFENDANT GOT YOU COVERED TECHNOLOGIES, INC'S MOTION FOR SUMMARY JUDGMENT

I hope you referred to the glossary. If you found these documents and their descriptions confusing, look at their definitions and go back through them; it will be more meaningful.

We now move on to learn about the sequence and events that occur in a lawsuit.

The Pattern of Litigation

CHAPTER NINE

A dispute or an accident occurs. "I'll see you in court, you so and so!" The aggrieved party hires a lawyer.

Most lawsuits follow a predictable path. Before a suit is filed, the lawyer interviews the client to find out what happened and decide if there is a supportable case. The lawyer should conduct some investigation to verify the facts. Under the ABA's Model Rule of Professional Conduct, Rule 3.1, "every lawyer owes an ethical duty to the client, the court and the adversary not to "bring or defend a proceeding, or assert … an issue … unless there is a basis in law and fact for doing so that is not frivolous…" Most states either have adopted this rule or have it with similar language.

Sometimes it is impossible to conduct a reasonable investigation before filing suit. If a client hires a lawyer shortly before the statute of limitations is to run out, the lawyer may just file a case quickly and then check out the facts before serving it. It is a reality, however, that some lawyers just believe their clients, pursue the litigation, and then have a rude awakening when the defendant comes up with a good defense that could have been foreseen with some legwork.

The investigation starts with the obvious. Hey client, tell me what happened. Remember the description from Chapter Six, The Lawyer-Client Relationship, describing how this goes. From there, say, in an accident case, it is common to contact witnesses, obtain a police report, visit and photograph the accident scene, inspect and photograph the accident vehicles, review key documents, etc. The lawyer will likely obtain medical records on the client's claimed injury.

Sometimes, the lawyer will contact the prospective defendant for information, doing so ethically. Whether initially or later, during the litigation, the lawyer might retain a private investigator. The investigator can help by locating witnesses and interviewing them, or finding out other information about the case through other means.

The lawsuit starts with the drafting and filing of a complaint. Under the Federal Rules of Civil Procedure, Rule 11, counsel is deemed to certify that any writing presented to the court has a proper legal basis, is not frivolous, and the facts and positions taken are supported after "reasonable inquiry." In California and in other states, a complaint may be filed on a "verified" or "unverified" basis. Verified means that the party has sworn to the truth of the allegations. Most complaints are unverified, which provides a lot of wiggle room as to the accuracy of the facts.

Once the lawsuit is filed, it is served on the defendant who now also must hire a lawyer. In an accident case, the defendant's insurance company might provide the lawyer. (Discussed in Chapter Five, How to Pick Your Lawyer.) The defense lawyer goes through the same process, interviewing the client, using other methods to obtain information from outside sources, and then responding to the complaint.

Responding to the complaint requires the lawyer to go through a group of considerations. Was the complaint served properly? If not, that defect can be challenged, and the judge could throw the case out if not corrected. Is the suit filed in the right jurisdiction or in the right part of the state or county? Does the complaint state a cause of action, that is, does it lay out the legal theory of the case, such as negligence, breach of contract, etc., and allege facts that if proven would amount to negligence, breach of contract, etc.? If not, the complaint can be challenged until it is corrected; sometimes, a complaint with improper allegations can even be thrown out if the judge agrees.

If the complaint cannot be challenged, an answer is filed. An answer to a complaint filed in federal court is also considered the defendant's representation that the denials of the alleged facts or the assertions of different facts are true. Each allegation must be separately responded to, which is also true in many state courts. An answer to a verified complaint in California must be answered allegation by allegation and must be under oath. An answer to an unverified complaint requires only a general statement denying all allegations and is not under oath (since neither is the complaint).

Answers also contain "affirmative defenses." A plaintiff's complaint consists of allegations, like "the defendant drove negligently and caused the plaintiff harm." The plaintiff has the burden of proof to establish these allegations with evidence; failure to carry that burden at trial means the plaintiff loses. Affirmative defenses in an answer are also allegations, though by the defendant. The defendant has the burden of proof at trial to support those allegations or lose on the issue.

An example of an affirmative defense is that the plaintiff, who has a legal obligation to take steps to undergo treatment to try to recover from an injury, fails to do so, delaying or preventing their recovery. This is called "failure to mitigate" damages. The defendant has the burden to show that failure. Another example of an affirmative defense in a civil case is that the case was not filed by the deadline to do so, which is a violation of the statute of limitations. In a criminal case, the defendant may have harmed someone but claims it was in self-defense. The criminal defendant has the burden to show that.

Once the complaint in a civil action is filed and the answer is filed, the discovery phase proceeds. As discussed in Chapter Ten, next, discovery consists of a group of available procedures to find out information the opponent has that may be used at trial to prove the case. Discovery procedures are established by statute.

The usual sequence of discovery is to send interrogatories (written questions) asking for information about the alleged facts, subpoenaing documents (like medical or business records), sending an injured plaintiff to be examined by a doctor, or inspecting an object or property involved in an accident or other dispute. The litigants do not have to wait for these other procedures to be done before taking depositions (live testimony of parties and witnesses), but depositions are often more fruitful when the information obtained through other procedures is already known and analyzed.

Nearer to the end of the case is when the parties usually take depositions of experts, retained to provide analysis and opinion about the issues in dispute. Experts are used in lawsuits to provide specialized knowledge on complex issues, helping the court or jury understand technical concepts and make informed decisions. In fact, there are some subject areas where expert testimony is required or the case can be lost, like medical malpractice or legal malpractice.

Most people are familiar with a variety of criminal justice television shows, like CSI or Law and Order. The plots often involve a forensic investigation. The conclusions made from the investigation are presented at trial by experts, like specially trained crime scene investigators who explain how fingerprints or blood samples are used to solve a crime.

In civil cases, experts serve the same function, though on different subject matter; they too, add a measure of science to the presentation, which can be persuasive. Whether criminal or civil cases, there are always experts having the same or similar qualifications but on either side of an issue. How then do we know which one is correct if they draw opposite conclusions on the same facts?

Deciding the question of which expert's opinion should be accepted often becomes an important part of deciding a case. In this regard, there is a reality of litigation about experts to keep in mind. There was a popular TV western show in the late 1950s called Have Gun Will Travel. It ran for six years and was about a gunslinger who could be hired to carry out a measure of justice on bad guys. Experts are supposed to base their opinions on sound analysis, their conclusions landing wherever the facts lead them, regardless of who hired them. Right. Not all the time. Many are hired gunslingers.

Here is the official federal court jury instruction on how to determine if you should accept an expert's opinion[1]:

> *"You have heard testimony from expert witnesses who testified about their opinions and the reasons for those opinions. This opinion testimony is allowed because of the specialized knowledge, skill, experience, training, or education of this witness.*
>
> *Such opinion testimony should be judged like any other testimony. You may accept it or reject it and give it as much weight as you think it deserves, considering the witness's knowledge, skill, experience, training, or education, the reasons given for the opinion, and all the other evidence in the case."*

In addition to discovery, lawyers can obtain information through means outside the statutory scheme of discovery, like interviewing witnesses, sometimes with the use of private investigators. (See Chapter Eleven – You Are Not Paranoid – They Really Are Following You.)

---

1 Most state jury instructions are worded similarly.

Along the way, the parties may have to file, or choose to file, motions asking, for example, that the court decide if the pleadings are acceptable, decide a discovery dispute, or dictate the timing of events in the case. In some cases, parties can bring motions seeking to decide the outcome of the case before the trial, like a summary judgment motion, discussed earlier.

Once discovery is done, the deadline for which is dictated by a case management order issued by the court or set by discovery statutes, the case goes to trial. Trials can be to a jury or to a judge (called a "bench trial").

A discussion of the pattern of litigation would not be complete without a discussion of how cases settle. Settlement can occur at any time, before the case is filed, anytime during the pre-trial phases, or even while the trial is going on. The usual timing, however, is that settlement negotiations happen once the parties have gotten substantially, or completely, through the discovery process. Courts encourage and favor settlements, of course, because a settled case is cleared off the crowded trial calendar. Judges will encourage, coax, and order settlement discussions. Sometimes, the court may have judges specifically assigned to conduct settlement conferences but nowadays, cases are often settled in private mediation. (See how a mediation works in Part Two, Chapter Twenty-Two.)

After the trial, the party losing the case has the right to appeal. Appellate procedures fall generally into two categories, writs and appeals. There are different kinds of writs, but a common type of writ asks the appellate court to decide an issue affecting how the case will be tried; inherently, this is done during the litigation, that is, before the trial. An appeal, by contrast, is typically after the outcome of the trial is decided (with some exceptions); that is, the party losing the case has the right to ask the appellate court to reverse or modify the decision of the trial court, or have the result thrown out and the matter retried. At the higher tier, a losing party can ask the highest appellate court to reverse the decision of the lower appellate court.

Now, let's get into greater detail about discovery and investigation.

The "Discovery" Process – Prove It, Pal

CHAPTER TEN

Methods of Discovering and Confirming the Facts of the Case

Discovery is the main process by which lawyers obtain evidence. Discovery procedures are set forth in statutes. The purpose of the statutes is to allow each party to prepare their case. In actual practice, the discovery process can be quite the war. The client will be asked to assist in preparing responses, and the lawyer decides the strategy about what information to provide and when, and when to challenge the sufficiency of the responses from others.

The intent of the discovery rules is that each side is entitled to know what the evidence will be at trial. The response must be made under oath so that it is deemed evidence that can be admitted at trial to prove a fact. The goal is to prevent trial by ambush.

The extent, or depth, of information that can be requested in discovery is that which is "relevant" to the issues in the case. The spirit of the rules requires that even if a party does not have the precise answer to a discovery request, information must be supplied that could lead to finding relevant evidence.

The Federal Rules of Evidence define relevant evidence as evidence having "any tendency to make the existence of any fact that is of consequence to the determination of the action more probable or less probable than it would be without the evidence." The California Evidence Code defines relevant evidence as "having any tendency in reason to prove or disprove any disputed fact that is of consequence to the determination of the action." Similar words, but expressing the same concept.

Let me translate this. Relevance, that is, what is "of consequence" to the outcome of the case, turns on whether it affects the establishment of a fact. Here is an example. Car one hits car two, and the passenger in car two sues the driver of car one for injuries. The defendant (car one) asks in discovery if the plaintiff in car two had been drinking alcohol. The plaintiff objects, saying the question seeks irrelevant information; the argument is that since the plaintiff was a passenger and wasn't driving, whether the plaintiff had been drinking does not affect how the accident happened.

However, the passenger's perceptions of what happened could have been impaired, affecting the accuracy of the testimony, and therefore, the information is actually relevant for that purpose. On the flip side of this, if the defendant in that same injury accident case asked if the plaintiff had had multiple divorces, that would be irrelevant to how the accident happened and would have no bearing on the claimed injuries or damages resulting from the accident.

Though the process of obtaining evidence in a civil case evolved from about the 16th century, the first comprehensive set of discovery rules came into effect in the U.S. federal courts in 1938, known as the Federal Rules of Civil Procedure. Many states then modeled their discovery statutes after the federal system, some using the same numerical organization. Both the federal system and the state systems dictate what, how, and when discovery can be used.

The basic discovery procedures are defined for you in the Glossary. In Chapter Nine, "The Pattern of Litigation," discovery is discussed in the context of how a lawsuit plays out. The timing associated with discovery is referenced in Chapter Eleven, under the subheading "<u>Deadlines – One of a Million Things that Keep Lawyers Up at Night.</u>" The point is that discovery is a big part of litigation. Let's flesh it out, at least as to the most frequently used discovery procedures.

Interrogatories

Interrogatories are questions. (Hence the root word, interrogate.) One party "propounds" (sends) a "captioned" document containing the interrogatories to any other party. (You saw the caption-formatted set of interrogatories at the end of Chapter Eight, a very simplified set of questions.) Typically, the questions are preceded by a set of standard instructions and, importantly, a list of definitions.

Interrogatories ask for things like the identity and whereabouts of witnesses, doctors, documents, etc. They may ask what evidence you have to prove or disprove the case. Let's examine a couple of interrogatories and see how lawyers handle them.

A typical interrogatory might say:

"Please identify all persons present on the property when the accident occurred."

This interrogatory seems easy to answer. The question obviously is about an accident someone is suing for. The information sought is, basically, "tell us who the witnesses to the accident are." Straightforward, right? Not so fast.

Even though the intent is to allow all parties to a case to get the information they need to evaluate and try the case, lawyers often look for ways to avoid or limit full disclosure of facts. Why?

In the movie *Liar, Liar*, Jim Carrey's lawyer character objects to an audio recording because it proves his client was unfaithful to her husband. When the judge asks why he was objecting, he shouts, "Because it's devastating to my case!"

Providing full and good faith disclosures of information might weaken a client's case, but you are supposed to provide it; that's the point. Yet, the lawyer might try to object to delay disclosure for strategic reasons. Often the information will be provided, though preceded by objections, but sometimes they refuse to provide anything. So, we need a few words about objections.

Lawyers are creatures of words, and, in perhaps the most often used objection, it is common to pretend not to understand the meaning of an interrogatory. Rather than provide the obviously requested information, they object instead, asserting that the question is "vague and ambiguous," meaning it is unclear what is being asked for.

I mentioned the use of definitions earlier. Including definitions in the instruction section of the interrogatories is intended to forestall objections. Let's break down our interrogatory example above, *"Please identify all persons present on the property when the accident occurred."*

- What does "identify" mean? Is the question asking for a description of a person?

- Is "persons" limited to people? Generically, that's what it would mean.

- What "property" are we talking about? A house, a condo, an apartment, or the common area of a condo or apartment?

- What constitutes the accident?

Not defining these words will be greeted with "Objection: Vague and ambiguous," or the more insulting version, "Objection: unintelligible."

The definitions below could solve the problem:

"The word 'IDENTIFY' as used in this set of interrogatories shall be deemed to require you to provide a name, address, telephone number, and email address." By telling the responding party exactly what you want, you eliminate any other meaning of "identify".

"The word 'PERSON' as used in this set of interrogatories shall be deemed to mean individuals or organizations." Without this clarification, you might get just information about people, not the companies that do business at the property, whose employees might have useful information.

"The word 'PROPERTY' as used in this set of interrogatories shall be deemed to mean 9876 17th Street, Los Angeles, California, the location set forth in the plaintiff's complaint where the claimed injury occurred." This definition makes it clear that the information you want pertains to the accident site. If the accident occurred inside an apartment, the location might be defined just that way: *"…shall be deemed to mean Apartment C at 9876 17th Street…"*

"The 'ACCIDENT' as used in this set of interrogatories shall be deemed to mean the sequence of events alleged in the plaintiff's complaint that resulted in the claimed injury in this case." This may seem unnecessary since the case is about an accident being sued for, but the extent to which the opposing lawyer might try to mislead cannot be underestimated.

Even though the intent of discovery is to foster disclosure, lawyers tend to look for advantage if they can get away with it. A question really might be a bit unclear, but information still should be provided in good faith, or a discussion between counsel should occur to get things clarified.

In addition to the requirement that the questions seek *relevant* information and that the type of information sought is clearly worded and defined, when you send the interrogatories can matter. Some interrogatories are legitimately premature. A plaintiff might send an interrogatory at the beginning of a case, before the defendant, has had a chance to gather information, that asks: "*Do you contend the plaintiff was not injured in the accident?*" The truthful answer is that the defendant does not have a clue. But the response has to be yes or no; if you say you don't know, then that lack of knowledge could be used against you since the plaintiff is the only witness on the subject. The correct response in that situation is to object that the timing of the interrogatory is unfair and premature, and that objection would be appropriate.

Responding to the interrogatories also requires careful thought. The responses are under oath and are considered evidence. They can be read to the jury. This is another skill the lawyer brings to bear in the process.

Requests for Production or Inspection

Under this procedure, the same rules apply; you can ask only for relevant information or information that could help you find relevant information. The same kinds of objections are available. The procedure can ask for documents or tangible things, or to be allowed to inspect tangible things or property. "Documents" will have a definition, to include contracts, emails, photos, text messages, etc. Tangible things might include a vehicle or a machine involved in an accident.

The lawsuit we will follow in Part Two is about whether the design and manufacture of a pool cover was dangerous and caused a near-drowning. In that case, for example, the plaintiffs will want their expert to have access to the defendant manufacturer's engineering designs. (This might be met with an objection that the designs are proprietary, as trade secrets. A motion might be needed asking the judge to solve the dispute.)

Everyone will want any photographs taken of the scene on the day of the accident. (You will see in the story that a key photograph ended up being the most important piece of evidence in the entire case.) The plaintiffs will want any documents that show when the pool cover was installed, when and how it was maintained, and whether there had been any safety problems with it before.

The documents can be obtained by asking for them to be "produced", that is, sent to the requesting party; either the actual documents or copies. Again, a captioned document called Request for Production of Documents will be sent to the opposing lawyer asking, "*Please produce all photographs of the scene of the accident, including photographs of the area before and after the accident.*" Or, "*Please produce the pool cover in use at the time of the accident.*"

The first request gets you the pictures, if they exist. The second is more complicated, which is why "inspection" of things or tangible objects is the alternative to "producing" them. As a practical matter, a party cannot send a bulky object to the opposing lawyer's office. Instead, the party that possesses the pool cover will say they will permit the opposing counsel to come look at it, photograph it, and inspect it. To further highlight the distinction between production and inspection, using an absurd example, suppose in an air crash case, one party asks for production of the airplane. Right, I'll send it by U.S. mail, postage due. Instead, the parties and their experts will go to where the wreckage is being held. In our Smithson case, the parties will want to see the property where the accident happened for a variety of reasons.

Subpoenas

Subpoenas command someone other than the parties to the case, under the power of the court, to produce something for a litigation or to appear and testify. Discovery methods like interrogatories and requests for production of documents are subpoenas themselves, but do not need to be hand-served on the party. The notice to the party's lawyer has the same power as if a subpoena had been served.

To compel a non-party to provide documents or to testify, a subpoena must be served, which means handing them the papers. Lawyers will subpoena a variety of records from nonparties that could prove or disprove a case, such as business records, employment records, and medical records.

For example, an early set of interrogatories to a plaintiff in an injury case will ask the names of the doctors who treated the plaintiff. Once the doctors have been identified, the defendants will subpoena the medical records to verify or dispute the extent of the injuries and provide them to their own medical experts for review and comment.

Ordinarily, your personal health information is sacrosanct. Those who do have access to your medical records must, by law, keep them inviolate. HIPAA, or the Health Insurance Portability and Accountability Act, is a federal law that protects patients' health information, passed in 1996. In addition, this information is protected by most state constitutions. (See, California Constitution, Article 1, §1) Related to this, California also has a physician-patient privilege by statute, Evidence Code §992.

However, if you are claiming an injury, the defendant is allowed to see your medical records and inquire into your medical history. The waiver of the privacy right as to your medical condition is called "tendering the medical condition into issue." The waiver, however, is not unlimited. The only medical information a defendant can obtain is what is directly put into issue; they can get records of your neck pain treatment, which you hurt in the accident, but they are not allowed to see records of, say, some kind of embarrassing urological problem. Here is one where it is a close question as to relevance and whether it has been tendered into issue: Suppose you slip and fall, hurting your foot, and you sue the property owner. Is the fact that you have had diabetic neuropathy, which can cause pain in the ankles and toes, fair game? It might be.

Part of your damages might also be that you missed work due to an injury. If you are claiming an injury prevented you from working, the defendant will want to see how much you were earning up to the time of the accident, etc.

Requests for Admission

This discovery method seeks to have a party agree to the existence of a fact or that an issue in the case should be deemed established before the trial. By contrast, an interrogatory asks for facts the opponent contends exist, and might be disputable, but at least you know what they think they can prove. With a request for admission, the requesting party wants to take a fact out of play, that is, establish it as true for the trial. A plaintiff might ask a defendant to admit that the defendant was negligent or that the defendant was exceeding the speed limit. A defendant might make similar requests, like asking for an admission that the plaintiff was negligent or was speeding, or ask the plaintiff to admit that the defendant's product, as designed, met all applicable safety standards.

Requests for admission are designed to cut down the need to prove certain things at trial. Whether or not the requests are admitted, denied, or objected to, it is important to comply with the deadlines. The court has the power to deem facts admitted; in essence, if a party does not comply with the rules, the penalty could be that the case goes to trial with facts the court has ordered into existence, even if they are simply not true. Here's how it could work.

The plaintiff wants to prove the defendant was speeding. The defendant fails to respond by the time limit to a request to admit the speed limit was exceeded. The defendant fails to respond, and a motion to deem the fact admitted is granted by the judge. If so, the jury will be told it is an undisputed fact that the defendant was speeding. Even if the defendant could later show, say, from his car's EDR (black box) that he was not speeding, he is stuck with it. It is a weird kind of penalty, but one that could mean winning or losing a case, so the lawyer must be on top of the rules and deadlines.

Depositions

A deposition is live testimony taken before trial. All counsel are present and have the right to conduct examination of the witness. The examination, that is the questions and the answers, is recorded word for word by a court reporter, who is specially trained to take down "shorthand" and is licensed by the state to do so. Before computers, court reporters would use old-fashioned shorthand, which was a method of rapid writing using abbreviations and symbols; it was invented in the 19th century. The reporter would then convert, or translate, the shorthand notes into readable text. Today, reporters use a stenotype keyboard interfaced with a computer that converts the input instantly.

Before any examination is done, the court reporter places the witness under oath, also something the reporter is licensed to do, just as in a courtroom. The lawyer who noticed the deposition, with rare exception, conducts the first session of examination, followed by the other lawyers, with multiple rounds if needed.

The questions are subject to objection, like written questions. When an objection occurs, the witness must still answer, and the objection may be ruled on by the judge later. On occasion, a witness's own lawyer may instruct the witness not to answer, and the matter can then be submitted to the judge for ruling.

The examination continues until all lawyers indicate they have no more questions. The length of the deposition varies depending on the complexity of the case and the depth of relevant information the witness may have. In California, the deposition of an individual cannot exceed seven hours unless agreed or ordered otherwise. The deposition of an organization has no limit. There are cases where depositions might last for days. In Part Two, I will bring you along to certain depositions, seeing the questions, the answers, and the objections, and you will see how the court reporter lays it out.

Medical Examinations and Obtaining Medical Records

A proper medical opinion to prove or disprove an injury claimed in a lawsuit requires a physical examination of the plaintiff and a review of medical records.

At the trial of an accident case, the plaintiff will testify about the injury and pain, as will the plaintiff's doctors. The presentation may also include a specially hired medical expert to testify to the diagnosis, necessary treatment, and the prospects for recovery (the "prognosis"). The treating doctor and the additional medical expert have easy access to any medical information needed just by asking the plaintiff or the plaintiff's lawyer for it. Naturally, the treating doctor has already seen the plaintiff and has a medical chart.

The defendant is also entitled to a medical professional to dispute the claim, but the defense-hired doctor is not the treating doctor and does not have free access to the plaintiff and all other information necessary to support a medical opinion. A thorough physical exam is crucial for gathering essential information about a patient's condition and can be vital for making an accurate diagnosis.

A plaintiff making a medical claim is required by statute to submit to an examination by the defendant's selected doctor. In fact, I would argue the very existence of the statute shows the law recognizes it is generally considered improper to give a diagnosis without a physical examination, especially when combined with a detailed medical history. Relying solely on a patient's reported symptoms may lead to missed or incorrect diagnoses.[1]

A plaintiff may claim a mental injury (like depression or post-traumatic stress disorder) either in combination with physical injury or by itself. If so, the plaintiff may be required to submit to a mental examination. Unlike a physical examination, a mental examination (in California) must be ordered by the court unless the parties agree to it. (Both physical and mental examinations are discussed in more detail later in this chapter.)

---

1 Campbell/Lynn "Clinical Methods: The History, Physical, and Laboratory Examinations" 3rd edition, Chapter 4. Walker/Hall editors.

There is no limit to the number of medical examinations in a federal court case, subject to oversight by the judge. In a California state court case, a defendant is entitled to one examination no matter the number of injuries claimed, unless agreed between the parties or if the court orders it.

In more complex cases, with multiple injuries, a plaintiff may intend to have multiple doctors testify at trial. A defendant will want medical testimony in each of the injury categories the plaintiff intends to assert. As an example, a plaintiff in a car crash may claim a back or neck injury, or broken bones (typically addressed by an orthopedic doctor), a head injury like a concussion (typically addressed by a neurologist or neuropsychologist), and severe emotional distress (typically addressed by a psychiatrist or psychologist). In such a multi-injury case, a court will typically authorize multiple examinations, and experienced plaintiffs' lawyers know this and will cooperate.

People who have been in an accident may need an ambulance, emergency room medical care, or they may proceed to a hospital on their own. Alternatively, people may live with an injury, not thinking it is that bad, but it turns worse, and then they go to a hospital or a doctor.

The first thing some people do is call a lawyer, possibly because they have no insurance and cannot afford medical care, and the lawyer can send them to a doctor familiar to the law firm, who treats them and agrees to be paid later, out of the eventual recovery. (In this situation, the plaintiff will agree to give the doctor a lien on any recovery.) Because payment can be deferred by seeing a lawyer-recommended doctor, some people who do have insurance will not use it. It is common in accident lawyer advertisements to say the lawyer will get the client to a doctor.

Another reason to go with the lawyer-referred doctor is that many doctors have experience serving as experts in litigation. This is true for doctors on either side of the case. Doctors will testify as experts to supplement their medical practice income; some may have a majority or all of their practice devoted to patients in litigation. This actuality can add some spice to the process of having a plaintiff examined. Even though doctors, whether they are just the treating medical provider or they are to be testifying experts, are supposed to make diagnoses free from any influence, the adversarial nature of what is happening can have an influence.

Let's discuss how defense medical examinations work, both for physical and mental injury claims.

Physical Examinations

Under Federal Rules of Civil Procedure, Rule 35, or under California Code of Civil Procedure, §2032.220, the examination allowed is called a "physical" examination. The process starts with a written request from the defendant, a form of notice on a captioned document, which requests that the plaintiff come to a selected doctor's office on a specific date and at a specific time to be examined.

The plaintiff's side will provide a written response indicating whether the examination will be permitted, but it usually contains objections and conditions seeking to limit the scope of the examination. The plaintiff often demands the right to have a medical professional, such as a nurse, attend the examination with the plaintiff.

For illustration, let's assume the case involves a claim of orthopedic injury. The orthopedic physical examination, depending on the body part at issue, will involve observation and physical tests. A range of physical tests are used, such as Tinel's sign, in which the doctor lightly taps a nerve to elicit a tingling or "pins and needles" sensation in the nerve's distribution, indicating potential nerve irritation or damage, such as carpal tunnel syndrome. Another example is a Hoffman's sign test, where a doctor flicks the nail of a patient's middle finger, and a positive result is observed when the thumb and index finger involuntarily flex, indicating a potential nerve issue in the neck.

If the case concerns neurology, like a head injury, an examining neurologist will conduct a similar examination and perform certain neurological tests. That testing is sometimes referred to a different specialist, called a neuropsychologist.

Following the examination, the defense doctor must prepare a written report, which is shared with the plaintiff's lawyer. The report will include not only the results of the physical examination, but also the examiner's review of other sources of information, like deposition transcripts or other medical records.

A medical examination can be a rather pervasive event. True, a plaintiff being examined is with a doctor, but not the plaintiff's doctor. So, there are limits to the examination, but your privacy can be invaded in other ways. Specifically, which of the plaintiff's medical records does the defendant and the defense doctor get to see? The answer is that they get to see anything that could be related to the injury claim you are making. The purpose is to allow the defendant a fair shot to determine if the claim is verifiable or disputable. Yet it can go too far, and lawyers regularly argue over the scope of the records sought.

Mental Injury Examinations

Accidents, defamation, intentional acts, and so forth can cause emotional distress. Emotional distress is mental suffering or anguish, a non-physical, psychological injury. A plaintiff may recover for both physical injury and the mental effect of being upset by an accident or having to go through pain and treatment. But mental injury claims often go farther than mere anguish, like actual diagnosable depression, exacerbation of existing mental problems, or even post-traumatic stress disorder.

The rules are a bit different to obtain a mental examination as opposed to a physical examination, at least in California. The party seeking the mental examination cannot simply send a notice and require the other party to appear at the office of a psychologist or psychiatrist. It must be either agreed to by the other party or a motion is required to obtain a court order.

A mental examination in litigation is very different from a physical examination as well. In a physical examination, the plaintiff's lawyer or a hired medical professional can attend. Not so for a mental examination; the law deems that there is a sensitive relationship between the mental health professional and the examinee that cannot be influenced by others present. The examination consists of an interview discussing the examinee's background and sources of the claimed distress. The examination may also include psychological testing.

Property and Evidence Inspections

Let's say you buy a pressure cooker, and it explodes, spraying you with scalding liquid. Of course, the pressure cooker is not supposed to do that. You sue, claiming the pressure cooker was defectively designed. The defendant is entitled to examine it. For the moment, it is sitting in your garage. The defendant can send your lawyer a notice to produce the pressure cooker for inspection by the defendant's engineering expert to examine it for defects, put parts under a microscope, or conduct tests.

Or, instead of a product, you are a property owner and your brand-new roof leaks. You sue the roofing contractor who refuses to make it right. The defendant contractor is entitled to have an expert inspect the property, and in some cases, to cut into the structure to see what happened. (This is another way your privacy can be invaded in a lawsuit.) Here is another example. Let's say your neighbor's contractor uses pile driving equipment that causes so much vibration, it damages the foundation of your house and causes cracks in your walls. During the suit, the defendant would be entitled to examine just about everywhere in your house to investigate the damage.

The discovery process, as you can see, provides a lot of different ways to obtain information to plan, evaluate, and try a lawsuit. In many cases, literally all of these procedures are employed and occupy most of the time between when the case is filed and the trial. It is a necessary, though costly, process, but if done fairly and thoroughly, it allows the parties to the litigation a fair opportunity to evaluate the case for settlement or take the case to trial.

Investigation: You are Not Paranoid – They Really are Following You

CHAPTER ELEVEN

Discovery is not the only method to obtain information needed for a case. Private investigators are often used for a variety of reasons.

Private investigation is a varied industry. Many investigation companies specialize in finding people. It often happens that witnesses will leave their jobs or leave the area, but their testimony may be important to the case, so they need to be tracked down. Investigators are also used to obtain information about a case by checking court records or public records, or by directly contacting a witness for information.

Investigators are also used to find information when fraud or gross exaggeration is suspected. People lie. People exaggerate. Can we agree that at least some people may present their claims falsely because they hope to score some money from their lawsuit?

Let's look at a hypothetical claim in which an investigator blew the case open.

Mr. Frauderick Jones files suit because of a vehicle accident. He goes to an orthopedic doctor complaining of back pain so severe that he can hardly get out of bed or out of a chair. He arrives at the doctor's office using a walker, driven there by his wife because he claims he can't drive. The doctor conducts tests and diagnoses a disk bulge in the plaintiff's lower spine. He prescribes physical therapy and pain medication. The plaintiff later says he cannot do the physical therapy because it hurts too much, and the doctor sends him to a pain specialist who prescribes further pain medication and injects his spine with steroids.

The plaintiff gives a deposition under oath, saying he can't leave his house, except to limp from his vehicle and go into his doctor's office using his walker, he is reclined or seated almost all day, and all he can do is watch television. He is in so much pain that the deposition takes three days because he can't last more than an hour a day.

He says he is unable to work in his job as a house inspector for a real estate company because that would require him to drive around, climb stairs, and do a lot of bending. He is only forty-nine years old and claims he may never work again. He is reluctant to have surgery on his back because he fears it will make it worse.

You are a juror, and this plaintiff comes to court making these claims about his inability to work, to leave the house, to drive, to do anything but watch TV, and is in constant pain no matter what the doctors try to do for him. He comes into the courtroom every day of the trial in a wheelchair. On cross-examination by the defendant's counsel, this is what happens:

> Lawyer: "Mr. Jones, you have testified the accident was caused by my client's bicycle running into your Dodge Ram pickup truck from behind while you were stationary at a red light, that you were able to talk to my client and the police officer who arrived while standing on the street after the collision, and that the conversation took at least 30 minutes before you got back in your truck and drove directly to the hospital."
>
> Mr. Jones: "Yes, that's true. The pain didn't start right away but got worse while I was on my feet."
>
> Lawyer: "Mr. Jones, you also say the pain got much worse overnight and quickly deteriorated since?"
>
> Mr. Jones: "Yes."
>
> Lawyer: "You are unable to work, you cannot bend without pain, you can walk only with a walker or a cane, and then usually only to go to the bathroom. When you do go out, your wife has to drive you and, wherever you go, which is rarely, you have to use a wheelchair, as you are sitting in right now. Is that right?"
>
> Mr. Jones: "Yes, that's my testimony."
>
> Lawyer: "That's your testimony under oath, right, Mr. Jones?"
>
> Mr. Jones: "Yes, sir."

Lawyer: "So far, all the treatment provided to you has not improved your condition. You tried but discontinued physical therapy treatment after one session, you have had three pain injections, you are on constant opioids for pain. None of these things has helped, is that correct?"

Mr. Jones: "Yes, that's right."

Lawyer: "You used to go bowling, you played on a softball team and did your own yard work. But you now cannot do any of that and have not done any of that since the accident. Is that also true? And remember you are under oath."

Mr. Jones: "Yes, my life has been shattered."

Lawyer: "Your honor, I have no further questions for the witness, but I would now like to call to the witness stand, Mr. Rocky Rococo."

Lawyer: "Mr. Rococo, what do you do for a living?"

Mr. Rococo: "I am a private investigator. I am licensed by the State of California as required by the Business and Professions Code."

Lawyer: "Did you conduct an investigation of Mr. Jones at my request?"

Mr. Rococo: "Yes, I did that on three occasions, September 25 of last year, this past January 12, and just 45 days ago, on February 9."

Lawyer: "Please tell the jury what your investigation consisted of."

Mr. Rococo: "On each of the three occasions, I parked my van across from Mr. Jones' residence. His house is on a corner lot and I positioned myself at an angle that allowed me a view of the front and a portion of the backyard. I simply watched his house to see if Mr. Jones was physically active at all. Of course, I could not and would not attempt to see into his house, but I waited to see what would happen if he came out."

Lawyer: "Did you observe Mr. Jones last September 25?"

Mr. Rococo: "Yes, I arrived at 8 a.m., and by 9 a.m., I noticed from my angle that there was some activity in the backyard."

Lawyer: "What did you see?"

Mr. Rococo: "I got out of my van and moved to a better position, and I saw Mr. Jones putting sacks of what appeared to be soil into a wheelbarrow, move the wheelbarrow to another part of the yard and then use a shovel to disperse the soil or whatever the contents of the wheelbarrow were."

Lawyer: "Did you observe Mr. Jones on January 12?"

Mr. Rococo: "Yes, on that date, I arrived again at 8 a.m. but nothing happened until about 7 p.m. At that time, I observed Mr. Jones exit through the front door, carrying a round-looking bag. He then opened the door to his truck and got in. No one was with him. It is a fairly large vehicle, a big Dodge Ram, so he had to step up into the cab, tossing the bag across the seat as he got in. I then followed him for 20 minutes until he arrived at Bowlarama on Cheshire Boulevard. After Mr. Jones went into the bowling alley carrying the bag, I parked and exited my vehicle and followed him in. I stayed for about an hour and during that time, I watched him bowl a few games with people he appeared to know."

Lawyer: "At any time, did you observe Mr. Jones using a cane, a walker, or a wheelchair?"

Mr. Rococo: "I did not observe that he did so."

Lawyer: "Did you observe Mr. Jones on February 9?"

Mr. Rococo: "Yes, at about 4 p.m., I observed Mr. Jones exit his house, get into his truck and drive away. I followed him to 'Batter Up' on Iago Street, which is a baseball batting practice facility. At that time, Mr. Jones put on a helmet, went into a batting cage, and hit balls for about 30 minutes."

Lawyer: "Mr. Rococo, we have only your word, though under oath here today, that Mr. Jones did all this, that he worked in his yard carrying heavy bags of what appeared to be soil and used a shovel, that he went bowling, and that he went to a batting cage, all without the need of a cane, walker, or wheelchair. Do you have any other proof of what you personally observed?"

Mr. Rococo: "Yes, on each occasion, I took video of my observations using a long-range lens."

The videos were played for the jury. Here are stills from the videos:

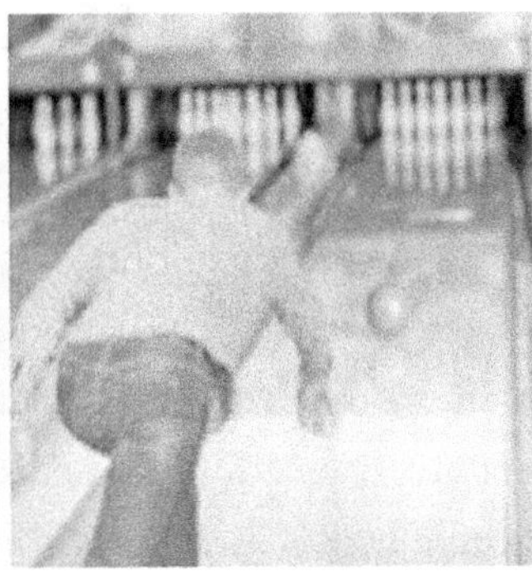

So, you are a juror. Would you give this guy any money? Unless you have seen something like this play out, your first impression on hearing that private investigators follow people and watch them without their knowledge seems sleazy. But so are false claims.

The kind of investigation illustrated in the Frauderick Jones hypothetical vehicle accident case is called "sub rosa," which is another phrase for surveillance.

If you are a plaintiff in an injury case and your case is presented fairly and truthfully, you have nothing to worry about, but you still could be the object of someone's private eye.

Deadlines – One of a Million Things That Keep Lawyers Up at Night

CHAPTER TWELVE

Once a lawsuit is filed, and after a trial date is set, it is subject to a set of deadlines that are imposed by statute or by a judge's orders. Unless the court rules otherwise, the parties must conduct the case, primarily the discovery process, by certain dates. I want to explain this regimentation.

Many states, like California, allow the parties to conduct the discovery process at their discretion, that is, it is self-executing, though within the bounds of the statutory rules and deadlines. The court also has the power to make "case management orders," often used to manage complex, multi-party matters, which can alter the statutory timelines. Some states require certain stages of a case to be completed before allowing discovery.

Federal Court rules have their own discovery limitations and deadlines unless the court allows otherwise. Most federal judges also issue a standard case management order applying to all their cases that set the overall case deadlines. The case schedule and deadlines set forth here are based on California rules.

In a normally busy litigation practice, a lawyer calendar may be crowded with trial dates, one after the other. The lawyers, however, are at the mercy of the judges who want to keep things moving. In turn, this means managing cases, particularly in the discovery process with an eye on the calendar. If deadlines are not well-managed, the right to implement discovery procedures could be cut off. Discovery deadlines and more are what keep lawyers up at night.

Here are the deadlines, very generally, in order of how the case develops, skipping some procedures not within the scope of this book:

1.   The complaint must be filed within the statute of limitations, which differs depending on the type of case.

2. Service of the complaint must occur on the defendants within sixty days of filing, unless extended by the court.

3. Before a defendant responds to a complaint, a plaintiff may amend without court permission. If the complaint has been answered, court permission is required to amend. (Seeking "leave of court" to do so. "Your honor, we are seeking *leave* to amend." As stated earlier, quaint old English stuff.)

4. An answer to a complaint or other challenge to it must occur within thirty days of service. The deadline may be extended under certain situations or by agreement.

5. If there is no answer, a default must be taken within forty days of service. A default judgment must be sought within forty-five days after the default is entered. Courts often do not strictly enforce this rule but rather will make an order extending the time to a certain date.

6. Cross-complaints must be filed when the answer is filed unless court permission is later obtained.

7. Discovery, in the form of interrogatories, requests for admission, document production requests, etc. may be propounded by the plaintiff ten days after the complaint is served, even before the defendant answers. Defendants may propound discovery as soon as they have been served.[1]

8. The deadline to respond to written discovery is thirty days, a few days more if served by mail or email. Missing the deadline can result in penalties, including fines, called "sanctions," or waiving the right to object to unfair information requests.

9. If no response is provided to written discovery, there is no deadline to move the court for an order compelling a response, other than the limitations imposed by the trial date. If responses are provided that are insufficient or contain improper objections, a motion to compel better responses must be filed within forty-five days.

---

1 The big verb for "send" is "propound". The plaintiff *propounded* interrogatories on the defendant. Sound heavy, doesn't it?

10. Motions, generally, must provide sixteen court days' notice (weekdays, not including court-recognized holidays). Briefs in opposition generally must be filed in court and served on all parties nine court days ahead of the hearing date. The moving party may file a reply brief, rebutting the arguments in the opposition brief, five court days ahead of the hearing. (An *ex parte* motion/application generally may be made on twenty-four hours' notice, unless a judge dictates otherwise, but a showing satisfactory to the judge of the reason for such urgency must be made.)

11. A summary judgment motion (aka MSJ), a completely different animal from ordinary motions, may be filed no sooner than sixty days after the defendant is in the case. A hearing on an MSJ cannot occur in less than seventy-five days from when it is served on the other party (more time is added if served by my mail or email) and must be heard no later than thirty days before the trial date. An MSJ also has its own opposition and reply deadlines. (An MSJ is an evidentiary procedure, as previously stated, and so has specifically required written sections and must be provided in statutorily prescribed formats.)

12. A plaintiff may serve deposition notices twenty days after serving the defendant.

13. A defendant may serve deposition notices upon answering.

14. Depositions may not be set less than ten days after notice unless agreed by the parties. More time is required if served by mail or email. More time is also required if the deposition notice seeks production of documents from a subpoenaed non-party.

15. No written discovery or deposition of a lay witness is permitted to occur within thirty days of the trial date unless the parties agree.

16. Expert witnesses must be "designated" (announced in a prescribed writing), but only if the designation is requested in writing by a party. The request (or demand) for designation of experts may be made no later than seventy days before the trial date. The written designation

must be made fifty days before the trial date. (There are variations in the statute.)

The designation document must identify each expert, explain the subject matter of each expert's expected testimony, describe the qualifications to give that testimony, and announce what the expert charges for the services rendered.

The designation document also must attach a copy of any report an expert prepared. Reports from all experts are required in federal court and in many other states. In California, non-medical experts are not required to prepare a report. (Medical experts hired by defendants must prepare and share reports after examining a plaintiff if requested by the plaintiff at the time of the examination.)

The deadlines listed in this chapter are plenty, right? There are more, and there are variations, but these are the most commonly faced in litigation.

This chapter's subsection heading includes the phrase "One of a Million Things that Keep Lawyers Up at Night." I hope you now have the idea. Once you have practiced litigation law for a time, you master these deadlines, though sometimes you still have to look up fine points. There are computer programs (tickler systems) to remind you of upcoming deadlines, and a good, professional legal assistant will also help to avoid a deadline disaster. But it happens anyway.

CHAPTER THIRTEEN

In this Part One, you have been given information to help you be informed about what to do if you have a legal dispute and need to hire a lawyer, or how to understand and participate if you are already involved in a lawsuit. If you are someone thinking of becoming a lawyer, if you are a law student, or even a young lawyer with limited experience, this information should help you understand the terminology, the pattern of litigation, and what may be expected of you at your law firm. For experienced practitioners, I hope you learned a few tidbits you didn't know before, or found value in thinking through the litigation phases you usually take for granted; and maybe, I hope, some of my observations about the practice and ethics of law caused you some reflection.

As I stated earlier, in Part Two that follows, we put together what we've learned by tagging along on a lawsuit that resulted from a dreadful accident. In the Smithson v. Family Swim Club and Got You Covered Technologies lawsuit that we will follow, we will hear what the lawyers think, why they make certain choices, and pursue certain strategies. We will watch them face off against each other, and address the court and the jury. (Part of the complaint for the Smithson lawsuit is shown in Chapter Eight, Essential Legalese.)

With the Smithson case, my goal is to show you what really happens, beginning with the accident, then hiring the lawyer, developing the case theories, conducting discovery, filing and responding to motions, and how the judge decides them, conducting settlement negotiations, and taking the case to trial. Along the way, the lawyers reveal their plans and strategies and talk or think about their concerns. You will see how the case plays out. Again, if the description of the accident that follows (though set forth quickly) is troubling, stay with the story because you will see that the narrative is more focused on showing you how the process works in the real world.

Ready to litigate a case and go to trial? Let's roll!

PART TWO

CASE STUDY

Smithson V. Family Swim Club, LLC and
Got You Covered Technologies, Inc.

Cast of Characters
(In Order of Appearance)

1. Anne I. Dewey – Lawyer and name partner in the firm of Dewey, Cheatem & Howe (DCH), representing the Smithson family (previously introduced in the discussion of hourly fees in Chapter Seven);

2. Issa Robert (Rob) Berry, Lawyer and associate with DCH, reporting primarily to Anne Dewey;

3. Frauderick Jones – A plaintiff faking injury (appearing in Chapter Eleven);

4. Paul Smithson – Successful salesperson. Married to Patty Smithson and father to Perry, Penny. and Peter;

5. Patty Smithson – Certified court reporter. Married to Paul and mother to Perry, Penny, and Peter;

6. Perry Smithson – Paul and Patty's eldest son, ten years old at the time of the accident;

7. Penny Smithson – Paul and Patty's daughter, eight years old at the time of the accident;

8. Peter ("Petey") Smithson – Paul and Patty's youngest child, five years old at the time of the accident;

9. Douglas N. Heels – Manager of Family Swim Club, LLC;

10. Phillip Y. Knight – Business owner, former member of Family Swim Club whose company also provided pool maintenance services;

11. Daphne Duckworth – 18-year-old receptionist at the Family Swim Club;

12. Sharon Little – Risk manager at Got You Covered Technologies, Inc. and wife of Noah Little;

13. Susan Dembach – General counsel at Got You Covered Technologies, Inc.

14. Parker "Skip" N. Havidyad – Lawyer and partner in the firm of Kaniver, Acostia, Wright, Wong, Grin & Barrett, (Kaniver firm) representing Got You Covered Technologies, Inc.;

15. Mary D. Wright – Lawyer and junior partner at the Kaniver firm, reporting primarily to Skip Havidyad. She is the daughter in law of name partner, Callum Wright, who left the firm years earlier to become a judge, now deceased;

16. Andrew "Drew" Delascard – Lawyer and associate at the Kaniver firm, reporting primarily to Skip Havidyad;

17. Riley B. Goode – Lawyer and name partner in the firm of Gotcha Goode, representing Family Swim Club, LLC.

18. Sasha Young-Greenhorne – Lawyer and associate at the Gotcha Goode firm, reporting primarily to Riley Goode;

19. Maxwell S. Nerdley II – Mechanical engineer, retained as liability expert for the Smithsons;

20. Holden De Monet – Vice-president of claims at Cambridge General Indemnity Company;

21. Hon. Maya B. Stickler – Judge of the Los Angeles County Superior Court, initially appointed in 2005 by the governor, Republican Arnold Schwarzenegger, and re-elected to the bench three times, all unopposed;

22. Noah Little – Vice president of engineering at Got You Covered Technologies, Inc., and husband of Sharon Little;

23. Marc Mewords – Mechanical engineer at Omnisis Laboratories, retained as liability expert for Got You Covered Technologies;

24. Samit Ramaswamy – Safety engineer at Safety Plus Accident Mechanics, retained as liability expert for Family Swim Club;

25. Ivana Brainsby, PhD. - Human factors expert;

26. Rocky Rococo – Private investigator;

27. Carlotta "Lottie" Cash – Senior Claims Specialist II at KMA Insurance Company, primary insurer for Got You Covered Technologies, Inc.;

28. Luke Askantz – Claims Supervisor at Bumbershoot Specialty Assurance Company;

29. Calum E. Ismael – Mediator with End It Resolution Services, a retired federal magistrate who served in the court's admiralty law division;

30. Docker "Stamp" Bates, of Techie-Doc Trial Support, hired by the parties to assist with electronic evidence presentation during the trial;

31. Jose Kanusee - Juror number 1;

32. Lois Price - First juror number 2;

33. Barbara Dwyer - First juror number 3;

34. Christopher P. Bacon - First juror number 4;

35. Paige Turner - Juror number 5;

36. Tish Hughes - Juror number 6;

37. Al Beback - Juror number 2;

38. Mack Burger - Juror number 3;

39. Jed Dye - Alternate juror number 1;

40. Freida M. Fider - Juror number 4;

41. Joanna Behere - Alternate juror number 2;

42. Anita Job - Juror number 7;

43. Sam Manila - Juror number 8;

44. Chip Monk - Juror number 9;

45. Duane Pipe - Juror number 10;

46. Jean Poole - Juror number 11;

47. Ken Reade - Juror number 12;

48. Benjamin Proctor, M.D., Plaintiffs' pediatric neurologist expert;

49. Crystal Ball, LVN, Plaintiffs' life care planning expert, CLCP (certified by the Commission on Health Care and CNLCP (by the Certified Nurse Life Care Planner Certification Board);

50. Robin Do, MBA, CPA, CFF. Plaintiffs' economist expert; and

51. Cameron Payne, M.D. J.D. M.S. MPH. Defendants' life expectancy expert.

How the Case Begins – The Accident

CHAPTER FOURTEEN

Paul Smithson is a successful buyer for a major department store, married to Patty since 2005. Patty works from home as a customer service representative. It is 2023, and they have three active children: Perry, age ten, Penny, age eight, and Peter, age five. Perry plays in soccer and baseball youth leagues. Penny is in soccer and ballet. Peter played T-ball and now wants to play soccer like his siblings. They are all in elementary school. The Smithsons do not have a swimming pool, but go to the beach when they can in the summer with the kids, a long drive, and a tiring day. They decide to join a private pool club nearer to home so the kids can go swimming more often and not take up an entire day. A friend tells them about Family Swim Club, known simply as the "club," about five miles away in the next town. On Saturday, November 11, 2023, the family drives to the club to check it out and maybe sign up.

The manager, Douglas N. Heels, shows the family around. There is an indoor pool, used year-round, and an outdoor pool, now closed for the upcoming winter. The kids are excited and quickly find the snack bar and the recreation room with a ping-pong table and a big screen television. Paul and Patty then follow Doug to his office, where they begin to fill out forms and talk about available payment plans.

Suddenly Perry and Penny are shrieking down the hallway, "Mommy, Daddy, where are you?! Where are you?" Patty rushes to open the door and sees the two older children. They are screaming for her to "Come quick, hurry, hurry!" Paul and Patty rush after them, Doug close behind. The kids run through the door to the outside pool yelling, "Petey, Petey!"

The pool is covered with a vinyl tarp, secured to the concrete edge by straps sown into the tarp material. The straps attach to metal anchors drilled into the deck about eighteen inches apart. Paul can vaguely see a shadow floating under the tarp near the edge. He starts ripping at the anchors while everyone around him is screaming. He yanks one of the anchors free, plunges his arms under the tarp, and pulls Peter from the water. Peter is unconscious and not breathing. Doug is on his cell phone calling 911.

Others now arrive, and an employee starts CPR, which goes on until the paramedics arrive, about eight minutes later. The effort causes Peter to spit up water and start a pulse. All necessary medical protocols are followed while Peter is taken to the hospital. During this process, the paramedics ask how long Peter was under the water. Paul and Patty believe they were in the manager's office for five to ten minutes. Perry tells his mother that he and Penny started to play ping-pong and thought Peter had gone to the other side of the room to watch television. They played for a brief time, realized Peter was not in the room, and went looking for him. They saw him through a window slip under the cover, ran outside, and tried to grab him. Then they ran inside. The paramedics prepared a report, eventually estimating that Peter was underwater for five to seven minutes.

At the hospital, Peter is alive but unresponsive. He is placed in the pediatric intensive care unit. Over the next few days, he moans from time to time, his eyes open occasionally, but he does not respond to his parents' voices. Peter remains in this state for weeks, though he starts to respond to some verbal cues. His parents have been camping out in the ICU the entire time; Patty's parents are caring for Perry and Penny.

The doctors eventually conclude that Peter has irreversible brain damage and will never recover. They tell Paul and Patty that Peter will survive for a time on a feeding tube, it will cost about $500,000 per year to maintain his existence, and his life expectancy is less than ten years. So far, with the emergency treatment and long-term residency in the pediatric ICU, the cost has mounted to about $1.5 million.

Hiring the Lawyer

CHAPTER FIFTEEN

Patty's parents advise Paul and Patty to talk to a lawyer when they are ready, though that was the last thing on their minds. They are convinced to see a lawyer when Patty's father points out that the costs they face may bankrupt them. They recommend Anne Dewey, of the law firm of Dewey Cheatem & Howe, or DCH, who was very patient and professional in helping them the previous year with a minor backyard beef with their neighbor. They arrange for Anne to visit Paul and Patty at the hospital. Anne sees Peter in his pediatric intensive care unit room, a pitiful sight with tubes everywhere. She and Paul find an empty room to talk; Patty won't leave Peter's side.

On hearing about the ordeal since the accident, the diagnosis, and eventual expenses for medical and caretaking, Anne tells Paul she can't imagine the emotional upheaval. She explains this conversation is completely privileged, whether or not the family retains her, or if she agrees to accept the case. Like any lawyer faced with a prospective client who suffers a catastrophic injury, she is not only sympathetic about what happened, but it is inescapable to her that this case could put her firm on the map.

The DCH firm is an eclectic practice. Anne handles homeowner-type cases, as Anne and Rob did for Patty's parents, some estate planning, some family law, and she is well-experienced in personal injury, but none as calamitous and potentially high profile as this one. Howie Cheatem specializes in corporate law, and Oscar Howe mostly does workers' compensation law, though he hasn't pulled his own weight in some time, which has strained cash flow. Anne has not thought through yet what kind of experts she will need, but knows the firm will have to commit a lot of money from its annual budget to handle the case properly.

Anne gently asks Paul to provide the details of what happened. As painful as it will be, it is important to understand the circumstances, the timing, the condition of the pool, the cover, and other aspects of the property. She is looking for information to support a claim of negligence against the club. How did Peter get outside? She will have to visit the property to think it through but wonders why the door to the outside pool wasn't locked if the pool wasn't in use. Paul cannot distinctly remember whether all the straps attaching the tarp to the anchors were in fact attached; he was in a panic. He does recall pulling the corner of the cover off. Anne now considers whether the anchors were properly attached and spaced, and whether the pool cover was adequately maintained. There must be an explanation of how Peter was able to slip under the tarp.

When Anne first got the call about the accident, she looked up the causes of brain damage from drowning. She learned that the timing of the sequence is important because brain damage can occur after about four minutes underwater. If less than four minutes, there still could be damage, but the chances of recovery are better. What everyone with knowledge of the accident says about the timing must be taken with a grain of salt, considering the trauma of the moment, but Perry and Penny saw Peter go under; that's when the timing sequence started. It is uncertain how long Perry and Penny spent trying to get to Peter before they hurried to their parents, but they probably realized quickly that they could not get to Peter. Anne assumes this was no more than a minute. It would have taken up to a minute to find the parents and for the group to hurry back to the poolside, and maybe another minute to extract Peter. It was possible, Anne thought, that Peter was under less than four minutes. Anne intends to obtain the medical records as soon as possible to understand the diagnosis that Peter will not recover. She is not sure it is accurate.

Paul asks how things will proceed and what his family's involvement will be; he's never been in a lawsuit before. He explains that everyone is highly traumatized and wants to know when Anne will proceed with the claim. Anne explains that there is a two-year statute of limitations from the date of the accident before they have to file suit on behalf of Paul and Patty. (As a minor, Peter's statute of limitations does not begin to run until he is eighteen, but he needs the money now for his care. She does not mention the likelihood that Peter might not make it to the age of majority.) She assures Paul they will proceed much faster than that because the sooner they can get to a resolution, the sooner the family might have funds for Peter's care, assuming the case has merit.

Anne gives Paul a brief description of how a lawsuit works, including that she will get a court order appointing him as guardian ad litem for Peter. Minors are not allowed to sue as themselves under the law and must be represented by an adult, who in turn is represented by a lawyer in court. He and Patty will have to contribute to and sign discovery papers from time to time, and he and Patty eventually will have to give depositions. She explains the deposition process, which elicits a look of fear from Paul. Anne assures Paul that all they have to do is tell the truth, but she will spend time with them in advance, going over the procedure in detail and discussing their testimony.

Before Anne leaves, she tells Paul she will be sending a retainer agreement to sign. She will accept the case on a contingency fee basis. Her fee for representing Paul and Patty will be 33% of any recovery if the case can be settled before experts give depositions close to the trial date. If the case settles after that point or goes to trial, the fee will be 40%. By statute, her fee for Peter cannot exceed 25%. The firm will pay all expenses, which the family will have to reimburse out of the recovery, only if the case is settled or won at trial.

The Case Theory – The Allegations that the Villain Did You Harm and Deserves to Be Humiliated in the Public Square

CHAPTER SIXTEEN

Legal Bases for a Negligence Suit with the Smithson Accident Facts

We are about to see how the plaintiff's lawyers think through how to present the lawsuit and what information they need to start the process. They consider what causes of action should be in the complaint they will file. This helps them determine who should sue and who should be sued. As a minor, Peter Smithson does not have the legal capacity to sue, so one of his parents must be designated by the court as guardian ad litem. The case obviously includes negligence as the reason for Peter's near drowning, but the parents were traumatized, too, maybe even Peter's siblings. They also want to allege product liability against the pool cover manufacturer if an expert agrees there is a case to be made.

As discussed earlier, negligence means carelessness. There was no supervision around the outside pool where the accident happened, but the pool cover was in place. Arguably, the door to the outside should have been locked, but it is also reasonable that if the cover was properly installed, Peter could not have fallen into the pool. On the other hand, a five-year-old was left alone to wander around exploring the place. Accidents happen on a "Murphy's Law" basis; anything that can go wrong will go wrong. It happens all the time.

Paul and Patty were not physically injured but certainly had emotional distress. Negligent infliction of emotional distress is a legal theory against someone who causes emotional harm as opposed to physical injury. Making an emotional distress claim is the only way for them to make a claim for their own damage, separate from Peter's. This is often called a "bystander claim," that is, someone nearby could make such a claim if they directly perceived the accident as it happened. The law limits such claims only to close family members, so the employees and other club members have no right to make claims even if they were distressed by what they saw.

Perry and Penny were right there when it happened and could be emotionally scarred. The lawyers will have to decide whether they, too, should be plaintiffs in the suit on a bystander theory, but the ultimate decision to include the kids in the case will be up to the parents.

Premises liability is a legal theory that property owners or occupiers are responsible for injuries on their property due to unsafe conditions they should know about. Premises liability is still based on negligence, but the negligence lies in the more general notion of failing to reasonably assure the property was safe, rather than the more direct act of opening an otherwise locked door and then leaving the area open and unsupervised. In this case, premises liability is included in the complaint as an "alternate theory of liability." It is subject to slightly different evidentiary proof, but here it may be ultimately unnecessary because the theory about negligently leaving the door open, depending on the facts that come out, seems enough to win the case, assuming the jury agrees it was careless to do so.

Product liability is a legal theory that holds designers (inventors or engineers), manufacturers, or sellers responsible for injuries caused by a product. The defects can be in the design or in the manufacturing process. Examples of a design defect might be that a vehicle is too top-heavy, giving it a propensity to rollover in an accident, or a chair design engineered with specified screws that were too small, which could cause the chair to collapse under the weight of an ordinary person. An example of a manufacturing defect might be that a chair manufacturer uses smaller, weaker screws than the design engineer specified, resulting in a collapse.

Some products cannot "design out" the possibility of failure in use, or even misuse, but the manufacturer has an obligation to include a warning or instruction for use of the product to avoid such failure. The act of improper design, manufacture, or failure to warn also qualifies as negligence, and so both theories are viable. The difference is that the evidentiary requirements differ between the theories; negligence requires a showing of lack of reasonable conduct (carelessness) while product liability requires a showing simply that the product did not perform as safely as would be expected.

Initial Strategy and Investigation

Anne and her associate, Rob Berry, discuss what causes of action should be in the complaint, what theory of negligence is supported by the facts, and whether it will be persuasive. Anne would like to file suit as soon as possible, but needs to understand more about how the pool cover works. Rob raises the idea of waiting to file the case. They really don't know if the child will recover from the permanent vegetative state, but this needs to be balanced against the possibility that witnesses' memories will fade somewhat as to important details. And what if Peter passes away?

Anne points out three reasons they need not wait and should proceed promptly. First, they have to send a letter to the club reminding them to preserve and not alter any evidence. This makes it clear to the potential defendant that they have an obligation to hold onto the pool cover because litigation is reasonably foreseeable under *Webb v. Special Electric Co., Inc.*, (2016) 63 Cal. App.4th, 167. So, if the club was thinking they might not be sued, the letter will make sure they understand. Once the letter goes out, the club will report the possible suit to their insurance company, and an investigation is sure to follow. Thus, waiting for memory to fade is not an important strategy in this case.

Second, Anne also thinks it is important to gain access to the premises and specifically the pool cover as soon as possible because their case theory may be affected by it. They definitely will sue the club, but do they have a case against the pool cover manufacturer or installer?

Third, if the complaint needs to be amended to make it a wrongful death case (assuming that grim reality), they can bring a motion with the court to do so as long as they act promptly.

Anne instructs Rob to write the letter right away, hire an investigator to check for witnesses and obtain their versions of what happened, and then retain an expert knowledgeable on pool covers. Because the club is private property, it is questionable whether they can just walk in to inspect the place and start taking pictures; Anne wants to handle this case without any cloud over their actions, so they will get the property and pool cover inspection by serving a formal notice of the intent to inspect the property under California Code of Civil Procedure §2031.010(d) once suit is filed.[1]

They have not yet started drafting the complaint. Once filed, a motion will be filed to appoint Paul as guardian ad litem. She decides to include both the club and the pool cover manufacturer as defendants, but does not yet know the identity of the installer. She could wait and "doe" them in later, but wants their name on the caption.[2] This is not crucial, but Anne feels this could be a case picked up by the press, and so the defendants might be motivated to settle sooner to avoid a prolonged, publicly followed litigation. She decides to call the club's manager and ask. He would be within his rights to refuse information at this point, but she ethically can talk to him directly until he is represented by counsel. If he says he is represented by counsel, she will have to end the call.

She waits a few days for Rob's evidence preservation letter to be delivered and then calls. The club's website shows the manager is Douglas N. Heels. She dials the number.

"This is Doug Heels; how can I help you?"

"Mr. Heels, my name is Ann Dewey. I am a lawyer, and I was retained by the Smithson family in connection with the accident that happened two weeks ago."

"Oh, yes, I got a letter from your firm. We haven't done anything with the pool cover; it's still in place, nothing has moved. After all, it's still the cold season, so that pool remains closed."

"Good, thank you. I ---"

---

1 Go ahead and Google this. This statute permits a request to another party to the case for production of documents (subsection (b)), production of an object for observation or testing (subsection (c)), and, applicable here, to enter land to inspect, test, etc. (subsection (d)). California law does not permit a subpoenaed or noticed inspection of property owned by a non-party to the case. When that happens, it can impede the workup of the case unless the third party agrees to allow the inspection.

2 If you go back to the complaint caption shown in Chapter Ten, you will see named defendants followed by "Does 1-50". If you don't know the identity of a defendant, you include them in the case anyway with the fictitious name "Doe," until you find out. This preserves the statute of limitations against them. When you find out, you file with the court a separate document called a "Doe Amendment" showing the exact name and serve them with the complaint and the amendment. Here's another movie reference. The use of "Doe" to name an as-yet-unidentified person goes back a long way. Check out "Meet John Doe," a 1941 film starring Gary Cooper and Barbara Stanwyck.

"Goodness, Ms. Dewey, we all here at the club feel so awful about what happened. The staff and the members have all been buzzing about it. Horrible thing. I haven't been here that long, just two years, but I am told we have never had an accident as terrible as this, certainly none since I've been here."

He speaks rapidly, sounding nervous.

"I was with the parents in my office, really nice folks, kids were running around a bit. And then all this ruckus starts coming from the hallway. We all rushed out, and Mrs. Smithson is saying, 'Show me, show me.' We found our way to the pool outside, and Mr. Smithson was putting his arms into the water at the edge, grunting. He couldn't reach the boy, so from what I could tell, he grabbed a strap and just ripped it off at the stitching. I have no idea how he did that; the straps are pretty solidly attached. He pulled the boy out, and oh my God. What a scene. I was behind all this, and luckily, my cell phone was in my pocket, so I called 911."

Heels sounds almost tearful as he's talking. Anne, expecting a brief call, only had a Post-it note to take down the names of the pool cover manufacturer and installer. She scrambles for a notepad and writes furiously.

"Mr. Heels, can you ---"

"Goodness, call me Doug, please. And as they carted the boy off to the ambulance, I have never seen looks like these on anyone's faces. Tears everywhere. It was dreadful. And, oh yeah, while all this was going on, the other kids were crying, 'Don't die, don't die!' The trauma these people had and what they are going through must be just awful. Sometime in there, some of our employees who heard the commotion came along with a few club members. Everyone seemed stunned. I know someone started CPR before the EMTs got there, but I don't remember who it was." Heels finally takes a breath.

"Doug, thanks for telling me all this. I very much apprec ---"

"Oh, no problem. We have all been talking about this ever since it happened. We wondered what we could have done to avoid the accident.

I mean, maybe the door to the pool outside should not have been propped open. Our maintenance guy, Javier, had been working out there and had just gone to find a tool for whatever he was working on. I mean, that door would have been locked otherwise."

"Wow," Anne thinks. She hopes he will testify to all this under oath.

"Doug, I called for three reasons. I ---"

"Oh, my goodness, I have been rambling on. You called me. How can I help you?"

(Heels has already helped to the point of proving the plaintiffs' case by blurting out the part about the open door.)

Anne says, "I first wanted to be sure you received our letter and that the evidence was being preserved. You already answered that one. I also wanted to know about the club's insurance. Have you notified your insurance company about the matter, and can you tell me the amount of insurance you have?"

"Yes, goodness, of course, I emailed the letter to my insurance broker immediately and then called to ask what the next step would be. I was told they would notify Cambridge General Indemnity Company about the accident. Let me look at my insurance file a sec. --- Yes, I have it. The liability insurance is $2 million. Was there another question?"

"Yes, " says, Anne. "Can you tell me the name of the pool cover manufacturer, who installed it, and when?"

"You want that? Goodness, let me see. That was before my time, though I know we didn't have the cover when the pool was installed many years ago when the club was built. I have to check another file." Heels pauses as he shuffles through papers. "Here it is. Oh, heavens, it was installed by Phil Knight, Knight Pool Company. That's Phillip Y. Knight. Phil's company used to do our pool maintenance. His guys would come once a week to clean the pools, check the filters, and do whatever else was needed. Once a year, they'd test all the equipment. He shut down, though. I'm not sure what happened, but his company had to file for bankruptcy. Too bad. Phil, - really nice guy, funny. We used to tease him, calling him 'Phly By Knight.' With a "Ph." He loved it. Turned out to be true, I guess." Heels chuckles softly at his own joke. "That's when we hired Javier Gonzalez."

"What document showed you that Knight Pool installed the cover?"

"I have a file on pool maintenance, and his business card is attached to it."

"Do you have the invoice for the work so we can see when they installed it?"

"Sorry, I do not."

"Do you think Knight Pool Company had insurance?" Anne asks.

Heels replies, "I don't know, but it wouldn't surprise me if he didn't. Phil had a lot of businesses and I'm not so sure he put a lot of money into any of them. Oh, and here's the name of the pool cover manufacturer, it says here 'Got You Covered Technologies'." And oh, my goodness, I should have asked from the start. How is the boy doing?"

"Doug, I have to tell you it's not good. We are hoping Petey will recover but it's been enough time that there may be permanent brain damage. I'm sorry to tell you that. But I want to thank you for all your help and honesty, and I am sure your insurance company will reach out to me soon so we can hopefully resolve this."

"Ms. Dewey, we all want the best for the Smithsons, and happy to help. Have a good day."

Anne reviews her notes to unpack all this information. Doug Heels seems to have made her negligence case. He said the door to the outside pool usually was locked at this time of year, but was propped open while Javier, the maintenance employee, worked outside. He left the door open to go to the restroom, fetch a tool, have lunch, or whatever, so there was no supervision around the pool as there might be when the pool was open for member use. Mr. Gonzalez's action, or in this case, inaction, in not closing the door when he stepped away, was arguably negligent and his employer, the club, will be vicariously liable for his conduct.

He didn't add much to help figure out the amount of time that passed while Peter was treated at the poolside. It now occurs to her that even though it might only have been three or four minutes until they got Petey out of the water, there is no information about whether the eight minutes of CPR until the paramedics arrived had restarted his breathing. If not, this would support the diagnosis that Petey may never recover.

While the case now appears to be on solid ground, there is only $2 million in insurance, not nearly enough to care for the child, much less to compensate for pain and suffering. Anne also has experience with Cambridge General Indemnity. Their reputation matches their acronym on the street, CAGI.

Since there is limited insurance available to the club to pay the claim, she considers whether to sue Knight Pool Company, but they are out of business and probably had no insurance. She will have to try to make a case against Got You Covered to get any more money out of this. At this point, though, she does not have enough experience with a mechanism like a pool cover to formulate a product liability theory, but hopefully, their expert can help.

A few weeks pass, and there is no word from Cambridge General. In a follow-up call to Doug Heels, she learns he has heard nothing as well. He provides her with a telephone number for Phil Knight. Mr. Knight confirms that his employees installed the pool cover equipment some years earlier. He had personally worked on the cover installation with two other employees, and they followed the manufacturer's instructions, measuring the distance between the anchors at 18" each and then drilling into the pool deck.

He had an employee clean the pools on a schedule, repair equipment as needed, and about a month before the accident, his employee inspected and tested everything to see if repairs were needed or equipment replaced. It was the end of the year for using the outside pool, so they also put the cover in place for the season. It was at that time that his company was about to shut down, so they also used that time to train the club's maintenance person, Mr. Gonzalez, on how to install and store the cover. He was not told there was anything wrong with the straps or anchors. Knight confirms his insurance had expired, confirms his bankruptcy, and says he expects to be discharged from all debts soon.

Rob has retained Maxwell S. Nerdley II as an expert in the case. He got Nerdley's name from a friend in another firm and explored his website before calling him. Maxwell Nerdley has a PhD. in mechanical engineering, and the website shows he has handled many catastrophic injury cases stemming from a variety of factual situations and involving many kinds of products. In the telephone interview, Dr. Nerdley admits he has not handled a case specifically where someone has gotten caught under a pool cover but he is familiar with the product, having worked on a case involving a pool cover retractor mechanism that injured a worker while using it. He told Rob he also could provide opinions at trial as needed on the negligence of the club and its employee since he also qualifies as a safety expert. His CV shows he has testified many times and mostly on behalf of plaintiffs against defendants. [3]

Months go by, still without any news from the club's insurer. Anne and Rob elected not to reach out yet to Got You Covered because they might react faster and more aggressively in investigating the matter and do so before Anne could get access to the property. It is time to start working on the complaint.

The Complaint – Alleging How You Did Me Wrong

Anne and Rob sit down to review his draft complaint. He has included four causes of action, negligence (against the club for failing to close the door to the pool and possibly for improper maintenance of the equipment – the latter theory to be fleshed out), negligent infliction of emotional distress, premises liability, and product liability (against Got You Covered).

Rob asks if Perry and Penny should be plaintiffs; they obviously are close family, perceived everything as it happened, and were clearly distressed by their reactions at the scene. Anne agrees that it's possible and will see if the parents want to put them through it.

After a detailed discussion with Paul and Patty, they decide not to include Perry and Penny in the lawsuit. This seems to be an emotional decision for the parents so Anne wants to be sure they will not change their minds after it is too late. She repeats her opinion that the children do have a viable case, though they seem to have gotten back to their routine, and are back in regular school session,

---

3 A curriculum vitae or CV, from the Latin "course of life," is a professional resume, usually containing much more detail than, say, a typical job application resume.

doing fine. She has the Smithsons sign a letter she prepares for them confirming their decision.

Months go by while Peter's condition settles in. On March 12, 2024, after it seems Peter clearly will remain in a permanent vegetative state, at a cost so far of about $1.5 million (paid by Paul's medical insurer), they file suit in Los Angeles Superior Court. When the summons is issued by the court, it is served with the complaint on Family Swim Club at its address by a licensed process server who hands it to the front desk receptionist on March 18, 2024. They have until April 17, 2024, to respond.

Got You Covered Technologies Inc. is a New Jersey corporation but does business in California, so it subscribes to a company whose business is to accept service of papers for out-of-state companies. Anne's secretary locates Got You Covered's agent for service through public records and has the process server deliver the papers. The agent's job is then to send the papers to the served company. The agent was served on March 20 and so Got You Covered Technologies has until April 19 to respond.

Responding to the Complaint – Hey, I Did Nothing Wrong and I Don't Owe You a Dime

CHAPTER SEVENTEEN

Family Swim Club Is Served with the Complaint

The receptionist at the club who received service of the Smithson complaint is Daphne Duckworth. She is 18 years old and about to start her first semester at the local community college; this is a summer job for her. She is Doug Heels' niece. Doug was not on the premises at the time, so Daphne placed it on the reception desk on top of a pile of club brochures that had also just been delivered. She then went to lunch with one of the lifeguards.

While Daphne was out, the mail delivery arrived and was tossed on the empty reception desk, landing on the same pile of brochures. She saw the mail on her return and put it on Doug's desk. She then scooped up the brochures and placed them in a file in the desk drawer. The lawsuit papers, having mixed with the brochures, had slipped her mind and were accidentally put in the drawer.

Got You Covered Technologies is Served with the Complaint

On March 20, Got You Covered's risk manager, Sharon Little, walks into the office of the company's general counsel, Susan Dembach, holding the Smithson complaint.

"Sue, we've got another one. This one's in California," says Sharon.

"Another drowning? Seriously?" Susan responds.

People getting caught under pool covers have sued the company five times in the last two years. The five cases are all filed in different states, all awaiting trial, and all seeking millions of dollars. The company's strategy so far has been to resist settlements because once they pay, they may have to settle them all for significant amounts. And, more, once those settlements are public, more suits could follow. Their current thinking is it's better to fight the cases because if they can win one of their more defensible cases, they could take the wind out of the sails of the other cases.

Got You Covered is controlling the defense of all the cases from within the company, which includes that Susan dictates the strategy to their litigation lawyers. The company has $50 million in insurance coverage, but the first $2 million for every individual claim is "self-insured.[1] That is, until they pay $2 million in attorney's fees or if the case requires more than that to resolve, the excess insurers usually do not get involved, though they may monitor the progress of the case.[2] Because there are five cases, all with high potential verdicts, the company could end up paying $2 million per case, or $10 million, a serious issue for the company.[3]

> "Okay, when is the answer due?" asks Susan.
>
> "Thirty days from today".
>
> "Well, we don't have a lot of litigation in California. I will have to get a recommendation for a top product liability lawyer. I'll call our insurance broker, who will probably call one of our excess insurers."

Two days later, Susan receives a recommendation and discusses it with Sharon.

---

1 Got You Covered's first $2 million is called a self-insured retention, or "SIR". It differs from a deductible because a self-insured company manages the cases directly, selects and pays its own defense lawyers, and pays the claims within the SIR. A "deductible" is more in the nature of a "co-pay" amount, but the insurer controls all decisions and the defense.

2 Liability insurance may be purchased at various tiers. The first (or ground floor) level of liability insurance is called "primary" insurance, which includes the insurer's obligation to provide you with a lawyer to defend a claim. (See "Insurance Defense," in Chapter Seven.) Additional insurance above that is called "excess" insurance and comes in different forms. There can be multiple layers of excess coverage depending on the insured's needs. If the excess insurance covers multiple types of liability coverage, it is referred to as "umbrella" coverage. For example, you would have liability coverage in a homeowner's policy – for a claim by someone tripping on your driveway, and you would have coverage in an auto policy – for a claim by someone you hit in a car accident. You can buy an umbrella policy to supplement your primary protection that would apply over both a homeowner claim or an auto claim. Here, Got You Covered has a self-insured retention of $2 million per claim and excess insurance (not umbrella) over the SIR.

3 Sometimes, a self-insured company can negotiate a lower annual cap for its exposure. There are many kinds of similar insurance arrangements.

"I was told to call a gentlemen named Parker N. Hava- Havi-, I can't even pronounce it. It's spelled H-A-V-I-D-Y-A-D. The firm is called - gee, they have a lot of partners who want their names over the door - Kaniver, Acostia, Wright, Wong, Grin & Barrett. Ever heard of this firm, Sharon?"

"Nope, but I see in their website that Mr. Havidyad specializes in product liability, has represented companies like General Motors and John Deere, and has enough trial experience that he belongs to ABOTA."

"Good, let's call him."

Parker "Skip" Havidyad calls his team into his office, five hundred square feet in a southwest-facing corner on the 57th floor in Century City. He can see Santa Monica and the Pacific Ocean. On a clear day, he easily can see the Catalina islands. There is a big screen television opposite the desk, on at all times, the sound off. Mary Wright has been with the firm for eight years and is now a junior partner. She has worked on Skip's team the entire time at the firm, his right-hand person. Her father-in-law, now deceased, was one of the founders of the firm and later became a judge. Drew Delascard is a first-year associate; he passed the bar exam in February after working at the firm the previous summer as an intern. He is still intimidated by "Mr. Havidyad," who can be gruff at times, and is often heard yelling on the phone.

Skip says, "We have a new case, a hot one. A five-year-old nearly drowned at a private pool club and is permanently injured. Terrible situation, and potentially an astronomical verdict. The boy got caught under a pool cover manufactured by our client, Got You Covered Technologies."

Mary remarks, "Ooh, that's not good. A boy gets trapped by our client's product – the phrase "Got You Covered" could be taken the wrong way."

Skip says, "Right. I think the name is because those covers are used not only to protect the pool from debris when not in use, but they also can be used as a kind of heat blanket. But good pickup. We'll think about filing a motion in limine to exclude a cheap-shot argument like that at trial, if it gets that far."[4] Skip begins to spew orders. Mary and Drew scribble notes. "Mary, take a look at the complaint. No way to challenge on the statute of limitations, right? How about whether they have stated the causes of action properly?"

Mary responds, "The complaint seems fine. They haven't alleged a claim for punitive damages, so I think we should just file an answer.

"Drew, we'll have you take care of the written discovery. We'll need all medical records we can get our hands on, including his pediatrician's previous records. And find us an expert on pool covers. But there will be a lot more. On the liability side, let's think about safety, mechanical engineering for the alleged pool cover defect, and possibly accident reconstruction. On the damage side, they'll need a pediatric neurologist for the brain injury, a life care specialist to chart out his needs and the costs of those needs for the rest of his life, an economist to total everything to present value, and a life expectancy expert. That would be the minimum, depending on his condition. We'll need to match them expert for expert. And also get an investigator to locate and interview any witnesses to the accident and look into the plaintiffs' finances.

"On it, sir," says Drew. He leaves the office.

Skip, to Mary, "When did I become a 'sir'? That was my grandfather, Parker Havidyad, the Massachusetts appellate justice."

"Oh, I don't know, Skip. Maybe act less like a military commander around the office?"

Skip smiles as she leaves.

Got You Covered Technologies files and serves its answer on April 16.[5] The answer includes forty-eight affirmative defenses, chief among them are allegations that the negligence of the club and the parents caused the accident.

---

4 A motion in limine (Latin for "threshold") is a pre-trial motion asking the court not to admit/ allow certain evidence. An example would be a motion to exclude from evidence that Got You Covered has other cases pending on the same subject matter - the fact that multiple cases exist should not be allowed to imply the product must be defective since those cases have not been tried and may be defensible. Another example might be to keep from the jury video of a news report of the accident because it might contain opinions not otherwise admissible into evidence.

5 Once a party "appears" in the case, such as filing an answer to the complaint, service of

Family Swim Club Is in Default for Not Responding to the Complaint

On April 23, Anne Dewey still has heard nothing from CAGI nor has she heard from a lawyer on behalf of the club. Got You Covered's answer has arrived along with a deluge of discovery items, including interrogatories, requests for documents, and a notice of intent to inspect Family Swim Club's premises and the pool cover. The inspection is scheduled for May 29 at 9 a.m.

Anne calls the Kaniver firm and is directed to Mary Wright. She explains that the inspection set for May 29 is premature since Family Swim Club still has not answered the complaint and she may have to file a default form. Anne says the plaintiffs also want to inspect the premises but there is no way to command them to allow the inspection until they are a party. Mary agrees to delay the inspection and will try to coordinate a convenient date in about a month.

She then calls Douglas Heels to ask if he has received contact from his insurance company and if he has sent them the complaint. He does not answer so she leaves a message. She follows up a few days later and still can't reach him. She emails. No response. On Friday April 26, she calls the main number and finally is told Doug is on vacation and will not be back for about a week. Anne calls again on May 6 and he picks up. He tells her he has not heard anything from his insurance company, but it seems to Anne he has not taken any affirmative steps to inquire.

> "Doug, I guess I am going to have to file a default against the club. I am overdue to do so as it is."
>
> "What do you mean, what's that?"
>
> "It means since the club has not answered the complaint we served; the club will not be able to respond once I do that and my clients will get a judgment without opposition. You can blame it on your insurer. You did send them the suit papers, right?"

---

documents on that party no longer requires personal delivery. It can simply be mailed or emailed to the party's lawyer attaching a statement under oath that it was sent to the correct address or email address, usually by a legal secretary. The "filing" of a document in court can be hand-deposited at the court clerk's office or most courts allow e-filing. In typical practice, law firms pay an attorney service to handle the actual digital transmission or hand-delivery as needed.

"What papers? We don't have anything like that."

Anne checks her process server's note and asks Doug, "Do you have an employee named Daphne?"

Doug replies, "Well, that's my niece. She was here for the summer. Back to school now. Why?"

"Because the papers were handed to her." Anne hears Doug gasp. He says, "I'll call you back."

Doug has his secretary start a search for the papers. He texts his niece asking about them. She texts back that she does not remember anything like that. The papers are not found. Doug calls Anne Dewey back and asks her to send the papers again. She emails them. Doug then forwards the email to his insurance broker, saying these papers had been served over a month earlier and must have been lost. The broker places Cambridge General on notice using a special form titled "Notice of Claim." Cambridge General has the papers in its system as of that day, May 6, 2024.

Weeks pass with no word on behalf of Family Swim Club. Anne gets the name of the broker from Doug Heels and calls. The broker hasn't received anything from Cambridge General either, but will try again. She also confirms that Family Swim Club has no excess insurance. Anne searches online for Cambridge General and finds out their corporate headquarters is in Boston. She calls the general number and asks to speak with someone in the claims department. She cannot reach a human being and so leaves a message. The message stated why she was calling, the name of the lawsuit, the name of Cambridge's insured, and the policy number she got from the notice of claim form. She can't leave a claim number since Cambridge needs to set up its file and assign the number.

She waits two weeks, no word. It is now June 17, three months since the complaint was served. She instructs Rob to file the default, a copy of which was mailed to Family Swim Club. The default was entered in the court's system on June 21, 2024. They will wait another 30 days, and if there is no response, they will seek a default judgment.[6]

---

6 A default filing prevents the served party from filing an answer. The default can be withdrawn by stipulation of the parties or on a motion to the court giving a satisfactory explanation for the delay. The longer the delay, the more likely the motion might be denied. A default judgment is a procedure whereby the plaintiff submits affidavits with proof of the complaint's allegations and

On July 31, 2024, as there is still no contact on behalf of Family Swim Club, Rob Berry files papers with the court seeking a default judgment. On August 5, 2024, Dewey, Cheatem & Howe receive a "minute order" from Judge Maya B. Stickler rejecting the default judgment papers on the basis that not all necessary documents were provided. Rob Berry starts the process of making the necessary corrections, but he will not be able to complete the process for a few days because he has to attend to other cases.[7]

On August 7, Anne Dewey receives a call from Doug Heels.

> "Ms. Dewey, I am calling to find out what is going on with the case. I got another set of papers from your office and sent them to my insurance broker. Did someone contact you."

> Mr. Heels, we have heard nothing. In fact, if not for a mistake we made in how we filed default papers, your company would have a multi-million-dollar judgment against it as we speak. The papers will be resubmitted shortly."

> Heels gasps, "A judgment? Goodness. I don't understand what's happening. I need to call my broker again."

Heels calls his broker and this time he is in hysterics. The broker has just returned after a lengthy vacation. He has not seen the default papers. He cannot find anything in his system showing the papers were sent to the insurer. He promises to get right on it.

The broker calls the claims department at Cambridge General and is forced to leave a message. He calls again and when the message kicks in, he hits zero and is directed to a general operator. He explains he must reach someone in the claims department immediately and asks for help while he stays on the line. At last, he is directed to the vice-president of claims, Holden De Monet. Again, he has to leave a message but does so at length, in detail, and at a considerable decibel level. An hour later, Mr. De Monet calls back.

The following morning, Anne Dewey receives a call from Attorney Riley Goode, of the Gotcha Goode firm.

---

the judge makes an award.

7 A "minute order" is a written decision or directive, filed in the court's record.

"Anne, Riley Goode here. I don't know if you remember me, but we had a case together a few years ago. I think you represented that guy who jumped up on the forks of a moving forklift, got hurt and sued the property owner."

Anne does remember that case. Taking that client's case was one of the worst decisions she ever made. This bozo shows up at a construction site hoping to get a day job and volunteers to work for a day as a showcase. The dummies running the job were short a worker so they let him hang around when they shouldn't have. Thinking he was helping, he saw a forklift moving a load that wasn't secured so he hopped up on the forks to hold the load in place with his body. Of course, he fell off. Anne thought she could get him at least a small settlement. Riley Goode won a summary judgment motion against her on the basis that her client was not supposed to be there, even though they did let him do some unpaid work and that at best it was a worker's compensation claim, not a civil claim. Great form on Goode's part to call after all this time and rub it in her face.

"Hello, Riley. Nice to hear from you. To what do I owe the pleasure?"

"Anne, I was retained in the last hour by Cambridge General to represent Family Swim Club. I'm calling to see if I can take advantage of our prior relationship to get out from under the default."

He believes we got along well in the forklift case, Anne thinks. The guy not only won the case, but he was also rather crass to Anne's client when he took his deposition and then tried to get costs of suit. It was a total loss to Anne's firm.

"Riley, have you been told how long CAGI's been sitting on this, holding up the case? Frankly, I am not inclined to let them out of the default. Had CAGI responded to this case promptly – Well, we all know this is their modus operandi."

"Anne, really? That's what you think? It was a paper-pushing error, nothing more."

Anne is not buying this. CAGI has to get hit on the head sometime for them to wise up and play fair.

"Riley, the default is filed. I would have had a judgment by now but for a picky court clerk who rejected our papers. That's how badly CAGI has failed to protect its insured, putting them in this jeopardy. You will have to bring a motion, and we will oppose it."

Anne thinks it serves Goode and CAGI right that they have to bring a motion. It will send a message that she's not fooling around with this case. The motion may not be heard for months because of the court's congested calendar, but this might put the defendant might in a disadvantageous position. She also believes that the co-defendant, Got You Covered, will line up against the club seeking to deflect liability in their direction. On the other hand, Goode could try to get out of the default by bringing an *ex parte* motion, which could be heard within a few days, but he would have to show this is an emergency. The fact that the default judgment papers are looming could be enough to qualify as an emergency. She'll wait and see.

Sure enough, the next morning Anne receives an email notifying her that Family Swim Club will be in court in three days to ask for relief from the default. While Gotcha Goode had the right to set the *ex parte* hearing the day following the notice, they set it for the following Monday, August 12, which was the date of the already-set first status conference with the judge. At that time, the judge will ask about certain details of the case and possibly set a trial date. The moving brief is attached admitting the insurance company's fault due to a systems logging error. The brief argues that even though more than five months have passed since the club was served, the club should not be penalized for the insurer's administrative snafu. It is a persuasive sounding argument since it tells the truth and basically pleads that fairness dictates there should be a trial on the merits.

Anne and Rob drop everything else because of the short deadline since the opposition brief needs to be filed in the court quickly so the judge can have a chance to review both arguments in advance of the hearing. Their brief sets out the timeline of efforts made over months trying to get the case started, the calls to the club, the calls to the club's broker, the frustrating attempt to contact Cambridge General by telephone only to have to leave messages, the obvious attempt by the club to get the attention of its insurance company, only, it seemed, to be ignored. Anne throws into the last draft a paragraph about past frustrations dealing with this insurance company.

The Family Swim Club's Motion for Relief from Default

While most motion hearings these days are handled by video conferencing, Anne decides to attend in person because of the importance of the potential outcome and to argue for a prompt trial date. The defendants are thinking the same thing. On the day of the hearing, August 12, there were twenty-seven other hearings already set on the court's calendar, consisting of motions and status conferences.[8] There are two other *ex parte* motions, all three added to the end of the calendar. All morning calendar hearings are set at 8:30 a.m. and so all counsel must be in the courtroom at that time even if the judge is not yet ready. At 9:15, preceded by two buzzes from the front of the courtroom, the judge enters the courtroom from her chambers.

> The court clerk: "All rise and face the flag of our nation, recognizing the principles for which it stands. Department 2 of the Superior Court of the State of California for the County of Los Angeles, is now in session, the honorable Maya B. Stickler, judge presiding. Please be seated."

The judge takes the bench.

Two hours later, all regularly scheduled matters are completed. Judge Stickler says, "the Court needs a break. We will reconvene in 15 minutes." She stands and leaves the room, all remaining attorneys standing in response. Anne calculates there are three remaining matters with only thirty minutes left. The court clerks must be let out by noon for lunch, a courthouse rule that is rarely disregarded by the judges. She assumes little argument will be allowed after all this waiting around.

The judge returns and calls one of the other two *ex parte* cases. The lawyers approach counsel table, which is set up horizontally to the judge's bench. The lawyer who brought the motion, representing the plaintiff, looks like he is

---

8 The judge will monitor and control the case by holding status conferences and issuing case management orders, among other things. The parties will have submitted information about the case addressing pre-determined topics, such as a brief statement of the nature of the case, whether any special circumstances may affect the work to be done, what discovery is anticipated, and when the case will be ready for trial. The goal is to allow the judge to set a realistic trial date to keep the case moving.

twelve years old. He goes to the wrong side of the table, where defense counsel were already standing. Plaintiff's counsel is supposed to be on the side closest to the jury box and defense counsel on the other end.[9] The judge directs him to the other side of the table; he moves to follow her direction by walking between the table and the bench to avoid going around the other lawyers.

"Counsel! What are you doing!" bellows the judge. You are not to step in the well!"[10]

The young lawyer stops, confused, and works his way around the other side of counsel table. He then asks the judge for permission to submit a summary judgment motion exceeding the limit of twenty pages. The judge asks how many more pages are planned. Now flustered, counsel says he will need approximately fifty pages. The judge asks counsel if he understands why the twenty-page limit exists. Counsel fumbles a reply. The judge asks if counsel understands the court's workload, including the number of motions that have to be read and analyzed on a daily basis. It is a rhetorical question; the judge does not wait for a reply. The judge is out of patience after a long morning. "Motion denied." The lawyers walk out of the courtroom, plaintiff's counsel looking at the floor, the other two stifling smiles.

The next *ex parte* matter is called, not Anne's. One lawyer steps up. The motion appears to be unopposed, so no one else is present. The moving party, a defendant, wants to delay the trial.

Judge Stickler says:

"Counsel, I see the other three parties to this case, including the plaintiff, are not present. Are you representing to the court that they do not oppose this motion?"

"Yes, your honor," says counsel.

---

9 Plaintiff's counsel, or in a criminal case, the prosecutor's counsel, traditionally sit closest to the jury because they have the burden of proof.

10 Historically, trials were held in the courtyard of the castle, where the well would be centrally located. In modern times, the "well" is the area between counsel table and the judge's "bench." (The "bench" is a large desk elevated and centered, facing the rest of the courtroom.) Both as to tradition and in some respect for the safety of the judge and staff, no one is allowed in that area, the well, without permission. "Your honor may we approach the bench?" is the traditional permission-seeker. Some courtrooms are configured in a way that there is no reason to walk into the well.

"Then why have the parties not signed and submitted a stipulation showing all agree to continue the trial?"

Counsel replies, "Your honor, the other parties told me they will not oppose the motion, but they do not want to be on record as agreeing to it."

The judge appears irritated and states, "So, what you are telling me is that the other lawyers in the case don't want their clients to know they agreed to this. They will go back to their clients, shrug their shoulders and say it was out of their hands? This court will not abide such game-playing. Either those folks get their clients' permission, or they need to get this case ready for trial. Your trial is scheduled for one month from today, your pre-trial conference with the court is set for next week, and your pre-trial motions and documents are overdue by a week. By code, your expert depositions are to be completed within two weeks from now. How many experts have been designated?"

Counsel now looks a bit shaken and responds, "All parties totaled, it is about twelve, your honor. Only two of those depositions have been taken so far."

The judge adopts a low but haranguing tone, "Nine months ago, all counsel in this case stood where you are now, and the court specifically asked if the current trial date was feasible. Could the parties be ready on time? I went around the room and asked each of you, and each said the current date was fine. And now what I'm hearing is the parties did not get discovery done in time, and none of you prepared and timely submitted pre-trial documents in violation of this court's standing case management order. And where, counsel, in your declaration supporting this motion, is the reason for the requested delay explained to the court? How is the court to know if this was an excusable situation or simply group inattention on a case-wide basis?"

"Your honor, we assumed the court would understand the problem."

"Right, you didn't put it in the declaration, and you 'assumed' (the judge elongates the word) the court would 'assume' (this, delivered with some snark) the need for delay was excusable. I've heard enough. Here is what the court will order now. First, the *ex parte* motion is denied. Second, the parties are to file pre-trial motions and trial documents per the court's previous order within seventy-two hours. Failing that, the parties will be sanctioned $5,000 each for each day the trial is delayed because of it. We will see you next week. Have a good day."

"The court calls the *ex parte* matter for Smithson v. Family Swim Club." State your appearances please."

"Good morning, your honor, Sasha Young-Greenhorne for defendant and moving party, Family Swim Club."

"Good morning, your honor, Anne Dewey for the plaintiffs, opposing parties."

"Good morning, your honor, Mary Wright for defendant Got You Covered Technologies."

"Good morning to you all," says Judge Stickler. "I think it's still morning for another few minutes. I have to apologize that you all had to wait this long. As you can see, this is a very busy courtroom, and it certainly would go more efficiently if everyone knew what they were doing."

The judge's demeanor has significantly changed from the earlier hearing. She begins, "I did read the moving and opposing papers here and I will say both sides did an excellent job of laying out the facts. I am assuming as well that the facts in each supporting declaration are true, that there was this five-month delay from the time of service due to some administrative error but also that the plaintiffs reached out in multiple ways, the defendant club did so, and even the insurance broker did so. I believe I understand the issue, and since we do not have much time, let me give you my tentative thinking on this."

The judge launches into her explanation. "Typically, a motion to be relieved from default brought within six months should be granted and we are still under six months. There is case law on this, and those cases were cited in the moving brief. However, I have to say the lengths to which plaintiffs' counsel went to try to get someone's attention were extraordinary, only to be met with a brick wall of silence. It strikes me that it's one thing for the suit papers to be sent by the broker to the insurer and they somehow got lost. But how do you also have a system where you leave telephone messages, and no one gets them, or it they got them, did not return them? Here is a severely injured child who needs financial help he can only get by moving a lawsuit along and trying to prove his case and then runs into this kind of incompetence. But given the case law, I do not think the court has much discretion.[11] A trial, rather than a denial of rights, is always preferable. Now, I see we are set for a status conference today, but I also do not need to hear further about the case since the facts are set out in the *ex parte* papers. Here is what the court will do instead of denying the motion. First, the motion is granted. The defendant Family Swim Club shall file an answer to the complaint within five calendar days. Second, I am setting the trial of this matter for six months from today, Monday, February 10. 2025. Your pre-trial conference, at which time we will hear all motions in limine, will be on Monday, January 27, 2025. If any of you think you cannot be ready under this schedule, speak now. Hearing nothing, that will be the order. Get busy folks. Have a good day."

After all that, Anne felt like she'd won the motion. She did not realistically think her opposition would be successful because of the six-month rule but in the end the judge seemed to penalize Family Swim Club for the delay by squeezing the litigation timeline. If the more experienced lead lawyers were there, they might have put up at least some fight. The younger lawyers, seeing the judge dress down others in the courtroom, may have been intimidated into keeping their mouths shut.

Anne also considered that the trial date six months away was more than fair. She had the option to seek an even closer trial date by bringing a motion, because parties older than seventy-two and in bad health, or parties younger than age fourteen, are entitled by law to priority in setting trial dates, with a

---

11 Note that the judge refers to her actions in the third person, as "the court." This is akin to the "royal we". The court is an overarching entity, and each courtroom is an extension of that entity. The language is steeped in tradition. Phrases like "May it please the Court" or "The Court finds…" are part of that tradition. Sometimes a judge will refer to themselves in the first person; they are people after all. Here, Judge Stickler does both.

maximum of one hundred twenty days. Given the amount of work that has to be done, she really needs more than four months to prepare the case for trial, so she decided not to bring that motion. But six months was a great result; otherwise, the trial could have been set a year away.

Sasha reported the outcome to Riley Goode and the insurer, who, though the case would have to be sped up, felt they dodged a bullet.

When Mary advised Parker of the outcome, he was not happy. He planned to file a summary judgment motion which requires two and half months' notice and must be heard no later than 30 days before the trial. And they need to conduct some discovery before they can know the motion has a chance to succeed. They need to step on the gas.

The fact that deadlines are missed creates the problems these parties just went through. Dewey, Cheatem, & Howe have a terribly injured child in a care facility and the family needs monetary help, even beyond Paul's medical insurance. Cases take long enough to get to the settlement or trial stage because of overcrowded courts. Anne Dewey is tearing her hair out trying to get the case moving.

At the same time, an ordinary business like Family Swim Club has employees who make mistakes. This one, where the receptionist unwittingly buried the papers, was a doozy. Things get compounded because anyone who could solve the problem can be busy or on vacation. Then, as in this case, you have to deal with gargantuan bureaucracies, like insurance companies, who lose things, who have employees who also make mistakes or may be overworked. To be sure, not all insurance companies suffer from the inefficiencies like CAGI does, but it happens.

Planning and Initiating the Case Strategy

CHAPTER EIGHTEEN

The answers are now filed, there are only six months left to the trial date, and the discovery process has started. As we saw in court at the time of the *ex parte* hearing, there is no guarantee the trial will be "continued" once the judge sets the date. [1]

Judges can treat some cases differently from others. In fact, let's address what happened to the young fellow in the earlier *ex parte* hearing before Judge Stickler. He wanted to delay the trial of his case, and it seemed he prepared and filed the motion as a courtesy for the other lawyers in the case, even opposing counsel. You can imagine his day was uncomfortable, not only in court after the judge came down on him like that, but when he got back to the office and told the others in the case happened, fire alarms would have gone off.

Actually, it is common that trial dates are delayed because the parties simply cannot get the discovery process done in time, often because of other cases that, for one valid reason or another, have a higher priority. There are judges, like Judge Stickler, who want to keep the parties' feet to the fire, maybe to force them to settle, but just as many tend to understand and allow one or more trial delays. Sometimes, you don't know what you're going to get, as Mrs. Gump said.

Until you have donned a robe and presided over a case, it is hard to speculate why some judges would rule as Judge Stickler did. To anyone in the courtroom, it may have seemed she was punishing the young lawyer, shooting the

---

1 Here's another lingo thing. In California, delaying a procedure, like a trial, a hearing, or a deposition, means to "continue" it. An order might say: "The trial is continued to X date." or "The hearing on today's motion is hereby continued to X date." In New York, delaying a court hearing is called an "adjournment." Dismissing a case in New York is to "discontinue" it; in California, it is simply a "dismissal". Go figure.

messenger, as it were. The fact is that poor kid was sent to court to be ambushed because the brief was poorly written, and he was not experienced enough to assert himself to the judge properly.

If the young lawyer was the author of the brief, then his boss sent him to the lions without spending any time checking it over and teaching him what needed to be in it. There are guides for how to do it, but there is often nuance that experienced lawyers better understand. The court must be provided with a satisfactory reason to make an order, especially on an *ex parte* basis. The brief, or more particularly, the supporting declaration to that brief, did not lay out the reasons for the requested ruling, and the ruling was within the framework of how judges deal with such issues.

There were multiple parties to that case, and no doubt some of the litigation activities were delayed because someone was in trial, or a witness took ill for an extended period of time - lots of things can happen. Instead of saying that, which would show the situation was out of the parties' control and thus excusable, the lawyers in the case must have talked about it and thought since they agreed, the court would just rubber-stamp it. Oops.

It did not help, and also seemed to irritate the judge, that no one else showed up, especially since they did not indicate their support in writing. It seemed like the judge would have been receptive to that. Even so, had the brief clearly set out the reasons for the delay, they might have gotten away with it. Oversight of the work product by the supervising lawyer could have helped.

For all we know, this may not have been the first time this group had disregarded the rules with Judge Stickler, and so she was already not happy with them. After Judge Stickler's ruling, depending on the complexity of the case, several lawyers will be pulling all-nighters to prepare all the documents the judge required before the upcoming pre-trial conference, including multiple motions, jury instructions, exhibit lists, witness lists, etc. Good luck to them.

In many courtrooms, particularly in populous regions, there may be several trials set to start every week. This is in part a function of how many cases are filed constantly. The courts, therefore, impose trial dates on all these cases immediately on filing or within months thereafter to keep the litigants moving along. Consequently, there may be several trials set to start each week in any given courtroom.

Most cases settle, so the courts can gamble on having multiple trials on the calendar, and if they do end up with more than one trial starting on the same day, the courts have the power to delay one of them at least until the first trial is completed. Another consideration is that most states have an outside period within which a case must be tried, or otherwise it will be dismissed. In California, the outside deadline is five years. If there are multiple trials set at the same time, the older cases will get priority.

The Smithson case trial date, now six months away, forces the case to fruition much faster than the usual couple of years it takes to work things up. Advantage plaintiff – maybe. Typically, plaintiffs want to get to trial fast; the sooner the trial date, the sooner the clients can be compensated if it's a winnable case, or the defendants will be ready to settle that much sooner.

Defendants, on the other hand, are ordinarily in no rush. The defense firms may be crushed with other cases or with personnel changes that constantly affect what cases have priority to work on. Plus, the longer the wait to trial, the less patient the plaintiff may become, possibly willing to accept less in settlement. There are lawyers who employ delay strategies as much as possible for that reason, especially when the impatience is expressed by opposing counsel.

The time squeeze imposed by Judge Stickler in the Smithson case is now mostly on the defendants who must conduct discovery to get the information needed to evaluate the merits of the case and report those conclusions to the respective insurance companies, where settlement decisions are made. The defendants will have to move rapidly.

After the *ex parte* hearing, Skip Havidyad, Mary Wright, and Drew Delascard meet to work on a discovery plan. They work backward from the February 10, 2025, trial date. Skip believes the discovery will show the spaces between the anchors were installed according to published engineering standards and therefore cannot be a design defect, if that is what the plaintiffs contend, which they have to find out in discovery. Since the installation was done by another company, not hired by Got You Covered, there can be no installation error defect blamed on Got You Covered. He hopes they just need to have their expert see the pool cover setup and file the summary judgment motion, supported by the expert's declaration.

They have their secretary reserve Monday, January 7, 2025, for the summary judgment hearing; this requires securing the date in the court's electronic system and paying a $500 fee. January 7 is as close to thirty days before the trial date as they can get. They must give notice seventy-five days before the hearing, plus two additional days if they serve it via email. If they email the notice, adding two days to the seventy-five-day minimum service time, the motion must be completed, filed, and served by October 22. They will need a couple of weeks to write the motion, so they decide they must get access to the property, hopefully no later than the end of September. It is now August 12.[2]

They also decide they need to take the deposition of someone from the co-defendant, Family Swim Club. Not only will they ask about the pool cover installation, but they also want to establish that the club is substantially or fully at fault (just as Anne Dewey had hoped). The jury will be tasked with assigning a percentage of negligence to any party they feel contributed to the accident. The higher the percentage attributable to the club, the less will fall to Got You Covered, assuming even that Got You Covered is found partially responsible. Also, the plaintiffs' interrogatory responses arrived, identifying Javier Gonzalez as the maintenance person. They want Gonzalez's deposition as well.

The expert Drew found, Marc Mewords, is a forensic engineer in the Orlando office of Omnisis Laboratories, a nationwide litigation expert firm. The firm provides litigation analysis services in most fields of science, employing approximately 250 engineers, laboratory technicians, construction professionals, and life science professionals. The company maintains elaborate testing facilities in many states, including three proving grounds and testing facilities for vehicle crash testing. Mewords has an undergraduate degree in mechanical engineering from the Technical University of Munich and a master's degree from Florida State University (60th-ranked in the country). He speaks with a modest German accent, which sometimes can impress jurors on the subject of engineering. When Drew spoke with the Omnisis case coordinator to explain

---

2 As you can see, the deadlines can be onerous and not paying attention to the schedule can be problematic.

what kind of expert was needed, he was referred to Mewords, who had worked on a Florida case with facts similar to the Smithson case.

Discussing the case with Drew, Mewords explained he has worked on many swimming pool cases; they tend to be clustered in states like Florida, and other southern states where there are more swimming pools. He has not had a California case, though the state has nearly as many residential swimming pools as Florida, which has the most. The subject matter of the cases includes diving board accidents, slip and falls, electrocution, and toxic water. While Mewords has worked on only one pool cover case in the past, he is aware that there used to be more such accidents, but industry standards improved, and cover design became safer.

Drew told Mewords they do not yet have much information about the pool cover system involved in the Smithson accident, only that the boy slipped under the cover off the edge of the pool. Mewords tells him that today's pool covers are tested for how much weight they can hold, which would be much more than a child, and that the attachment systems, sometimes with straps sewn into the fabric and secured to drilled-in anchors, usually do not have any space between the fabric and the edge. Drew promises to organize a conference call with the in-house designers at Got You Covered, and eventually, Mewords will have to travel to California to inspect the scene of the accident, hopefully before the pool needed to be reopened for club member use.

Now that the trial date is set and after the discussion in Skip's office, Drew contacts Marc Mewords to find out his availability to come to California for the inspection of Family Swim Club. He also contacts Sue Dembach and arranges for someone from the engineering department at Got You Covered to attend and help Marc Mewords with the company's design history. Sue will confer with Sharon Little, but she believes the best candidate is the head engineer, Noah Little, who happens to be Sharon's husband.

Drew has his secretary send out three discovery notices. The first, a notice of intent to inspect the Family Swim Club property, setting it for September 10, the second, a notice for the deposition of Family Swim Club, setting it for September 11, and the third, a notice for the deposition of Javier Gonzalez, setting it for September 12. The inspection notice sets forth the intent to enter onto the Family Swim Club property for the purpose of "examining, testing, and photographing the property, the subject swimming pool, the pool cover, and its connectors."

Sasha Young-Greenhorn is also busily working on the case for the club. Riley tells her not to worry about a mechanical engineering expert, since co-defendant Got You Covered will take care of that, but they do need a safety expert, someone who can determine if the warning signs around the pool were sufficient and take a look at the overall circumstances. Riley believes the client is exposed to liability because there should have been no way for the child to slip under the pool cover. If this was an installation error, they would be stuck with the poor workmanship of Knight Pool Company under the premises liability cause of action, but he hopes a case can be made against co-defendant Got You Covered, so they will have to contribute to a settlement. He tells Sasha to hire a human factors expert to consider how to argue that the parents are substantially at fault. He gives her some names of experts he used in the past. Human factors is a field that focuses on how people interact with their environment. Human factors advice also applies to how to incorporate safety features into equipment, processes, and the environment in general. Applied in accident forensics, these experts can comment on memory lapses, impaired judgment, and inattention.

She hires Samit Ramaswamy, who, according to Riley, is their go-to guy for safety. He helped them successfully on many slip and fall and trip hazard cases. He does a good job on the adequacy of safety training and signage. She then calls human factors expert Ivana Brainsby, a PhD in cognitive science. Sasha also receives Kaniver's discovery notices and obtains calendar availability from Mr. Ramaswamy and Dr. Brainsby. She calls Doug Heels, who advises her that the parties are welcome on the property any time, but Javier Gonzalez is on holiday to see his family in Mexico and will not be back until the end of September.

Doug asks Sasha for an explanation about the company's deposition. Sasha explains that a deposition may be taken of a person or an organization. Taking the deposition of an organization requires the notice to list the topics of the examination, and then it becomes the obligation of the organization to produce a person "most qualified", or "PMQ", to provide information about each top-ic.[3] She emails the deposition notice to Doug, which lists the topics as follows:

1. Family Swim Club's safety policies and procedures for the use of the club's facilities by members.

2. Family Swim Club's maintenance procedures and schedules for the repair and upkeep of the swimming pools and swimming pool equipment.

3. The purchase and installation of the pool cover.

4. Family Swim Club's investigation into the accident.

   On review of these topics, Sasha asks Doug, "Who in your business knows the most about these topics?"

   Doug replies, "Well, I am the manager of the place, and I know a lot of this information, maybe not everything. The club operates a good-sized property, three swimming pools, a hot whirlpool, saunas in each locker room, and a small fitness room with weights and exercise equipment. We also serve food from our snack bar. But Javier is really the one who takes care of all the equipment and does a lot of the cleaning."

   "Then Doug, you should be the witness."

   "Swell."

The next day, Rob Berry serves a notice on behalf of the plaintiffs for the deposition of Got You Covered's PMQ, setting it for September 30, which is after the club's PMQ deposition but before the Gonzalez deposition can be taken due to Mr. Gonzalez's unavailability. The topics are:

1. Got You Covered's corporate history.

---

3 In California, Code of Civil Procedure, section 2025.230 states organizations must produce the person "most qualified to testify on its behalf as to those matters to the extent of any information known or reasonably available to the deponent." In practice, the term "most qualified" is often stated as "most knowledgeable;" the phrases are used interchangeably – also referred to as "PMQ" or "PMK." However, the witness designated does not actually have to be personally knowledgeable, but if not, the witness must obtain information from others or from company files sufficient to provide information on the specified topics.

2. Got You Covered's pool cover designs for the last 10 years.

3. Anticipated life spans for each pool cover design.

4. Marketing material used for each pool cover design.

5. Prior litigation regarding Got You Covered's pool cover designs.

6. Standards followed for Got You Covered's pool cover designs.

7. Quality control for Got You Covered's production of pool covers.

The notice also asks Got You Covered to produce, to explore with the witness, all documents that explain the corporate history, which show the engineering details of the design, and so forth, relating to the rest of the categories. The notice schedules the deposition for October 3.

Mary and Drew come into Skip's office on hearing him yelling down the hall. Skip is raging. "How dare those SOBs set a deposition of our clients knowing a key witness is unavailable until later! They know we wanted the club people's depositions first, and they are now taking advantage of the fact that we are powerless to take them right now. This stinks." Expletives fly. He throws his pen across the room, just missing Drew's ear.

Mary knows Skip is the kind of control freak who is easily frustrated and quick to anger when his plans are stymied. "Skip, I think we will be okay. We already discussed that the property inspection is the key event for us. And we will get the club's PMQ before our client's deposition. I suggest we wait until a few days before our client's deposition date and then serve an objection based on the inconvenience of counsel. Eventually, we will have to produce a witness once our motion is filed since the other parties will be entitled to explore whether the motion can be successfully opposed." She is practiced at delivering points like this to Skip, laying it out calmly.

Skip harrumphs at this but takes a deep breath and waves them out of his office. Drew retrieves the pen and places it on Skip's desk, then quickly slinks out the door behind Mary. "I don't understand that guy, Mary. He could have taken my eye out!" Mary, still in pacification mode, speculates that a close trial date on such a big case can be unnerving and encourages Drew to just live through it – and next time he should keep his head down. Drew laughs apprehensively.

After two days of annoying, interrupting emails, back and forth, back and forth, and around and around, among all the lawyers, and because of the number of calendars to coordinate, the lawyers finally get on a Zoom call. They agree the property inspection will take place on September 26, the person most qualified deposition of the club will take place on September 30, and the Gonzalez deposition has to wait until October 4. They agree that the Got You Covered PMQ deposition will wait until about mid-October. But Drew realizes his client should testify no later than about October 15 so the other parties will not have the summary judgment motion papers until a week later, which would prompt, perhaps, more careful preparation on the part of the other parties.

Drew counts up the number of emails it took to work this out – 17, either those he drafted or incoming. Some of the emails were paragraphs, others were simply a few words, like, "Ok, I agree." Since the computer entry system allows no less than one-tenth of an hour per task, he records 1.7 hours, totaling $595 in legal fees.[4]

---

4 I want to comment on a pet peeve. I am going to show my age, but here goes. We are used to, and reliant on, our electronic means of communication; texting, emailing, instant messaging. In a busy world, it can be done on the run, saves time, and is easy and convenient to use. Until it isn't. There are times when a personal touch, like voice contact in a telephone call, achieves much more and does so more efficiently. Look at what happened here. All the lawyers in the case will read at least the 17 emails, each of them (those of them who will bill on an hourly basis) will invoice their clients almost $600 to work out this scheduling problem; their clients will be collectively billed about $2000, depending on their hourly rates. Any one of them could have been the one trying to herd the cats here, sending an email proposing a conference call. The call would have taken ten minutes. With the emails to organize the call and the time on the call, which likely would have included fewer lawyers, the total charges could have been less than $1000. Yet, some people are so accustomed to communicating electronically, the telephone option does not even occur to them; using the telephone does not even register with them. I have actually instructed lawyers working for me to "call" opposing counsel for some purpose – using the word "call" in the sentence. Following up, I asked what opposing counsel said. The response was "Oh, they haven't responded to my email yet."

Carrying Out the Discovery Process

CHAPTER NINETEEN

September 26, 2024 – Property Inspection at Defendant Family Swim Club

At 9:30 a.m., people begin arriving at Family Swim Club's parking lot, awaiting the 10 a.m. start time and for someone to announce themselves as the organizer. Sasha Young-Greenhorne arrives a few minutes before the hour and waves everyone over toward the front door, asking them to sign their names on a page held by a clipboard or to attach a business card. The group consists of Rob Berry and his expert, Max Nerdley, for the plaintiffs; Sasha Young-Greenhorne, her expert Samit Ramaswamy (a safety specialist), Ivana Brainsby (human factors expert), Doug Heels, Mary Wright, her expert Marc Mewords, and her client from Got You Covered, Noah Little.

Rob asks Sasha if Mr. Heels would show them where the recreation room is, where his office is, and the route taken from the office to the outside pool. Sasha is not required to allow communication with her client, but agrees to allow Doug to comply in the spirit of cooperation, advising him not to provide much detail.

In the recreation room, each of the experts begins taking photographs, videos, and measurements of the room. They want to be able to help a jury understand the physical layout of the building and try to recreate what could be seen from what vantage points. Jurors are sometimes bused to an accident site to view it during a trial, but it is not a common procedure, so there is no guarantee the judge will allow it.

At this stage, only the plaintiffs' lawyers know the details from the children about how long it took to do anything or go anywhere, or that they actually saw

Peter slip under the pool cover; the interrogatory responses identify the children as witnesses but not what they witnessed. Both the plaintiffs' lawyers and the club's lawyers are aware from their respective client interviews that the parents were in Heels' office when the accident happened; Got You Covered's lawyers do not yet know this and will learn the sequence of events during the deposition process.

The troupe is then taken to Doug's office; the photographing of the premises continues down the corridor and inside the office. Mary asks Doug where he was when the accident happened, but Sasha asks Doug not to respond, politely admonishing Mary not to ask questions directly of her client. All then are shown the pool.

As they approach the door to the outside, Doug uses a key to unlock the door. The experts make a note of this. The pool is covered, with all straps in place, attached to anchors drilled into the concrete. The pool deck is concrete but covered by artificial grass. All anchors are in place. Max Nerdley uses a digital force tension pressure tester to determine the strength of the strap connections; some need to be disconnected in the process.

Rob Berry has the information from Paul Smithson about where he ripped out the strap. Nerdley tests that spot and five others. Marc Mewords observes the testing and takes notes, and then measures the distance between the anchors, occasionally pulling at them. He finds and photographs the product information label, showing the name of the manufacturer and serial number.

It is clear to the defense group that the scene is not as it was at the time of the accident. There is no space at all at the edges for the child to slip through. There had to be a change or repairs to the pool cover system. Rob Berry asks Sasha if the strap, pulled out by Paul Smithson, exists and where it is. At Sasha's request, Doug brings the strap out to the group, and all photograph it extensively. Sasha does not permit Nerdley to conduct a tensile strength test because it might damage the evidence, and no destructive testing was included in the inspection notice.

The inspection concludes at 2:30 p.m.

September 30, 2024 – Deposition of Douglas N. Heels as Person Most Qualified for Defendant Family Swim Club

At 9:45 a.m., Mary Wright logs in to the Zoom link provided by the court reporting service. The deposition she will take today, of the person most qualified at Family Swim Club, whom she understands will be Doug Heels, will be taken methodically and will take most of the day. She is joined by Drew Delascard, who will observe for learning purposes and take notes to help her summarize the testimony for her client and insurance representative. She had prepared a multi-page outline to be sure she covers all the necessary topics in detail. The court reporter is on screen, as is the video technician; there will be both an official transcript taken by the reporter and a video recording of the event to use as needed if the case goes to trial.

Within minutes, the other lawyers check in, including Riley Goode, Anne Dewey, and Rob Berry. Paul Smithson also logs on but keeps his camera off. Anne offered Patty the chance to listen to the testimony, but Patty felt she might not be able to hold up emotionally. Paul felt the same way, but Anne pressed that at least one of them should participate in case the witness says something they know is incorrect and could prompt her about it.

Doug Heels logs on at 9:59 a.m. Mary has the videographer begin the session and all are asked to announce their names for the video record. The reporter has Doug raise his right hand and swear to tell the truth. Mary begins the examination.

Mary starts by asking Heels if he has a history with lawsuits and if he has testified before. He has not.

> Question, by Ms. Wright. Mr. Heels, because you are new at this, I want to take a few minutes to be sure we make a good clean record of your testimony as the court reporter takes it down and will eventually have it made up into a transcript. I ask you to speak clearly and use words instead of gestures, nods or shrugs. Say "yes" or "no," instead of "yeah" or "un-unh," okay?[1]
>
> Answer: Yes, of course."

---

1 When a deposition transcript is prepared, the examination is set forth as appears here, by question and answer ("Q" and "A") to identify who is speaking.

Q. Don't guess if you truthfully don't know the answer but you might be shown photos or documents that will help you remember some things. And we expect you will do your best to provide information if you do not recall specifics, and to estimate things like dates and times to the best of your ability. Do you understand?

A. Yes.

Q. You are here designated as the person most qualified, sometimes called the person most knowledgeable, on certain topics, including the club's safety and maintenance procedures, the history of the pool cover, and your investigation of the accident. Have you seen the deposition notice with those topics, and are you the best person in the company to provide information on them?

A. Yes.

Q. Is there anyone else in the company you feel might have more detailed information to respond on these topics?

A. Goodness, no, I'm the guy. I mean, Javier knows some of this, but I can help you.

Q. The deposition notice also asked you to provide certain documents. These documents include anything written on the topics. Counsel Goode, is the witness producing any documents in response to the notice?

By Mr. Goode: No, any documents responsive to that would have been produced when we answered the interrogatories and document requests weeks ago.

Q. By Ms. Wright: Mr. Heels, no documents were produced about any of the topics earlier in the case. Can you explain that?

A. Well, my goodness. Let's see. We don't have a safety policy or procedure in writing and never did as far as I know. We did change from a maintenance company named Knight Pools and hired Javier Gonzalez, so I don't know if Knight had anything in writing. As for the purchase of the pool, that was before my time, and I could not find any files about it. As for the accident, nothing was written down.

Q. Finally, Mr. Heels, before I get into the facts of the case, I want you to be aware that the court reporter who swore you in is licensed by the State to do so. She has the same power to put you under oath as if you were in a courtroom. Do you understand that the testimony you are giving right now is under oath and carries with it the penalty of perjury if you are not truthful throughout the deposition?

A. Yes, I do.

Q. Mr. Heels, do you understand what perjury means?

A. Yes, I could get into trouble if I lie.

Q. Do you understand that committing perjury, lying under oath, is a crime?

A. Yes, ma'am.

Mary always makes sure a deposition witness understands they are under oath. It is important to especially emphasize it here because of the information she obtained the previous day from Marc Mewords and Noah Little at the accident site. She has a trap planned for this witness.

The deposition proceeded at length, covering the history and employee hierarchy of Family Swim Club, the purchase of the property by the founders thirty years earlier, the sale of the business fifteen years ago, the number of members, the cost of membership, the use and deployment of lifeguards, and how the operation changes seasonally. It was established that at the time of the accident, November 11, outside activities are more limited as the weather in Southern California gets chillier. The volleyball, shuffleboard, and bocce ball courts remain open but are not used very much.

The outdoor pool is closed annually by October 15, depending on the weather. The process of closing up the pool is to pull the cover, which is stored by rolling it up on a cylindrical spool in the summer, over the pool and attaching the straps to the anchors. The anchors are screwed into the deck when not in use to avoid a tripping hazard. Heels is aware of the procedure from watching others do it, but he has not done it himself. He does not know how careful Mr. Gonzalez is in this process.

Heels describes what happened on the day of the accident. The Smithsons arrived at the club, and he showed them around. He recalls Mr. Smithson was happy they have a fitness room, and Mrs. Smithson liked the setup of the recreation room for the kids. The kids were exploring the recreation room when the parents followed them into his office to discuss membership. Mary continues with the examination:

Q. Did the Smithsons agree to the fee?

A. Yes. I pulled out our membership contract, and we started to fill it out together. They were interested in a payment plan. They were going to use a credit card to be charged monthly.

Q. Mr. Heels, earlier, in response to written discovery, you produced a copy of the contract. I am sharing it on the Zoom screen, and I am marking it as an Exhibit to the deposition. Is this the contract you and the Smithsons filled out?

A. Yes, that's Mr. Smith's signature on page 2.

Q. Mrs. Smithson's signature is not here. Did she sign it or not?

A. I don't remember, well, I guess not. That's when all hell broke loose. At about that moment, there was screaming coming from outside the office, and Mrs. Smithson jumped up and ran out the door. We all did.

Q. Did Mrs. Smithson ever sign the contract?

A. No.

Q. Did you ever run the credit card?

A. No, I did not.

On further questioning by Mary, Heels describes how the group ran down the corridor to the pool. He was behind the Smithsons and the two children. The boy, Perry, pointed to the spot where he saw Peter fall in.

Q. Describe what you saw.

A. Mr. Smithson seemed to move around quickly, trying to see the boy in the water. He tried to get his arm under the pool cover and then started pulling at a strap.

Q. The pool is a rectangle. Can you tell us where along the edge he was pulling at the strap?

A. Yes, it was at a corner. The southeast corner, I think. And oh, my goodness, it seemed like it was one of those situations where somehow you get extra strength, and he yanked the strap right off. You could hear it rip. He was then able to pull the boy out. I was on the phone calling 911 while all this was going on.

Q. Who else was present during this sequence?

A. Mrs. Smithson was holding onto the other two kids who were screaming, and she was, I guess, whimpering. I think some other club members had come out to see about the commotion, but I don't remember exactly who. At some point, Javier showed up. I remember that he was trying to help with the boy.

Q. What words do you recall anyone saying while all this was happening?

A. When Mr. Smithson was trying to do CPR, and then the EMTs were there, I recall the little girl saying, "Don't die, don't die." She kept repeating it.

Q. Mr. Heels, I am going to show you a photograph of the pool cover,

taken yesterday. I will make it an exhibit to the deposition.

She puts it on the screen.

Q. Mr. Heels, can you see the photo on the screen?

A. Yes.

Q. You were present yesterday at the group inspection at Family Swim Club's premises, right?

A. I was.

Q. This photo shows the current condition of the pool cover?

A. Yes, it does.

Q. Mr. Heels, when we started the deposition earlier, we talked about the oath you took and that you are required by law to tell the truth. Do you recall that discussion this morning?

A. Yes.

Q. Mr. Heels, please answer this question. Is this the pool cover that was in place when Peter was in the water?

A. No, we replaced the entire system about two months ago, and we replaced some high-maintenance grass around the pool with the artificial grass you see in the picture, which also covers the concrete deck. We were able to use most of the previously drilled anchor holes.

Anne Dewey, taking notes furiously, thought he seemed oblivious to the egregious admission he just made. The club had completely destroyed the evidence, even after a warning not to, and they did so during the lawsuit. Max Nerdley had realized yesterday that the new cover was indeed a Got You Covered product, but the serial number, as well as its seemingly pristine condition, showed it was recently installed. She was sure the Got You Covered people came to this same conclusion because Rob Berry told her they were acting conspiratorially while looking at the identification tag on the cover. Well, they obviously did since Mary Wright had planned this part of the examination for maximum effect. This testimony was vastly different from Anne's discussion with Heels before the lawsuit started.

Mary presses on:

> Q. Mr. Heels, where is the old pool cover, the one that was on the pool when the accident happened?

> By Attorney Goode: Objection: Calls for speculation, and it is irrelevant and not calculated to lead to the discovery of admissible evidence.

> By Attorney Wright: Counsel, those are improper objections. The question was crystal clear. If the witness does not know the answer, he can say that, and the whereabouts of the evidence is fair game.

> By Attorney Goode: I've made my objections.

> By Attorney Wright: Mr. Heels, you may answer the question. Why are you hesitating? Do you need the court reporter to read the question back to you?

> By Attorney Goode: Now, you are harassing the witness. I am instructing my client not the answer the question.

> By Attorney Dewey: Wait, you're what? You are not going to let him answer about the destruction of evidence? It's completely relevant.

> By Attorney Goode: Anne, there is no reason to shout.

> By Attorney Dewey: Mr. Heels, are you refusing to answer the question? Are you going to follow your attorney's instruction?

> By Attorney Goode: Doug, don't respond to that. Counsel is out of control. Anne, you need to calm down, and it's not even your turn to ask questions.

> By Attorney Wright: Mr. Heels, did you take any pictures or video of the scene, that is, while the old cover was in place, whether on the day of the accident or later?

> By Attorney Goode: Objection, compound, and irrelevant. Instruct the witness not to answer.

By Attorney Wright: That's it. I am stopping the deposition and will file a motion to compel the witness to respond. And I will be seeking sanctions.[2]

The attorneys bicker back and forth for another few minutes, and the record is closed.

Mary Wright really does not need to bring a motion to ask further questions. She has what she wanted. The club looks really bad, and she knows from the previous day's inspection that there is no evidence to hurt her client. She will discuss with Skip whether to bring the motion.

To Anne Dewey, it was amusing to see Goode squirm. He went over the line by instructing the witness not to answer the question about destroying the evidence. His reaction confirms her observation of Heels, that he did not seem to understand he'd done anything wrong. Goode recognized it too and acted to protect his client from further evidence of culpability as best he could. Goode must not have known his client upgraded the pool cover and the surrounding area.

She is concerned, though. The witness never actually answered whether the old pool cover still exists in storage somewhere or was discarded. It is important to the plaintiffs' case against Got You Covered to at least see the strap and to be able to see the actual installation. She will re-engage with Goode soon to see if he will relent and produce his witness for further examination, since she must do that before a motion can be filed. The motion, seeking to complete the deposition, is sure to be granted if for no other reason than she was not given a chance to examine the witness on behalf of her clients.

---

2 A word about "sanctions," which has opposite meanings depending on its usage. Using the same Latin root, to sanctify means to make holy. The Latin word for saint is "sanctus." As a verb, a government may "sanction," say, a new environmental initiative, officially approving its implementation. (In Chapter Ten, I referred to your health record using a different word with the same root, "sacrosanct", an adjective essentially meaning sacred.) Used as a noun, a government might impose "sanctions" on another government in the form of a boycott to try to force compliance with a policy. In law and in other contexts, sanctions are a form of punishment, similar to the meaning of politically boycotting a country. The court may impose monetary sanctions, a kind of fine, on Mr. Goode for improper actions in the discovery process. As we will see, destruction of evidence could result in an "issue sanction," where the court may "deem" that some portion of the case is decided against Family Swim Club, which is another version of what could happen, as mentioned earlier, if you don't answer requests for admission.

Soon after the deposition, Paul and Patty call Anne, asking what just happened. Anne explains Mr. Goode seemed to be caught unaware that his client had changed the pool cover and took steps to protect the company by intentionally interfering with the deposition. Mr. Goode might get in some trouble with the judge, but eventually, the deposition will be completed. Even so, this looks very bad for the defendant club, and the situation could help them win the case against them. She said, though, that the case against defendant Got You Covered could get more difficult than it already is.

Anne calls Rob Berry into her office and instructs him to prepare two motions. She will contact Riley Goode about rescheduling the rest of the deposition, but Rob could get started on a motion to compel it. The second motion will ask for permission to amend the complaint to seek punitive damages. The basis for the motion to amend the complaint will be that the destruction of the evidence was a willfully bad act.

October 4, 2024 - Deposition of Javier Gonzalez-Rincon, Employee of Defendant Family Swim Club

Mr. Gonzalez is a native-Spanish speaker, and gave his deposition through an interpreter. The deposition proceeds, and Mr. Gonzalez describes his background, his skill set as a handyman hired about a year or so ago at Family Swim Club, and his daily routine. He knows nothing about the change of the pool cover or the area surrounding the deck, and he was surprised to see it when he returned to work. He is asked to describe the old pool cover, which he said was blue and attached to the anchors in the concrete deck in a similar way to the new cover.

> By Ms. Dewey: What were you working on around the pool area before the accident happened?
>
> A: I put the old pool cover on not long before this accident, and I had trouble unwinding it from the reel. I had other things to do in the meantime, but that day I wanted to repair the winding mechanism.
>
> Q: Here is a picture of the new pool cover we showed previously to Mr. Heels. Is the reel what we see that blue cylinder at the back of the pool area?

A: Yes

Q: Please explain what you were doing and why you were not there when the accident happened.

A: I was trying to get the spool handle to work better. It was getting stuck. I needed a tool, so I went to get it.

Q: Where was the tool?

A: First, I went to the maintenance area at the back of the property, but then I remembered it was in my truck.

Q: How long did it take to find the tool and return to the pool area?

A: Maybe five minutes.

Q: What happened when you came back?

A: There were a lot of people there and a lot of commotion. I saw the boy on the ground and the father pressing on his chest. The EMTs showed up after a few minutes.

The examination continues in this vein as Anne goes carefully through the sequence.

Q. Mr. Gonzalez, how did you get access to the pool area? Wasn't it locked up?

A. Yes, it was locked, but I have keys.

Q. Let's take this step by step. You intended to repair the reel, so you went outside to the pool area by unlocking a door? This is a self-closing door, right?

A. Yes, I pushed the door open and walked through. I thought I might have to go back and forth for tools, so I propped the door open with a bucket.

And there it was. Anne used the information she had gotten from Doug Heels in their first telephone call. She saw on the Zoom screen that Riley Goode's head dropped when this answer came out; another detail his client had not told him. Anne was feeling good about things at this point, confident she had established negligence on the part of the club; it was negligent to walk away from the outdoor pool area, leaving the door propped open to an area that would usually be supervised while in use by members.

Anne finishes her examination, and Mary Wright says had a few questions. Mary asked for more details about his routine and what he knew about other accidents. He did not know much, only that sometimes people slip on wet spots; there had never been a diving accident because the lifeguards do not allow the members to do that, and there are signs everywhere that show diving is against the rules.

> By Ms. Wright: Mr. Gonzalez, was there any conversation among the employees or with Mr. Heels after the boy was taken to the hospital and everyone had left?
>
> A: Yes, some. Everyone felt very bad. Mr. Heels said he was afraid the family would sue.
>
> Q: When Mr. Heels said that, how did you react?
>
> A: I thought maybe I might be in trouble, so I took a picture.
>
> Q: You did what?
>
> A: I took my phone out. This was after everyone had walked away from the pool area.
>
> Q: How many pictures did you take, and what did you take pictures of?
>
> A: Just one. I took a picture of where the boy fell in.
>
> Q: Did you give the picture to Mr. Heels?
>
> A: No. No one asked me for it, and I really just took the picture for myself.
>
> Q: Do you still have that picture?
>
> A: It should still be on my phone.
>
> By Ms. Wright: Mr. Goode, I would like to go off the record and ask you to have the witness retrieve the photograph and produce it now as an exhibit to the deposition.
>
> By Mr. Goode: All right, let me see what I can do.

The deposition resumes fifteen minutes later.

By Ms. Wright: Mr. Goode, do we have the picture?

By Mr. Goode: I am putting it on the screen now.

Well, thinks Anne. Another break. We now have at least a chance to reconstruct what the area looked like, and maybe Max Nerdley can use this in developing the case against Got You Covered.

Mary Wright's examination continues with many questions about the straps, the grommets for the straps, and the anchors. The witness saw the strap that was pulled out and threw it away that day. He was asked if all the straps were attached to all the anchors, how tight to the surface the cover was, and whether anything could be slipped underneath. Riley Goode objected to this last question as calling for opinion and not fact, but allowed the witness to answer. The answer was that when fully attached, the cover was flush with the concrete coping, and it would be hard to even put your hand underneath it.

To Anne, this meant only one thing: the cover was not fully anchored down; it could not have been. Someone could be lying. She suspected the corner of the cover shown in the picture was already disengaged, which is how Peter fell in. Paul didn't have to pull the cover up from the concrete; he must have been able to grab the corner of the cover in his hands, which gave him leverage to pull the cover open for better access to Peter, who had floated farther underneath. Why didn't the witness say he also had done something with the cover itself, not just the rollup mechanism? When Mary finished her examination, Anne asked the direct question:

> Q: Mr. Gonzalez, I asked you earlier what you had done that day, and you said you needed to work on the rollup mechanism, but the picture we now have shows a corner of the pool cover is flapped open. Why was that corner open?
>
> A: I don't remember, ma'am.

After the deposition, she calls Paul to ask if he remembers more about what he did to pull Peter out of the water.

"Anne, I remember being panicked and ripping at it. I remember seeing his shadow under the cover a little farther from the corner and tried to grab him, but had to pull the cover off to reach him."

Anne says, "So you remember you were at a corner of the pool?"

"Yes," he replies.

She emails him the picture from the deposition while they are talking.

Paul says, "Wow, I just don't remember it being that open, but I guess it must have been."

The Expert Phase of the Case –
Have Gun - Will Travel

CHAPTER TWENTY

Experts are used in lawsuits to provide specialized knowledge and expertise on complex issues, helping the court or jury understand technical concepts and make informed decisions, especially when the case involves matters outside their expertise. In fact, there are some subject areas where expert testimony is required or the case will be lost, like medical or legal malpractice cases. You may be familiar with the variety of criminal justice television shows, like CSI or Law and Order. The plots often involve a forensic investigation, and the conclusions made from the investigation are presented at trial by experts, like specially trained crime scene investigators who explain how fingerprints or blood samples are used to solve a crime.

In civil cases, experts serve the same function in a variety of subject matters and also add a measure of science to the presentation, which can be persuasive. As we have seen, there are always experts having the same or similar qualifications but on either side of an issue. How then do we know which one is correct if they draw opposite conclusions on the same facts? Here is the official federal court jury instruction on how to determine if you should accept an expert's opinion[1]:

> "You have heard testimony from expert witnesses who testified about their opinions and the reasons for those opinions. This opinion testimony is allowed because of the specialized knowledge, skill, experience, training, or education of this witness.
>
> Such opinion testimony should be judged like any other testimony. You may accept it or reject it and give it as much

---

1 Most state jury instructions are worded similarly.

weight as you think it deserves, considering the witness's knowledge, skill, experience, training, or education, the reasons given for the opinion, and all the other evidence in the case."

In our Smithson case, each side will offer expert opinion testimony on how long Peter will survive in his permanent vegetative state, on tubes and wires. The cost of caring for Peter includes the facility where he was placed, the medical treatment he needs, the medicine, etc. Experts might disagree on what should be charged for these costs, but once determined, the amount of damages in that category is the sum of the charges over time. An important factor, then, is how long will Peter survive.

If he survives many years, the damage figure is higher. If he succumbs earlier, the cost is less. The plaintiffs' experts, unsurprisingly, will testify that Peter will last longer than the defendants' experts. Whose opinion do you accept? The experts on either side may agree that determining how long someone will survive in a permanent vegetative state is difficult and depends on various factors like the cause of the brain injury, the severity of damage, age, overall health, and quality of medical care, but generally, most people in a vegetative state have a life expectancy ranging from 2 to 5 years, with survival beyond 10 years considered uncommon, an analysis derived from medical studies.[2]

Where the expert opinions on either side will likely diverge would be in more subjective aspects of the opinions, like the expectation of the quality level of care, whether there were pre-existing major health problems, Peter's young age, etc. Sometimes, a jury has to choose from such competing opinions based on the credibility or qualifications of the witnesses. A neurologist is clearly qualified to give a life expectancy opinion in this circumstance, but what if the neurologist on one side has only limited experience with patients in a permanent vegetative state, and the other side has the neurologist who conducted "the" study on the subject published in the New England Journal of Medicine?

So far, we have seen the parties hire experts on the subject of liability; who was at fault. These experts, Max Nerdley, Marc Mewords, Samit Ramaswamy,

---

2 Medical Aspects of the Persistent Vegetative State, The New England Journal of Medicine, June 2, 1994. https://www.nejm.org/doi/full/10.1056/NEJM199406023302206

and Ivana Brainsby, all testify for a living. Their job is to investigate a claim within their field of expertise and provide opinions as to who may be at fault.

Nerdley is a mechanical engineer, meaning his focus is on how things work, particularly why mechanical devices or systems fail. He has worked on many different device and system failure cases; a kind of jack of all trades. He tends to be hired by plaintiffs in injury cases, which could suggest a bias in how he interprets evidence. From a cynical perspective, he can be portrayed as a gun for hire for litigants trying to prove a device or system is defective. This bias, of course, can be portrayed against either side; an expert who always works for the defense is subject to the same scrutiny.

Mewords is also a mechanical engineer. He is employed by a large company with a lot of engineering resources. He is a counterpart to Nerdley's expertise but has a bit more experience with pool cover cases.

Ramaswamy is a safety engineer. He is generally qualified to give opinions on the pool cover because the cover design is supposed to be safe, that is, it is intended not to allow anyone to slip under the connectors. But he was not necessarily hired about the function of the pool cover; rather, he was asked instead if the actions of Family Swim Club were unsafe. He will also provide opinions about whether the parents acted responsibly for the safety of their children. As we have already seen, it will be difficult to defend the club for leaving the door open and, it seems, for leaving the pool cover unattached in one corner.

Brainsby is a human factors expert. Much of what such experts do is to comment on whether a machine or system is safe based on tendencies in human behavior. In this case, she was hired to make a case against the parents for neglect.

The depositions of these experts will not be taken until much closer to the trial date. In federal courts and in many states, the timing of expert depositions is dictated by the case management order, but this phase almost always occurs near the end of the discovery period, since the experts will form opinions based on the percipient witness discovery completed earlier.[3]

In California, the timing is set by statute. First, disclosure of experts must be requested in writing, and that request is made seventy days before the trial

---

3 "Percipient" witnesses, also called lay witnesses or eyewitnesses, are those who provide the facts of the case; that is, they are the people who "perceive" what happened or who have information that could lead to finding information supporting relevant arguments at trial.

date. The written disclosure must be made 50 days before the trial date and will include a discussion of the subject matter on which each designated expert will testify and the amount of fees they charge, among other things, and it will attach any available reports authored by the expert on the case. (More deadlines, right?) The expert depositions are taken following the disclosure.

As we move to the next phase of the case, you should know that several additional percipient depositions were taken beyond Doug Heels, as the person most qualified for Family Swim Club, and its employee, Javier Gonzalez. The plaintiffs took the deposition of the person most qualified for Got You Covered Technologies on the topics of the cover design, comparison to older and more recent designs, and the extent to which the company provides instruction for installation.

The defendants, Family Swim Club and Got You Covered Technologies, took the depositions of Paul and Patty Smithson to get their versions of what happened, to learn more about Peter's current care and condition, and to assess how their lives have been impacted by the accident. They took the deposition of Phillip Knight to inquire about the details of the original installation. They also took the depositions of the kids, Perry and Penny, but not before the judge was asked to intervene. Paul and Patty did not want their kids subjected to the case, especially in a situation where all these strangers would be grilling them.

Anne Dewey knew that Penny's outburst at the scene ("Don't die, don't die!") would be emotionally impactful at the trial, but she could get that into evidence from Doug Heels, who already testified about it. She filed a motion for a protective order, asking the judge to forbid the depositions of the young children. Judge Stickler, wanting to protect the children, also recognized that they might be able to add substance to the issue of how long the accident sequence lasted because they are the ones who realized Peter was missing and then saw him slip under the pool cover. She ordered that the deposition would be limited to one hour each, and the subject matter would be limited to what happened, nothing about what they may have observed about their parents or Peter after the day of the accident.

The defendants also took the depositions of the emergency responders who arrived at the scene and attended to Peter. Five of Peter's medical professionals gave depositions, including the emergency room physician, the chief nurse of the pediatric intensive care department at the hospital, the main pediatric neurologist overseeing Peter's condition, and the main clinical nurse specialist at the chronic care facility where Peter was transferred.

On behalf of the plaintiffs, Dewey Cheatem & Howe retained, in addition to the pediatric neurologist specializing in coma cases (expertise which includes permanent vegetative state patients), a life care expert to testify and sum up the cost of that care and other needs for the rest of his life. They will also need, eventually, an economist expert to testify and sum up all the monetary damages and how the jury should apply that number in present dollars.

The defendants agreed to share medical and damages experts, including a neurologist, a life care expert, and an economist.

Let's get back to the case.

Motions – Here Comes the Judge

CHAPTER TWENTY-ONE

The Motion to Amend the Complaint

No motion was necessary to schedule the balance of the Family Swim Club PMQ deposition, though threatened by Anne Dewey. When she contacted Riley Goode to "meet and confer" as required before bringing a motion, he agreed to a new date and promised to allow his witness to answer questions about the upgrade to the pool cover system. Riley knew he crossed the line by instructing his witness not to answer legitimate questions. He did it intentionally, though, because he needed time to confer with Doug Heels.

Doug had not told him enough detail about the case, and certainly did not tell him about the upgrade. Had Doug told him about the plan to change to a new cover, Riley would have immediately invited all parties to inspect the old cover before it was changed out. Now, his client faces a possible issue sanction for destroying evidence. At least, now, he can coach Doug to answer the question truthfully, but hopefully in a way that eases the impact. In the end, he will do his best to avoid a case-crippling sanction, but he already knows his case is probably lost because of the Gonzalez testimony about leaving the door open and because the pool cover was not secure; otherwise, the boy could not have fallen in. Thankfully, the second Heels deposition did not take place until after the Gonzalez deposition, so he and Heels had that information and would not be blindsided.

A different and bigger problem was that the plaintiffs filed a motion to amend the complaint to add a claim for punitive damages. The motion is scheduled for November 15, 2024. Here is the court's ruling on the motion, which lays out the contentions of the parties and the court's reasoning:

The court has considered the plaintiffs' motion for leave to amend the complaint to add a claim for punitive damages, the opposition brief filed by defendant Family Swim Club, against which the punitive damages allegations are alleged, and the plaintiffs' reply brief. No briefing was filed by defendant Got You Covered Technologies, apparently having no interest in the outcome of the motion. The court also heard oral argument.

Moving parties on such a motion must make an adequate showing on two issues: 1) that the motion was filed promptly to avoid prejudice to the other parties who, if the amendment were allowed too close to the trial date, might not be able to conduct discovery on the issue; and 2) that the added allegations sufficiently state facts which, if proven at trial, would support a claim for punitive damages under the law.

The facts upon which the plaintiffs now bring this motion are that defendant Family Swim Club tampered with and/or destroyed evidence. This information was learned at the deposition of Family Swim Club's person most qualified on September 30, 2024, and this motion was filed promptly thereafter. The court finds no unnecessary delay in starting the deposition process. Therefore, the plaintiffs have satisfied the first issue as there remains adequate time to conduct discovery unless the court allows an extended process to challenge the adequacy of the amendment.

On the question of whether sufficient facts have been pleaded to support a punitive damages claim, ordinarily, the court might grant the motion to amend the pleading because it was filed promptly and allow the defendant to challenge the pleading as insufficient later. However, considering the close proximity of the trial date and that the defendant included in the present briefing an argument that there are insufficient facts to support the punitive damages claim, the court will rule on the issue now.

The court finds that destruction of evidence, if such occurred, may justify some form of sanctions, including an issue sanction, and it is presumed the plaintiffs will bring a motion to impose such sanctions as part of the motion in limine process at the time of trial. The allegations of the proposed addition to the complaint state that the destruction of evidence was intentional and malicious, but the briefing offers no specifics about why the destruction of the evidence was intended to harm the plaintiffs. The transcript of the deposition of Douglas Heels, as person most qualified for the defendant, shows there was no malicious intent to destroy the evidence; even though he admits he received a letter and had a telephone call in which he was admonished to preserve the evidence. He explains the directors of Family Swim Club had budgeted and scheduled the upgrade to the pool cover, scheduling it while Mr. Heels was out of town in the month before the letter and the call. Though the pool work was on his calendar, Mr. Heels credibly sets out in his testimony that he simply forgot to call his lawyer about it when he learned about the planned project on his return to work. To support a claim for punitive damages, the pleading must show specific facts amounting to "malice" as defined in the law. "Malice," by code and case law is despicable conduct intended to hurt the other party. The court finds based on this testimony the proposed amended complaint to contain insufficient facts to rise to the level of malice.

The motion is denied. It is so ordered.

Maya B. Stickler, Judge Presiding

Defendant Got You Covered Technologies' Motion for Summary Judgment

Tasked with the project to file a summary judgment motion for Got You Covered Technologies, Drew Delascard dove in headlong, weeks later proudly presenting Mary and Skip with a 48-page draft. "Are you kidding me? I'm not reading this! Mary, take this kid out of here and tell him what the California Rules of Court are! And hurry up, we don't have much time left before it has to be filed!" As Drew was tip toeing out of Skip's office behind Mary, a common situation for him, he hears Skip loudly thump the printed-out brief into his trash can.

When they were in Mary's office, she opens the California Rules of Court to Rule 3.1113, turns the book around, slides it across her desk toward Drew and points to the sentence that says, "In a summary judgment or summary adjudication motion, no opening or responding memorandum may exceed 20 pages."

"Oh," he says, "as long as it took me to write what I did, it could take that long to edit this down."

Mary replies, "No, it won't. Whatever your weekend plans, cancel them. We need to get this out. And I guess you should email me updates every few hours, and I will edit on the fly, from wherever I am."

"Have you written the other required components for the motion?" Mary asks. Seeing the blank look on Drew's face, she flips the pages on the court rules to Rule 3.1350 and says, "Read subdivision (c)."

Drew reviews the rule, which states:

> **(c) Documents in support of motion**
>
> Except as provided in Code of Civil Procedure section 437c(r) and rule 3.1351, the motion must contain and be supported by the following documents:
>
> (1) Notice of motion by *[moving party]* for summary judgment or summary adjudication or both;
>
> (2) Separate statement of undisputed material facts in support of *[moving party's]* motion for summary judgment or summary adjudication or both;
>
> (3) Memorandum in support of *[moving party's]* motion for summary judgment or summary adjudication or both;
>
> (4) Evidence in support of *[moving party's]* motion for summary judgment or summary adjudication or both; and
>
> (5) Request for judicial notice in support of *[moving party's]* motion for summary judgment or summary adjudication or both (if appropriate).

When Drew looks up, Mary continues, "You have only written the memorandum of points and authorities, which is subpart (c)(3). You still need to write the notice, the separate statement of undisputed material facts, make the list of evidence, and decide if you need to use a request for judicial notice to make any of the supporting evidence admissible."[1] "Have you drafted the declaration of Noah Little to support the theory of the motion?"

Drew does not answer this question, as the answer is obvious. He had not been given any guidance on how to prepare this complicated motion. And now several of his upcoming personal plans are jeopardized. "Mary, I will dig into this as soon as I come back from lunch. Several of the associates are taking the new interns out. And I think the group was planning to go for a drink at about 5 today. But we have another problem. I am supposed to attend a wedding on Saturday in Santa Barbara, so I will lose the entire day, and tomorrow too, because I need to be up there for other wedding activities. And I was planning to stay over at the hotel Saturday night because I shouldn't be driving for hours to come home late that night, uh, after the party. So, it's now Thursday, but I hope to have this all buttoned up for you by Sunday night after I drive back."

He doesn't give her the detail that he has a hotel reservation for tonight through Sunday, but that seemed inherent in what he said. He really wants to be in Santa Barbara tonight because the wedding attendees are supposed to be golfing tomorrow at a well-known country club.

Mary is flummoxed. Drew did not tell her he would be out of town for the weekend, not that he was required to announce his personal weekend plans, but he did not say anything about not coming to work on Friday. Was he just not going to show up? Plus, he's had weeks to work on this motion and seemed to have geared his time to the last minute. He has given no thought to the need for editing, and the editing time is now compressed because so much more writing is needed on parts of the motion that should be done already.

Trying to maintain her composure, she utters through very tight lips, "Drew, I am not sure what to say. For starters, it would be very ill-advised for you to take two hours to entertain the interns at lunch or to go drinking with them tonight, especially since you will not be able to work on the project tomorrow, Saturday, or a substantial part of Sunday, with Monday as the deadline to file the motion,

---

1 A request for judicial notice allows the court to accept a fact as true without requiring proof. It can be used to introduce evidence that is generally recognized as true, such as laws, court records, commonly accepted facts or facts not reasonably disputable. Easy examples might be a local geographical reference, like an Interstate runs north and south or east and west; or that water freezes at 32° Fahrenheit.

with both me and Skip needing time to edit and our secretary needing much of Monday to prepare the motion to be filed and served."

"Are you saying I shouldn't go to the wedding and lose my deposit?" He has no intention of allowing this to happen, regardless of her response.

Mary thinks he has not thought much about the deadline problem and obviously has no intention of giving up his plans. He should have planned his time to have this motion ready for me much sooner, and he doesn't even seem to realize that. Now the entire project is going to fall on my shoulders. Goodbye weekend. To boot, Drew seems oblivious to how this situation could affect our view of his progress in the firm. If Skip were sitting in on this conversation, he would have fired him on the spot, regardless of HR rules. I have no time to think about Drew's status right now. The priority is not committing malpractice and getting this motion completed.

"Drew, you are a licensed professional. You can make your own choices. You know this is not a 9-5 job, nor is it a Monday to Friday job. Go to lunch, go for drinks, go to the wedding, but you need to get your projects done timely." She picks up the phone as a sign that he should leave.

She calls her husband to say he will have to take care of the kids himself over the weekend. She has her secretary postpone a deposition scheduled for Friday. She pulls up the draft of the motion and starts working on some of the other needed documents. The notice of the motion takes only a few minutes. She decides no request for judicial notice is required. The evidence list cannot be finalized until the declaration is written and can be put together by her secretary.

The three big tasks at this point are editing down the memorandum of points and authorities, drafting the declaration, and refining the complicated separate statement document.[2] The highest priority is the declaration, if only because Noah Little has to approve it. He is on the East Coast, and she does not even know if he is available on Friday. She calls Noah, who picks up but says he is in an airport, but will be able to review and sign the declaration on Monday. This is going to be close.

---

2 The separate statement of material facts component of a summary judgment can take different forms in different jurisdictions, but in California, the rules specify a specific matrix, or table, setup listing each fact that makes up the story of the case and cites to a specific item of evidence, which in turn is listed in the Statement of Evidence Component.

Mary sends Drew an email about what she is doing so he won't duplicate it. She asks him to work on the editing and to come talk to her about his progress at 4 p.m. It is now 12:30, but he responds – from his desk, not his phone. He has apparently decided not to go to lunch with the gang.

The theory of the motion is that Got You Covered Technologies should not be held liable for what happened to Peter Smithson because there was nothing wrong with the design of the pool cover, and the accident would not have happened if installed and maintained properly. Mary starts typing Noah Little's declaration, saying he is one of the designers of the system, and identifies the installation method accommodated by the design (with straps pulled through grommets in the cover material that attach to anchors drilled into a concrete deck). The spacing of the straps and how they attach to the anchors is in accordance with all recognized national standards.

The implication of the motion will be that the design did not cause the accident, but it had to be that a flap of the pool cover at the corner of the pool was left open; the motion attaches the picture produced by the pool maintenance person, Javier Gonzalez. She re-reads her work, makes an electronic folder of the design plans showing the applicable standards, and emails the declaration to Noah. She copies Drew to let him know she has drafted the declaration and to give him guidance on the separate statement.

By 3:30 p.m., Mary opens the points and authorities document to determine the extent of what is needed to edit it down. She sees that what Drew did is to over-explain the law of summary judgment motions, which, under usual circumstances, requires only a few paragraphs citing the basics about what the court should consider.

She realizes Drew had not used the firm's extensive cache of templates, which he could have used to lay out the skeleton of the points and authorities and the matrix format of the separate statement. He was doing this essentially from scratch. She sends Drew a copy of a previous summary judgment motion to help him as a guide, including the separate statement from that motion. Drew has also included as his main argument section a complicated dissertation on the application standards, like the American Society of Testing Materials

(ASTM). From about fifteen pages of technical jargon, all he needed was a few references, like this one:

> ASTM F1346-23 establishes requirements for safety covers for swimming pools, spas, hot tubs, and wading pools (hereinafter referred to as pools, unless otherwise specified). It includes performance tests to demonstrate the compliance or noncompliance to requirements stated for safety covers. The standard also includes marking requirements for all covers—something that covers, protects, or shelters, or a combination thereof, a swimming pool, spa, or hot tub. When correctly installed and used in accordance with the manufacturer's instructions, ASTM F1346-23 is intended to reduce the risk of drowning by inhibiting the access of children under five years of age to the water.

He could then attach Got You Covered's installation instructions and show, with Noah's declaration, that the installation conformed.

Mary and Drew meet and 4:00 p.m. He will work on the separate statement until about 6:00 p.m., but then he has to go home, pack, and leave for Santa Barbara. He will not make any progress on the memorandum of points and authorities until Monday. Mary realizes this will be what she needs to work on over the weekend, and maybe they can finish it together on Monday, the 21st.

It is Monday morning. Mary was able to cut down the 50-page brief by Sunday morning, but it had to be substantially re-constructed. In addition to including a lot of flowery language and technical jargon (without explaining it), Drew's sentence structure and punctuation were also questionable. She had it down to twenty-two pages and needed to find a way to delete just a bit more. She decided they could take some liberties with the font size and reconfigure some sentences, finally getting the document down to twenty pages.

Yet, Drew would not make it in. He texts that he has not gotten back from Santa Barbara because he was in an accident and may not be in until late Tuesday. Exasperated, Mary continues working on the motion and sends Noah Little a draft of his declaration, asking for any edits he wants and to get him to sign the declaration. She needed to get the finished product to her secretary no later than mid-day. Noah, it turns out, is on an airplane. When she finally reaches him after he lands, she implores him to immediately find a Wi-Fi connection and work with her on the document Getting this motion filed in time would be close.

Noah did have some suggestions to add, and by noon, their secretary was emailing them that she probably would need authorized overtime to finish the filing; they had until midnight to electronically file it, but the attorney service that did the actual filing also needed to be on call after hours. She gets the motion papers to their secretary by 3 p.m. There is nothing more to be done unless the secretary has questions.

Mary is at home with her family, watching television at about 10 p.m., when her secretary calls to say she is having problems with the document. She is working as fast as she can. Mary gets ready for bed but knows she cannot relax until she hears that the motion was successfully filed. All she needs now is to find out that the court's electronic system is down. Mary stresses while staring at her cell phone. At 11:57 p.m., an email pops up on her phone informing her that the motion was filed. Mary emails a thank you to her secretary.

Anne Dewey arrives at the office the next day, to be met by Rob Berry. "Guess what? Got You Covered filed a summary judgment motion. It came in by email last night at 11:53 p.m. They each peruse the motion and Anne directs Rob to call Max Nerdley to see if there is a way to defeat the motion. If Got You Covered's motion is successful, the only compensation available to the Smithson family will be Family Swim Club's $2 million insurance policy, unless there is another source of funds available. As a practical matter, the $2 million is all there is.

Max Nerdley tells Rob he believes he can help them defeat the motion. The only hard evidence of what happened comes from the description of Mr. Smithson having to rip open the pool cover, the photograph taken by the maintenance guy, and the inference that the corner of the cover was unattached. He has enlarged the photograph as best as possible, and he thinks the reason why the pool cover was unattached is because the connection to the coping failed or the cover tore somehow. They get on a Zoom session, and Max puts the photograph on the screen.

Max puts an arrow on the screen pointing to one of the grommet spots and says, "See how there is no grommet at this point, like the others you see above that? That suggests something has broken off. It would be better if we had the cover to examine closely, but under the circumstances, I could say there is the possibility the grommet was improperly embedded or assembled into the cover during manufacture. Your case theory would have to change from a design defect to a manufacturing defect."

The plaintiffs' opposition is served and filed on this theory, supported by a declaration from Max Nerdley. Got You Covered's reply brief, filed two months later, argues the plaintiff's theory is too speculative because the entire argument rests on a blurry photograph. The reply brief goes on to argue that the absence of access to the hard evidence, that is, the ability to examine the pool cover, evidence which is now destroyed, should not be held against Got You Covered, and further, that the plaintiffs should not now be allowed to change their theory from a design defect to a manufacturing defect.

January 7, 2025 – Hearing on Got You Covered Technologies' Motion for Summary Judgment

Judge Stickler issued a tentative ruling on Friday, January 3, setting out her thinking based on review of the briefing on Got You Covered's summary judgment motion. She acknowledged that the evidence the plaintiffs submitted in opposition to the motion, primarily consisting of expert Nerdley's declaration, was almost entirely based on a single photograph from which it was very difficult to see the condition of the grommet. She also expressed concern that the plaintiffs had responded to interrogatories earlier in the case, contending a design defect, saying nothing about a manufacturing defect. The judge's tentative decision would be to grant the motion. This document was sent by the court clerk via email to the parties for them to prepare to argue about it at the January 7 hearing.

The judge begins:

"Good morning, counsel. This is a serious case, I recognize that. I wanted to be sure you all had a chance to consider my thinking on this before you got here. I assume Ms. Wright that Got You Covered Technologies will submit on the tentative ruling, saving time only to respond to the plaintiffs' oral argument this morning."

"Yes, your honor."

"Ms. Dewey, the floor is yours."

"Thank you, your honor. As we all know, summary judgment cannot be granted if there is a triable issue of fact, that is, if there is an inconsistency in the facts, it is improper for the court to decide the case; it must be left to the jury. The plaintiffs argue on this motion that there is such a triable issue of fact. On this, I have three points to make."

"First, it appears in the tentative ruling that the court relies on the fact that it is hard to see the evidence of the grommet failure in the photograph of the accident scene. Yet, the court has been provided with testimony from a qualified mechanical engineer that HE can tell what's wrong. I submit to you that it is not for the court to dismiss the expert's opinion because the court can't see it. Rather, the jury should be allowed to decide if Mr. Nerdley knows what he is talking about.

"The case authority cited in Got You Covered's opposition brief all center on not allowing expert testimony when it is speculative. The kind of speculation mentioned in those cases is, for example, where an expert relied on a photograph that an object was not the right size as designed, but the photograph did not show the full length of the ruler used to measure the object. That evidence was deemed unreliable.

Anne continues, "What no one can dispute here is that there is something wrong with the physical connection at the crucial spot, otherwise it would have the loop, or ring, connector like the other grommets have. Mr. Nerdley tells us in his declaration that he has seen this kind of failure before and included photographs from another case showing how grommets fail, including tearing of the surrounding fabric or that the strap material can wear out prematurely and rip. It is a fair inference that one of these two failures occurred. "This is not a case where the evidence is unreliable. Rather, the evidence requires interpretation, and that is exactly what the jury should be asked to do, not this court.

Anne rolls on to her next point: "Second, I certainly understand Got You Covered's concern and, no doubt, frustration, that the pool cover was not maintained. This was an egregious spoliation of evidence, but it was not the plaintiffs who did it, and neither was it Got You Covered. So, I suggest to the court that while Got You Covered argues that speculative evidence should not be held against Got You Covered, the plaintiffs have the same problem. I am saying that issue simply should not be considered on the question of whether evidence is speculative in deciding the motion.

"And finally, your honor," Anne exhales a breath, "the reply brief argues, and the court notes that the plaintiffs answered discovery earlier in the case, contending a design defect. The court should know that those interrogatory responses were early in the case, before we had the subject photograph. The law does not require a party to amend its discovery responses on finding new information unless asked in a subsequent set of discovery, which did not occur here. The plaintiffs were absolutely allowed to change the case theory after that point. On this, I will cite to the court *Biles v. Exxon Mobil Corp.* (2004) 124 CA 4th 1315, and C.C.P. §2030.070 and C.C.P. § 2031.050."

Anne is getting to the end of her argument: "In closing, there is clearly a triable conflict in the evidence, and the plaintiffs should not lose their chance at a jury trial given that an expert has interpreted the photograph. Let Got You Covered cross-examine him on it at trial, but it certainly should not be decided here. Thank you, your honor, and with that, I will submit the matter."

The attorneys continue to argue back and forth on specific points, but not much is added to what has been said or what was set forth in the briefs.

Judge Stickler: "Thank you both for your excellent briefing and cogent argument. The matter stands submitted, and the court will consider the arguments further. A final ruling will be sent by the court by the end of the week."

On January 10, the court issues the ruling, emailed to the parties by the court clerk, which states:

The Court, having heard and considered the arguments of the parties, both through briefing and oral argument, now rules on the motion for summary judgment filed by Got You Covered Technologies, Inc. and opposed by the plaintiffs.

This case, filed by the Smithson plaintiffs on March 12, 2024, alleges plaintiff Peter Smithson, a minor, suffered catastrophic injury by becoming trapped under a pool cover owned and maintained by defendant Family Swim Club (not a party to the present motion) and designed and manufactured by defendant, moving party, Got You Covered Technologies, Inc. Peter's parents, Paul and Patty Smithson, sue for infliction of emotional distress.

Got You Covered Technologies asserts in its motion that it is not liable for a design defect and supports the assertion that the evidence is insufficient to establish a case by simply using a single photograph of the subject pool cover. The motion argues that the photograph, taken on the day of the accident by an employee of

Family Swim Club, cannot establish a product defect. The photograph, the motion argues, only shows a corner of the swimming pool where, supposedly, the child fell in, and the fact that a portion of the pool cover is only partially attached to the pool deck is not conclusive of fault in any way. Got You Covered Technologies uses the photograph to show that the cover attaches to the deck according to industry standards and that if the cover were fully secured, the accident could not have happened. The evidence supporting the motion includes the declaration of Got You Covered Vice President of Engineering, Noah Little, who sets forth the applicable design standards and explains how the pool cover is to be secured if done properly. The court finds, based on this evidence, that Got You Covered Technologies has satisfied its burden of proof that the cover was properly designed and that the design would prevent an accident. As such, the burden shifts to the opposing parties, the plaintiffs, to submit evidence demonstrating a triable issue of fact.

In their opposition, the plaintiffs argue that they do not necessarily contend, as they once did in response to written discovery in this case, that the cause of the accident was solely the design of the pool cover. Instead, the plaintiffs now contend there was a manufacturing defect. The opposition is supported by the declaration of mechanical engineer Dr. Max Nerdley. Dr. Nerdley explains how the pool cover attaches: a metal connector attaches to a metal grommet manufactured into the pool cover material, through which is threaded a strap, and that strap attaches to metal anchors drilled into the concrete deck bordering the swimming pool. Dr. Nerdley, relying on the same photograph as the moving party, points to one of the locations on the pool cover where a metal connector should be visible extending from a grommet, but it is missing. Though out of focus, the photograph does show that something was previously there. Dr. Nerdley concludes that the material around the grommet failed and supports this conclusion, citing other sources that indicate when these grommets fail, it is because they were not properly attached during the manufacturing process.

In Got You Covered Technologies' reply brief, it is argued that Dr. Nerdley's opinion is speculative and thus inadmissible under *Sargon Enterprises, Inc. v. University of Southern California* (2012) 55 Cal.4th 747. Under *Sargon*, the court is considered a "gatekeeper" and must make an initial determination, before a jury is allowed to hear an expert's opinion, that the opinion is not based on speculative facts. Got You Covered Technologies argues that the poor quality of the photograph on which both the moving papers and the opposition papers are based renders speculative the evidence on which Dr. Nerdley relies.

The photograph is not completely clear, but both sides agree it is the swimming pool in question, that it was taken on the day of the accident, that the pool cover is a product designed and manufactured by Got You Covered Technologies, that the manner of installation is as described above, using grommets, and that grommets can be seen in the photograph. Got You Covered Technologies' argument for speculation is that it is hard to see the specific grommet on which Dr. Nerdley bases his opinion, and this is why he should not be allowed to talk about it.

It is not for the court to determine how the grommet and metal connector were damaged. It is sufficient that it is no longer in its manufactured condition, something neither side disputes, and thus it is a fair inference that it was damaged. Dr. Nerdley provides examples and writings showing how grommets on swimming pool covers become damaged. The court concludes that its gatekeeper function would exclude the opinion if there was no reasonable basis to know if the grommet was damaged. That is not the situation here.

Got You Covered offers two other arguments: that the plaintiffs should not be allowed to change their theory from a design defect to a manufacturing defect, and that there is evidence that

Mr. Smithson damaged the grommet trying to save Peter. The court finds that the evidence supporting the manufacturing defect theory was obtained after the inconsistent discovery position was taken. Since there is no obligation in the law requiring the plaintiffs to amend their discovery responses and there was no request for them to do so, the court rejects the argument in that regard. As to whether Mr. Smithson damaged the grommet, whether it was already damaged, or whether Mr. Smithson should have been physically able to damage the grommet if properly manufactured, this is for the jury to decide.

The motion is denied.

Maya B. Stickler, Judge Presiding

Settlement – Not Rolling the Dice

CHAPTER TWENTY-TWO

As you have seen, there is a pattern to litigation. The case starts with the allegations in the complaint and the response to them in the answer. Then, the fact-finding starts in the discovery stage, where each side gets to know what evidence there is to prove or disprove the allegations. That is, how do the facts that come out develop into the story of what happened? The lawyers for each side analyze these facts, get input from experts as needed, and decide if the facts support a credible argument to the jury why the dispute should be resolved in their client's favor.

Juries and, often, judges, are unpredictable. Facts can be gray, meaning they can be subject to interpretation. Any lawyer will tell you that going to trial is a risk; the proverbial roll of the dice. Cases thought to be sure-fire winners are lost (like rolling snake-eyes), and cases are won even though they seemed weak (like rolling a seven). Because trying cases can be a gamble, when you add in factors like high expense, that parties (and their insurers) want to manage risk, and because lawyers are good at what they do, most cases settle. Settlement can be negotiated at any time during the case. As mentioned earlier, many claims do not even reach litigation as they are settled before that happens. The main pattern, though, is that the facts need to be fleshed out during discovery before the parties are ready to negotiate a settlement, which can take years.

The three main ways cases settle are by direct negotiations between the parties, in settlement conferences, and in mediation. Settlement conferences occur at the courthouse with a judge acting as the intermediary. Settlement conferences can be ordered by the court (a "Mandatory Settlement Conference," or "MSC") or they can be voluntary ("VSC"). The judge presiding over the case normally does not handle the settlement conference to keep the trial judge free of any unintended pre-conditioning about the case that could seep into the trial. Some courts have judges dedicated to the settlement process, or even outside mediators, but the trial judge will otherwise send the case "down the hall" to another judge for settlement purposes. In federal court, the presiding judge often orders the parties to attend an MSC with the assigned magistrate, a kind of assistant judge.

The impediment to court-conducted settlement conferences is that some judges are better at it than others, and often a judge will not be able to spend the time needed for a fully explored negotiation. But that didn't stop some judges in the early days of mediation, the '70s and '80s. Several judges in the Los Angeles County Superior Court volunteered to preside over settlement conferences. They got really good at it, some going on to be successful private mediators.

One judge in particular would hold settlement conferences at 7 a.m. on Saturday mornings in Burbank, California. He did this for two reasons: to avoid interfering with his weekday trial calendar and because any group of lawyers willing to come in that early, much less on a Saturday, must be motivated to settle. His big schtick was to point at the clock over his desk, where all the numbers were made up of numbered dice, and use it as a prop to convince a party reluctant to settle that going to trial was too much of a gamble. At the approach of noon, he would point to the hands on the clock and dramatically say, "Do you really want to roll the dice?" He was quite the character.

Private mediation, or as it is known formally, Alternate Dispute Resolution ("ADR") has become a huge industry, especially in litigation since the early 1990s. There are many mediation firms, some national. There are schools that teach mediation. Mediators, often referred to as "neutrals," tend to consist of former judges and lawyers, though there are some businesspeople who succeed at it.[1]

---

1 There are many publications on the subject of negotiating. A good one that gives a history of using an intermediary to resolve disputes is A History of Alternative Dispute Resolution, The Story of a Political, Cultural, and Social Movement, by Barrett, 2004 Published by Jossey-Bass. You will see that mediators, of a kind, existed in Ancient Greece, that ADR was prevalent in the U.S. as the industrial age awakened in the second half of the 19th century, on into labor disputes in the 20th century, and so on.

We are now going to see that the Smithson case is ready for negotiations. We will watch how the lawyers decide on, plan for, and carry out the mediation process.

It is January 7, 2025. Dewey, Cheatem & Howe have dodged the bullet of Got You Covered's summary judgment motion. It is now a month to the trial. Experts have been disclosed, and the depositions of those experts will be taken over the next two weeks. Now would be the time to try to settle the case. Anne Dewey thinks Defendant Family Swim Club's insurance company must be shaking in their boots over the Gonzalez testimony that seems to establish liability against their insured.

The club has only $2 million in insurance, so the club surely must be pressuring the insurer to settle for the policy limit to avoid exposure to the club's assets. Anne needs to discuss with her clients whether to demand the policy limit in settlement or whether to set up a mediation.

Anne meets with Paul and Patty to discuss the situation. She advises them that the case has a verdict potential in the tens of millions of dollars, but the ability to recover such a sum may be unrealistic even with a judgment. The easier path to establish liability is against Family Swim Club, but it is questionable whether the club has any significant money available over the $2 million insurance limit; pressing the club for an amount greater than the available insured might just force them into bankruptcy. Chances are the Smithsons will have to accept the policy limit if it is offered.

Even if they settle with the club, she explains, it may be difficult to get a substantial offer from Got You Covered since Got You Covered's representatives obviously believe the club is the villain here, and their product worked just fine. They also discuss that there is an evidentiary problem with Max Nerdley's opinion that the grommet or strap material failed, since the picture taken by Javier Gonzalez is all they have. They were fortunate to defeat Got You Covered's summary judgment motion, so maybe that will loosen Got You Covered's purse strings. The Smithsons understand the analysis and agree to mediate.

Across town, Riley Goode knows he has a bad case and recognizes his client's policy limit is all they have, and that a verdict in the case could easily exceed that amount. He has given that opinion to Carlotta ("Lottie") Cash, the claims person to whom he reports at Family Swim Club's insurer, KMA Insurance Company. Riley counseled the Board of Directors at Family Swim Club about the exposure in excess of their available insurance limit.

A letter was written by the Board Chairperson to Lottie Cash questioning why KMA has not tried to settle the case to protect the club by now, given that negligence seems to have been established. Lottie and Riley discuss their options. Since there is no assurance at the moment the plaintiffs will accept the policy limit as a full settlement with Family Swim Club, Lottie authorizes Riley to suggest mediation, and that he has full authority to pay the policy limit, but if he has a chance to save anything off that amount, he should try to do so.

Later that day, Anne receives an email from Riley Goode proposing a mediation and quickly accepts the invitation. A round of emails follows with each side suggesting mediator names. Scheduling won't be easy because many mediators are booked for months ahead.

Parker "Skip" Havidyad and Mary Wright also receive the email. They see that the plaintiffs and the co-defendant are ready to mediate, but they feel their situation is different. It was disappointing that their summary judgment motion was denied, but they are confident they can persuade a jury not to accept Dr. Nerdley's view of the evidence.

Skip and Mary set up a Zoom conference with Holden De Monet, at Cambridge General Insurance Company, Sue Dembach and Sharon Little, at Got You Covered, and Luke Askantz, the claims person for Got You Covered's second-level excess insurer, Bumbershoot Specialty Assurance Company. Holden is an old hand at case evaluations and has a reputation for fighting claims to the last minute, hoping the other side will weaken; he often refuses to settle. Luke has been following the case since Sharon Little put him on notice of it but has not asked for much information to date.

During the conference, Skip tells the group his view that the case is very defensible, but like many cases they handle, the monetary exposure if they lose is very high, possibly $30 million. Got You Covered has the first $2 million of exposure under its self-insured retention. Cambridge's policy limit is $8 million. Bumbershoot's policy is $15 million above Cambridge's.

At the mention of a $30 million potential exposure, which would take all of Bumbershoot's $15 million policy, and more than the $25 million total available, Luke perks up and says he thinks mediation is a good idea.

Holden begins to speak and takes over the meeting for the next ten minutes, adamantly urging that the case should not be settled. The chances at trial are excellent, he argues, because Got You Covered's product met all required standards, the pool cover had been dislodged or was partially detached by the user, Family Swim Club, the parents may be found substantially at fault, and the expert for the plaintiffs is a known, biased gun for hire. Luke is nevertheless nervous. It's easy for De Monet to take that risk with Bumbershoot's money.

Sue points out that the judge seemed to accept the plaintiffs' expert's opinion, so there will be a trial, and the jury will hear it, and even though the jury will be instructed not to decide the case based on sympathy, they still might do so, considering the tragic condition of the child.

She adds that the first $2 million is Got You Covered's exposure anyway under the self-insured retention, so Got You Covered favors at least trying to settle the case. She lets them know that defense costs have depleted the $2 million SIR, reducing the available SIR by about $500,000 at this point. She adds that another $500,000 may be spent to get the case through trial or appeal. Therefore, the exposure will be that much closer to Cambridge's policy threshold. She appeals to Holden based on this situation that Cambridge really ought to support an attempt to settle the case.

Holden is dismissive, stating he will not object to mediation, but they should not expect a contribution from Cambridge, in essence, telling them to settle the case if they can within the remaining $1.5 million SIR, or the case is going to trial. Luke makes a note for his supervisor that Bumbershoot may have to pressure Cambridge to settle the case below Bumbershoot's coverage layer.

Following the Got You Covered conference call, Mary emails the other lawyers to say that Got You Covered will participate in mediation if it can be scheduled soon. Everyone in town knows most of the most well-known mediators are heavily booked up. Because the judge was clear that the trial would not be delayed, they may have to go with a less experienced mediator to find someone with a more open schedule.

After contacting various mediation companies, the group agrees on recently retired Judge Calum E. Ismael, from End It Resolution Services. His bio shows he was a magistrate judge in federal court for twenty-five years. He worked in the admiralty law division, so his experience would be geared toward cases arising from the use of ships, ports, and waterways. Though the cases derive from maritime law, they still involve accidents. As a magistrate, the presiding federal judge would refer discovery disputes to him for resolution and would order parties to him for settlement conferences. Therefore, he must have a reasonable amount of mediating experience.

Judge Ismail has recently left the bench and set up a mediation practice, and so he has some availability on short notice. Skip Havidyad called his partner in the Long Beach office, who handles maritime cases occasionally, who advises that Judge Ismael has a reputation as calm and level-headed, fair, and straightforward. The good news is he has a cancellation in his schedule. The mediation is set up for the first available date, January 25, 2025, during the expert deposition time period and just before the final status conference with Judge Stickler.

The Mediation – January 25, 2025

The mediation is set in the downtown Los Angeles office of End It Resolution, on the 45th floor of the Monolith Tower. Since the pandemic, many mediations are conducted on Zoom, but the parties agreed that an in-person session would be best for this case. The out-of-town participants are on a video feed, including Sue Dembach, Sharon Little, and Lottie Cash, all of whom are on the East Coast. Luke Askantz is not in attendance but said to call him if needed. Holden De Monet refused to participate. The parties are placed in separate rooms. Anne, Rob, Paul, and Penny are together in their own room.

Each party has submitted mediation briefs in advance to the mediator, setting out the facts of the case and providing details and arguments they believe should be considered in the negotiation process. The parties have paid in advance their equal share of the $10,000 fee.

The plaintiffs' mediation brief, which has been shared with all parties, includes a detailed description of Peter's neurological injury, his current condition, the care and treatment process, attaches a report from a life care planner showing Peter's care and treatment needs, and attaches a report from an economist showing the total cost to care for Peter for the rest of his life. The total comes to $1.5 million per year.

The brief goes on to claim Peter is expected to survive at least ten years. The brief then describes what Paul and Penny are going through, portraying it as watching the slow death of their child on a daily basis that will go on for ten years. They also provide a "day in the life" video. A day in the life video, often prepared by a professional production company, is a kind of video diary or documentary of how a severely injured plaintiff struggles to deal with everyday tasks since the accident, including basic personal hygiene, cooking, tending to surgical wounds, getting dressed, etc. The goal is to show the negative effects of the injury. The plaintiffs state in the brief that they will settle the case for $50 million.

Sasha Young-Greenhorne submitted a mediation brief on behalf of Family Swim Club, approved by Riley Goode. It was not shared with the other parties so that it could be candid about the liability problem and to inform the mediator of the policy limit problem. The defense position is that Peter will not survive more than a year or two at most.

Mary Wright submitted Got You Covered's brief without sharing it with the other parties. The brief was written as a very one-sided argument for why Got You Covered is sure to obtain a defense verdict. Despite that they might point the finger at each other during the trial, Gotcha Goode and the Kaniver firm have agreed to share all damage-related experts, so Got You Covered's brief makes the same argument about Peter's life expectancy.

Judge Ismael visits each room briefly at the start of the session for introductions; his first substantive visit was in the plaintiffs' room. He expressed sincere empathy to the Smithsons, and he quickly sees they might be emotionally ill-equipped for the long day ahead, which will focus more on numbers than the condition of their youngest son.

Judge Ismael smiles at the plaintiffs and begins, "Patty and Paul, let's spend a few minutes talking about how the day will go. First, you should know that my role here is to be as impartial as possible. I will give my opinion on the strengths AND weaknesses of each party's case, but my efforts will be to try to move the parties toward a settlement, not try to play favorites for anyone. Okay? You understand?" Nods of understanding. "I expect this will be a long day, and no doubt you both will be on a bit of a roller coaster as the parties go back and forth, making arguments for their case and responding to offers and counter-offers that might at first seem insulting. The idea is to go back and forth, and have you gradually decrease the amount you will accept, and the other parties will gradually increase what they are willing to pay. If we can't get to a number all agree on, the case will proceed to either another settlement discussion or to trial. Understood?"

Nods.

The judge continues, "Your lawyers, Ms. Dewey and Mr. Berry here, have asked for $50 million. I am here to tell you right now, this case cannot settle for that amount; only a jury can give that to you. The reason is that there is not enough insurance between the defendants to get there. Anne and Rob know that it is a starting point. You and your lawyers will be talking about your moves during the day, and I will chime in as needed. Okay, let's dig in and get going. Your number is out there, so the defendants owe you an offer. Make yourselves comfortable. There's coffee and snacks in the central area, and lunch will be brought in. I will see you in about an hour."

In Family Swim Club's room, Riley and Sasha are waiting. Lottie Cash can be seen on a large wall-mounted screen. After some small talk, the judge digs in with, "All, this is a terrible case for you. You recognize that, don't you?"

"Yes, your honor, we understand," says Riley, who then launches into a discussion of prior trial results he and Sasha found in public records showing defense verdict after defense verdict in cases where the jury blamed the parents for neglecting a child who was injured. Riley also emphasizes the limited life expectancy and how that should affect where the numbers land.

"Mr. Goode," says Judge Ismael, "What percentage of negligence, in your opinion, should be attributed to the parents?"

Riley responds, "More than 50%".

The judge stifles a smile; he knows this is pure advocacy. Even though the jury is not supposed to let emotions affect their reasoning, there is no way, in his opinion, the parents will be faulted much if at all, especially considering the evidence that the door was left open, the area left unsupervised, and the pool cover likely was damaged. He replies, "You saw the plaintiff's evaluation demanding the defendants pay $50 million. In today's high verdict climate, do you think that's unreasonable?"

Riley answers, "Considering at least some percentage of negligence will fall on the parents and possibly some on Got You Covered, I think that's high, but an eight-figure verdict would not be surprising."

Judge Ismael says, "Let's do the math using your percentage. And let's lump all the plaintiffs together to make the numbers easier; we know the bulk of the verdict would be for Peter and less on the parents' emotional distress. So, assume the verdict potential of the case is half what the plaintiffs are demanding, $25 million, and we'll put your suggested 50% on the parents. The verdict would come out to about $12,500,000, and assuming each defendant is tagged with 25% of the fault, your client faces a verdict of about $6,250,000. You still have insufficient insurance. How will your client pay the difference?"

Riley shakes his head and says, "Ms. Cash is prepared to pay a substantial sum in settlement, but none of us, on our side, see this as a policy limits case."

The judge says, "Well, I can't force you to pay more than your evaluation, but I doubt you will be able to get out of here for less than the $2 million policy limit. I have my doubts right now that you can even get it for the limit, since the plaintiffs have not indicated they will do that. I will be back after I visit with the other parties, but I'd like you to think about the policy limit situation and expect a question about what assets your client has over the policy limit that it might commit to the settlement."

When the judge is out of the room, Riley and Lottie realize that, coming to the mediation under the assumption that the plaintiffs would take the insurance money, the mediator's last comment is troubling. There is no one here from the client, Family Swim Club, to explain what the exposure over the available insurance means if they get a high verdict. This is an issue that will have to be addressed, but for today, they will continue to try to settle for the policy limit.

Having planted the seed to get Family Swim Club off the idea any money can be saved off the policy limit, Judge Ismael knows Got You Covered's position has much more justification so it may take some time to get them to make a solid offer. In Got You Covered's room, Skip Havidyad and Mary Wright are seated at the table. Sue Dembach and Sharon Little are on screen. The judge starts with, "Good morning, all. Sorry to make you wait, but I have now conferred with the plaintiffs and with Family Swim Club. You should know the Smithsons are very honest, upstanding people, and in my view, the jury will not allow any discounts on the basis that they, for some reason, do not like them. That said, I do understand your client's position that the majority of the problem is with Family Swim Club." The judge goes through the numbers with them the same way he did in the co-defendant's room.

Skip Havidyad, who can come off a bit stuffy in how he advocates and tends to adopt a mid-Atlantic accent stemming from his New England roots, starts, "Your honor, it must be said first that we are reluctant to even be here. Our client made a perfectly effective, properly designed, and properly fabricated product. The plaintiffs have sued our client only because they have deep pockets, and we intend to resist as much as possible. We are here because this will be an expensive trial, and we can justify a contribution to a settlement only in an amount that approximates the cost of getting our defense verdict at trial."

"Well, Skip – may I call you Skip? My first question is: How much insurance is available?" Skip tells the judge about the $2 million self-insured retention and adds that only $1.5 million is left after defense costs incurred to this point. He does not mention the insurance above that, though it is no secret; Got You Covered had to provide that information in response to interrogatories, and the plaintiff's brief included the number. The judge finds it a bit unsettling that Skip decided to hold that back, regardless of any negotiation strategy. The judge starts his next question while looking at Skip, but turns toward the screen to finish, "Is Got You Covered prepared to pay the amount remaining on its SIR?" Skip quickly jumps in to say that he would like to confer with his clients before answering that question, but reemphasizes that they have come to the mediation to make a cost-of-defense settlement.

The judge already knows how much insurance Got You Covered has because the plaintiffs' mediation brief talked about it, but he asks his next question just to see what they will say. "Can any of you tell me how much insurance there is above the SIR? That was not covered in your brief."

Skip says, "Your honor, there is insurance above the self-insured retention, but those carriers have not given us any authority to offer money from those policies."

Judge Ismail takes a moment to think about this and concludes that the reason the insurers are not participating in the mediation means either the insurers in fact will not pay any settlement contribution or, as a tactic, they decided not to attend to give the impression that the SIR is all the defense team can justify. This is a problem for the negotiation because higher-level insurers are often motivated to pressure the insured or the insurers below them to pay; that way, they may be able to avoid a contribution. Their absence prevents that dynamic from happening, at least for now.

"Though your client does have a reasonably defensible case, I will grant you that, do you deny the verdict potential is very high?"

"Not at all," replies Skip.

"Have you considered the joint and several liability problem?" When the judge says this, he notices quizzical looks from the Got You Covered people on screen. They are not insurance people and may not have come across this issue in other cases. Certainly, the Kaniver firm must have addressedupperlevel this issue with them before today. Seeing Skip hesitate, the judge says, "Skip, why don't you explain it in case anyone here is not sure how it works?"

"Certainly," says Skip. "In California, a verdict is cut down by a percentage of the plaintiff's negligence. In this case, the child will not be held to a percentage, but the parents' negligence will affect both the child's recovery and their own emotional distress claims. Damages divide into two categories: non-economic, or pain and suffering, and economic, meaning the life care costs we saw in the plaintiffs' mediation brief.

"For the pain and suffering, a defendant only pays the percentage of negligence found against them. The balance of the verdict amount, for the hard costs of medical treatment, life care, lost earnings, etc., must be paid by any party who is found negligent in any percentage, no matter how small. The "joint and several" phrase means the plaintiffs can decide which defendant has to pay those hard costs regardless of how negligent they were. It is known as the 'deep pocket' law."

"Thank you, Skip. You see, Sue and Sharon, the exposure to Got You Covered will not be calculated by the simple fact that Got You Covered may be minimally liable. Let's calculate how that might work using the numbers we discussed at the start of this session. The judge stands and goes to a whiteboard mounted on the wall. He picks up a marker and begins to write it out.

"Assume a $25 million verdict and the parents are found as much as 50% at fault for a net verdict of $12,500,000. Assume also that Family Swim Club is found 49% at fault and Got You Covered is found only 1% at fault. Let's say the total economic damages, the cost to care for the child, are $3 million, much less than the plaintiffs will ask the jury for. So, the verdict would be $9,500,000 for pain and suffering and $3 million for life care.

"At 1%, Got You Covered would pay $95,000 against the pain and suffering. But all $3 million in hard cost would fall entirely to Got You Covered under the joint and several liability doctrine because the co-defendant will not have enough to pay it. We know that Family Swim Club only has $2 million in insurance and most of that will go to pain and suffering. Therefore, the total liability is $3,095,000 using conservative numbers. This is the minimum exposure you are looking at unless you get a clean defense verdict, so you really need to be sure before risking a trial.

To drive home the problem they caused by not having their insurers participate in the mediation, the judge says, "So, I think it is supportable to say Got You Covered's exposure extends above its SIR, but there is no decision-maker here to address that. But I'll let you think about it a bit. I was just told that lunch is here, so let's take a break for that, and I will pick things up with the plaintiffs, circling back to you later to give you a chance to digest this." With a smile, he adds, "To digest lunch too."

Judge Ismael stops in at the plaintiffs' room, intending to be brief, to let them know he is working on the defendants. He asks, "Have you all considered whether you will accept Family's Swim Club's policy limit?"

Anne Dewey straightens up and, with a set jaw, begins to talk about the potential for a cover-up. "Your honor, we have what I believe are two important lies coming from Family Swim Club. Mr. Heels covered up that they intended to upgrade the pool cover system. The court rejected our attempt to plead a claim for punitive damages but acknowledged, even invited, a pre-trial motion seeking an issue sanction. We believe the issue sanction will be severe. So severe that liability could be established against the club on the lost evidence issue alone. But it's more than that. I believe we will still get punitive damages with a post-evidence motion once the judge hears how all this came down.

"But also, we now have the testimony of their employee, Gonzalez, who says he was working on the rollup mechanism and left the pool area to retrieve a tool. Yet we have the photograph that shows the pool cover was fully anchored down except for the open corner where Peter fell in. Rotating the spool mechanism could not be done with the cover anchored down to the pool deck. He has to be lying!"

"Anne, I am not sure I agree with how you've characterized Mr. Gonzalez's process that day, and I am not sure you can bet a lot on the punitive damages possibility. But as important, how does that affect the defendant's ability to pay a judgment, with or without punitive damages?" asks the mediator.

"Well, we will force them to sell the club and pay the judgment that way. It's a thriving business. And the organization also owns the property, I checked. So, we will get that too."

"Do I have your permission to argue this to Family Swim Club, that you will contend their employee is misrepresenting what happened?"

Anne replies, "No, I am not comfortable with that. I want them to be unprepared for that revelation at trial."

Judge Ismail is struggling with Anne's intensity on this point, but remains patient. "Anne, I think there are two problems with that. First, I can't exert much leverage if I can't use the argument, so that does not advance the negotiation ball. And second, I do not think you will be able to keep that interpretation of the facts from them all the way to trial because your expert has to provide some input about Mr. Gonzalez's actions as part of his presentation."

"Judge Ismail, why don't we just try to get an offer from them and see where it goes?"

Judge Ismael heads back to Got You Covered's room to see if they have reconsidered what they will offer after the joint and several doctrine discussion.

Skip begins, "We do want to try to settle the case, but we remain convinced the case is defensible. That said, we are prepared to make a one-time substantial offer. The offer is $250,000."

Meanwhile, Riley Goode and his clients have also decided to make an offer. They came to the mediation hoping to get a policy limit demand from the plaintiffs, make one counteroffer trying to save a little, but if needed, they would pay the entire limit. That demand did not materialize. They have now decided, in the best interest of the club, to just make the full policy offer and see what happens. They tell this to the mediator when he next appears. "Mr. Goode," says Judge Ismael, "I hope this works, but there is a lot of heat in that room. They still think they can get punitive damages and take over your client as compensation, forcing a sale of the business and the property. I will do my best to get them to accept your offer."

On hearing that the club has put up its full policy limit and Got You Covered offered $250,000, Anne and Rob have a heart-to-heart with the Smithsons. The Got You Covered offer is discouraging. They go over the options and work on whether settling with the club and trying the case against Got You Covered makes sense. They lay out how a $2 million settlement, with Family Swim Club alone, would be distributed, understanding that Got You Covered's offer is not nearly enough to settle with them. They estimate it as follows:

Settlement fund:	$2,000,000
Peter's Settlement:	$1,800,000
Parents' Settlement:	$200,000
Attorney's fees (Peter at 25%):	$450,000
Attorney's fees (parents at 33%):	$66,000
Costs so far:	$100,000
Reimbursement of medical ins. payments:[2]	$1,000,000
Total to Peter:	$250,000
Total to parents:	$134,000

The Smithsons now realize the impact of the fact that Family Swim Club has so little insurance compared to the magnitude of their damages. They are not crazy about the complicated option of winning the case and somehow selling off the property. And who knows how long that would take. But considering the case against Got You Covered is not a sure thing, they feel they have no choice but to go to trial. They tell Judge Ismael that since Family Swim Club

---

2 So far, medical insurance has paid for Peter's care, which must be paid back because the medical insurer has a lien on the case. Anne will negotiate with them to accept less, but it will still take a lot off the top. The assumption here is that $1 million of the $1.5 million in medical costs will have to be reimbursed.

does not have enough insurance, they want to keep their feet to the fire longer to see how things play out. And since Got You Covered is offering so little, they are ready to end the mediation.

The judge advises them to stay with it for a couple more moves. $250,000 can't be Got You Covered's last offer, but the plaintiffs should lower their demand and see what happens. The plaintiffs authorize the judge to counter with a demand of $25 million, the full amount of Got You Covered's available insurance plus its remaining self-insured retention, less any costs so far that might have diminished the SIR.

This news creates a lot of problems in the Got You Covered camp. By making a policy limit demand, a decision must be made whether it is in the best interests of Got You Covered to insist that CAGI and Bumbershoot pay the demand and avoid a judgment, even if they think they have a good chance to win the case. They also have to think about what it would mean to abandon their earlier strategy to try for limited settlements to avoid setting a high price for their other pool cover cases elsewhere in the country.

They decide not to make any further offer, but plan to write to their insurers demanding that they pay the demand. If the insurers refuse to pay, then a verdict in excess of the insurance money could possibly force them to pay the full amount regardless of the policy limit if that decision not to pay and protect their insured is deemed unreasonable. They ask the mediator to get the plaintiffs to leave the demand open for 30 days. The plaintiffs agree, and the mediation ends with no settlement.

Trial – Rolling the Dice

CHAPTER TWENTY-THREE

The Right to a Jury Trial

The right to a jury trial also has its seeds in early civilizations, though it faded in the Middle Ages and resurfaced with the Magna Carta. It is specifically assured in the U.S. Constitution.

While the concept of a jury trial was well established in English common law, the initial draft of the U.S. Constitution did not explicitly state this right. In fact, there were several rights the framers of the Constitution thought were fundamental in giving power to the people, so including them was unnecessary. Others argued vehemently about when and whether juries were necessary, whether they should apply to both criminal and civil cases, etc. However, given the political climate at the time, concerns were raised about whether the government might take steps to curb certain liberties just won in the Revolutionary War if they were not in writing. This concern meant the Constitution could not be ratified without assuring those rights, like freedom of speech, press, and religion, and of course, the rights to be confronted by witnesses against you and to have a case resolved by a jury of your peers.

These individual liberties became the Bill of Rights, a series of constitutional amendments adding to the list of "inalienable rights" contemplated in the Declaration of Independence. The Constitution was then ratified in 1791 after four years of debate. The Sixth Amendment to the Constitution assures the right to a speedy and public jury trial in criminal matters. The Seventh Amendment assures the right to a jury trial in civil matters.

Up to this point, we have seen many of the procedures and processes that make up a lawsuit. We have looked at deadlines, the discovery process, and motions. We have heard how lawyers analyze their cases, how they plan and carry out the pre-trial litigation activities, and explored how settlement of case are negotiated to avoid a trial.

Having a jury trial is not mandatory, though. One of the important decisions that can arise in many cases is whether to ask for a jury. In our system, with some exceptions, a jury trial is a constitutional right, but it can be waived. A trial without a jury, that is, that the judge will be the decider of the facts as well as the law, is sometimes called a "bench trial." Depending on the nature of the case, and perhaps from concern that a jury will not understand the complexities, the decision whether to have a bench trial is a part of the strategy considerations. If either side wants a jury, though, then that decides the issue.

Counsel, Why Is My Case Taking So Long?

In our hypothetical Smithson case, we have a situation where one party was kind of punished for delaying the start of the case, so the judge gave them a rather close trial date. In addition, the minor plaintiff would have been entitled to an even closer date had lawyer Anne Dewey decided to go that route. In reality, cases can take years to get to trial. This is because of congestion in the courthouse and because it just takes a long time to get everything done.

The rules contemplate that written discovery, for the most part, requires thirty days for response. The reality is that the pace of business in a law office, and for clients as well, means many discovery campaigns are in progress constantly. It is now rare for a lawyer not to ask for extra time, sometimes months, to respond to written discovery.

Similarly, depositions rarely proceed on the day they are first scheduled. It is not unusual for a negotiation to occur over available dates, requiring coordination of the calendars of several lawyers, a process that itself also can take weeks and months; and the "negotiation," such as it is, can break out into legal warfare, over whose client should testify first, whether the deposition of a certain person should be permitted, etc., requiring a judge to step in.

When it comes to motions, the reality is that you can't get a hearing date on a judge's calendar for months because of the high caseload in the courtrooms, even for the simplest of motions. As for summary judgment, it is normal that all the depositions in the case need to be done to know if it has a chance to succeed, and since a lot more lead time to the hearing is required, the necessary discovery needs to be accomplished long before the trial date. It is also true that many, if not most, trial dates do not stick; the parties agree to delay the date or, if not, a motion to delay the trial is commonplace. So, you get the idea; the wheels of justice are indeed slow, and this is the reason.

To non-lawyers, the fact that cases can take years may give the impression that the system is wholly inefficient and unnecessarily delays the resolution of disputes. I tend to agree that the system is substantially inefficient, but no one has yet found an overarching way to grease those wheels.

Trial Preparation

In today's world, trials are an interesting but also tedious process. For the lawyers, weeks, if not months, of preparation are often needed. Trial preparation requires that the percipient discovery is completed; a month of two before the trial, the lawyers may still be learning what the other side is going to. Full explanations of the expert opinions on all sides must be obtained and analyzed. The experts' opinions often reveal the exact way the opponent interprets the evidence, and that process typically occurs at the end of the percipient discovery process, close to the trial.

In addition, leading up to the trial, pre-trial motions are being prepared, along with other requirements the court may impose. The lawyers are making outlines of what they will ask during the voir dire process, what they will say in the opening statements to the jury, how they will conduct the direct examination of their own witnesses, how they will conduct the cross-examination of adverse witnesses, and, at some point, they need to prepare closing arguments.

There are other considerations. If the expense, complexity, and verdict potential of a trial warrant it, parties can test the facts and arguments in front of practice jurors, called "mock" jurors. There are different levels of this exercise. One option is to have a full trial (or mock trial), which is very expensive. Another way to go is to have a mock trial of just particular issues. The least expensive choice is to simply show the evidence to the mock jurors and ask for their input (called a "focus group" process).

The feedback from a mock jury exercise enables the lawyers to understand whether a certain argument or approach is effective or should be modified. It can also help them understand the monetary verdict potential. There are highly professional companies that assist in the mock jury process, arranging and paying for members of the public to give their time to do this. The professionals who operate these companies have special knowledge about juror tendencies and juror psychology.

There is still more to the trial planning process. There are professional jury consultants. They will help to decide what kind of people may be best suited for your case issues. Jury consultants will work with the lawyers during the jury selection process and beyond, helping to decide the fitness of jurors based on their behavior and answers in the voir dire process. John Grisham authored a great story in Runaway Jury. In the movie version, Gene Hackman played a top-of-the-line jury consultant (who also happened to be the villain).

All this preparation leads to the motion in limine hearing. The motions, if granted, can have a significant effect on the outcome of the trial. Say, a plaintiff seeking to be compensated for a car accident injury has, earlier in life, been convicted of a felony. The defendant's lawyer will want to bring this out because some jurors may be unwilling to trust the testimony of someone who is capable of committing a crime.

A motion in limine by the plaintiff's lawyer will ask the judge to order that the felony cannot be used against the client at the trial. Generally, if the crime was far in the past, even a violent crime or burglary, but the plaintiff has led a normal, upstanding life since, the judge might exclude the felony from evidence. On the other hand, if the crime was one of deceit, like lying under oath, passing a bad check, or committing some other kind of criminal fraud, the chances are the felony will be allowed into evidence.

Conduct of the Trial

Before the trial starts, often a few weeks before the actual trial, witnesses and evidence, the parties will have filed motions in limine, that is, they will ask the judge to exclude certain evidence as unnecessarily prejudicial and would cause needless side stories, or to resolve certain legal issues that might affect how the jury is instructed on the law, or perhaps to curtail expert opinion that does not meet the standard for admissibility, among other things.

Once the judge has ruled on pre-trial motions, the trial date arrives. Quite often, the courtroom is not available; perhaps another trial took longer than expected and is still in progress, or multiple trials are set on the same day. If so, the trial will be delayed, perhaps days or weeks, and during that time, the lawyers are juggling the schedules and availability of witnesses, including experts and doctors. Sometimes, the trial is rescheduled for months later, requiring all the motions and scheduling to be rebooted.

The trial starts with jury selection. The court's staff has arranged for scores of people to be summoned to serve as jurors, who assemble in a central area and are given orientation and training on what they will be doing. The number of prospective jurors sent from the jury assembly area to a courtroom depends on the size of the case. If a case has many parties (and thus many lawyers are involved) and will last a long time, many in the group will legitimately be unable to serve, so many are excused; therefore, more people need to be there to hear what the case is about.

Prospective jurors learn what the case is about during voir dire process. That process consists of posing questions to the jurors intended to determine if they can be fair in deciding the facts, but they will be told the basics of the case as part of the questioning. The judge will also read them a statement, on which the parties have agreed, setting out the essential facts and the contentions of the parties. After the voir dire questioning, the lawyers get to reject a certain number of jurors, as explained below.

Depending on the case and the jurisdiction, the jury in a civil case generally consists of twelve people, often fewer in federal court. But people have emergencies, they get sick, they misbehave by failing to follow the rules, or sometimes, they just disappear. To ensure a jury of twelve will be there at the end of the trial, extra jurors are selected, called alternates, who will fill in if an already seated juror is excused for some reason. Usually, there are two or three alternates. They listen to the case with the first twelve, take notes, etc., but they do not go into the jury room for final deliberations unless they are needed to replace an excused juror. If that happens, the deliberations must start over again.

Once the jury is empaneled, the conduct of the trial can be a daily grind. First, the lawyers give opening statements describing to the jurors what they are about to hear and see. Then, the witnesses are called to the witness stand and sworn in. The attorney who calls them to the stand will then conduct "direct examination," followed by cross-examination by the other lawyers in the case. Often, a lawyer may call a witness known to be hostile or otherwise adverse to the client, in which case the lawyer is allowed to ask the questions as if in cross-examination.

Direct examination is straightforward, somewhat open-ended questioning of one's own witness. The questions cannot suggest the answer. For example, a lawyer may ask his client or a favorable witness: "Mr. Witness, please explain to the jury where you were headed when the accident occurred." The witness may answer: "I was on my way to my daughter's school." The follow-up question would be: "What happened when you turned onto the street where the school is?" The response might be: "The defendant went through the stop sign and hit me broadside."

Cross-examination is the questioning of an adverse witness seeking to challenge the accuracy or truthfulness of what was said on direct examination. Cross-examination can be conducted with leading questions, that is, questions that suggest the answer.

Cross-examination of the direct testimony above by the opposing lawyer might go something like this:

"Mr. Witness, you know my client says it was you who blew the stop sign, don't you?"

Answer by Mr. Witness: "Yes, I understand that's what she says."

"Isn't it true, Mr. Witness, that at the time of the accident, you were headed to your daughter's school, it was 2:45 p.m., fifteen minutes after your daughter would have been finished with school that day, you were late to pick her up, and she was standing there waiting for you in the rain all that time?"

"Well, in answer to your question, yes, I was running late, but if you're suggesting I ran a stop sign because I was in a hurry, I deny that."

Using the cross-examination method, the lawyer was able to load multiple facts into the question and also suggest what the lawyer wants the jury to hear, that Mr. Witness was careless because he was in a hurry, something he would not say if simply asked an open-ended question, like, "Mr. Witness, tell me whether you were in a hurry."

When the plaintiff is finished presenting all the intended evidence to support the claim, the plaintiff "rests." The phrase, of course, is idiomatic in our culture: "I rest my case." If the plaintiff's evidence was not sufficient to meet the evidentiary burden, that is, if it has not presented facts sufficient as a "preponderance of the evidence," or whatever the evidentiary burden is on that case, the defendant can move the judge for a "nonsuit," which in some courts may be called a "directed verdict." By any other term that may be used in other states, a nonsuit is a finding that the plaintiff has no case, that is, that the plaintiff has not proven the case sufficient to satisfy the burden of proof.

Once the plaintiff rests, and if no nonsuit motion is granted by the judge, the defense starts its case. The defense evidence will consist of facts contradicting or attempting to disprove the evidence the plaintiff has already offered, and will offer evidence on certain defense contentions (defenses) asserted, on which the defendant now has the burden to produce evidence that "preponderates," to have the jury decide the contentions in their favor. Nonsuits on the defenses, once the defense rests, are possible. Very often, though, the defense evidence will come out in the cross-examination of the plaintiff's witnesses, so the defense case can sometimes be presented in less time.

Once the defense rests, the plaintiff will have a chance to put on "rebuttal" evidence. That is, since the plaintiff has the burden of proof, the plaintiff may offer evidence not presented in the case in chief that refutes evidence offered during the defendant's case, or evidence that a witness was untruthful (called "impeachment").

Once all parties have rested, the lawyers give closing arguments. This is followed by the judge reading to the jurors as many as a hundred pages of jury instructions. Jury instructions are the rules the jurors must follow in deciding the case. They are told they are the judges of the facts, they are the judges of the credibility of the witnesses, and how to determine which of the competing expert opinions may be more useful or persuasive to them. The jurors are told how to calculate damages. They are also provided a verdict form, a kind of questionnaire, to guide them in deciding each applicable legal issue.

After that, the jury retires to a jury room. The alternate jurors, those designated to hear the case but who will not participate in the deliberations unless someone is excused, are to remain in the jury assembly area until called upon.

Okay, the lawyers and parties in the Smithson case have been waiting patiently for us, so let's see how this will unfold.

The Smithson Trial Begins
With Pre-Trial Motions

CHAPTER TWENTY-FOUR

Up to this point, the plaintiffs' negligence case against Family Swim Club is based on Mr. Gonzalez leaving the door to the outside pool open while going to his truck for a tool, and leaving the pool area unsupervised. This allowed little Peter Smithson access to the danger while he wandered around exploring the club while his parents met with Doug Heels, and his siblings played in the recreation room. The plaintiffs attempted unsuccessfully to add punitive damages to the case based on the club's replacing the pool cover system and throwing it away, but remember, the judge anticipated a pre-trial motion might be filed asking that the club be penalized for doing destroying the evidence.

Anne Dewey was disappointed with the previous ruling and thinks this is an issue for appeal if needed after the trial. Yet, she still intends to ask for an amendment to the complaint to add punitive damages after the evidence is all in. The motion will be on the theory that the club not only failed to preserve the evidence, but she remained convinced that Mr. Gonzalez covered what happened; Mr. Gonzalez testified in deposition that he was working on the rollup mechanism at the other end of the pool, but Anne thinks he had to have been doing something at the corner of the pool; that is, he is the reason the corner of the pool cover seen in the photograph is not secured. She found it suspicious when he said he could not remember why the cover was open at the corner - he had to have done something to it. And it has never been explained how he could be working on the rollup mechanism if it was attached to the anchor system. She is anxious to argue this in her motion in limine.

On the other side, Family Swim Club filed a motion in limine, which, if it is granted, will all but ruin the plaintiffs' chances to add punitive damages. The motion in limine announces its strategy from the opening line in the motion, "With this motion, defendant Family Swim Club concedes responsibility for the accident that is the subject of this case." The motion goes on to say that while Family Swim Club will accept responsibility for the accident, there will still be evidence and argument that the parents should have been more attentive.

By admitting fault, the club argues, there is no need for the jury to hear evidence of how the accident happened. Without the details of the accident, the jury would not hear about the destruction of the evidence, and thus, there would be no basis for punitive damages. The strategy is couched in an argument that since no proof of negligence is necessary, it would be a waste of time, and the parties could proceed directly to damage evidence, shortening the trial.

Anne Dewey and Rob Berry were stunned on receipt of the club's motion. The positive to be taken from the admission of fault is that they'd won the case on liability against the club, needing only to prove the extent of the damages. The negative is that if the court grants the motion and prevents evidence of the details of the accident, they will not be able to cross-examine Javier Gonzalez on his apparent cover-up, the punitive damages attempt would be foreclosed, and the request for an issue sanction would no longer be necessary.

It was a smart move by Gotcha Goode. And the club had nothing to lose by this move because they would have been found liable anyway, would still be exposed over the policy limit, and would still be subject to the issue sanctions problem. The result, if the judge grants the motion, is that the plaintiffs would now have to reconsider taking the club's insurance money, dropping the case against the club, and making the trial all about Got You Covered.

The plaintiffs opposed the club's motion by directly calling it out as a tactic to escape the issue sanction. Their opposition brief suggested that if the court is inclined to grant the motion, then the issue sanction requested, that the club be found liable, is no longer necessary. Instead, the plaintiffs pointed out that an important result of discarding the pool cover made the plaintiffs' case against the other defendant, Got You Covered, harder to prove, which is highly prejudicial, especially considering that Got You Covered was in a better position to pay the large, anticipated judgment. Therefore, Anne and Rob propose that a fitting penalty would be to bar Family Swim Club from arguing the parents' negligence, effectively striking an affirmative defense in their answer to the complaint.

It was a further eye-opener when they received an opposition to the club's motion from the other defendant, Got You Covered. Ordinarily, a co-defendant does not take sides in a motion primarily between the plaintiff and a co-defendant. This is especially true where the co-defendant volunteers to accept at least some percentage of responsibility. However, how much negligence is attributed to the club will affect how much of the non-economic damages that will be allocated to each defendant; the more that goes to the club, the less Got You Covered will have to pay if any negligence is assigned to them. Therefore, the Kaniver team felt that percentage could only go up if a jury were to hear the entire sequence of Family Swim Club's stupidity. So, they decided to try to assist the plaintiffs in keeping the heat and focus on the club.

Got You Covered Technologies also filed a motion in limine, seeking to bar the testimony of plaintiffs' expert, Dr. Max Nerdley II. The basis for the motion is that the plaintiffs' entire case against Got You Covered depends on Nerdley's opinions, and those opinions are much too speculative. The argument is that it is nothing more than a guess to say that the pool cover was improperly manufactured from a mere blurry photograph.

On receipt of Got You Covered's motion, Anne and Rob view it as nothing more than a re-hash of their failed summary judgment motion, when the court decided the jury would be allowed to consider the blurry photograph. The concern remains, though, that the plaintiffs' case against Got You Covered Technologies is fully dependent on expert Max Nerdley's theory. The opinions given at his deposition were that the design using a strap threaded through a grommet was acceptable years ago, but is no longer the industry standard; now they just use straps sewn into the cover material. His testimony was also that regardless of the use of grommets, the only way the grommet could have torn out, as seen in Mr. Gonzalez's photograph, is that it was improperly fabricated; it should not have failed, so there must have been something wrong done at the factory. They will add the supposition that Mr. Gonzalez had to have been working on the cover that day because the cover was open at the corner, despite that he said did not remember that.

Got You Covered also filed a motion in limine to preclude the so-called "reptile theory" argument. This approach was based on a theory published by a neurophysiologist and a lawyer. The theory suggested that by highlighting safety violations and potential threats to the community (including the jurors themselves), attorneys can trigger the "reptilian" part of the brain responsible for survival instincts, hoping to bring out a strong reaction that could lead to higher damages awards. In response, defendants in an injury case want to have the judge block the use of the argument rather than having to try to convince the jurors that what the plaintiff's lawyer just told them was a clever manipulation, and that is not the way to view the damages.

It is January 27, 2025. The lawyers arrive at the courtroom for the pre-trial conference. The trial begins in two weeks, and the court's rulings today on the motions in limine will affect how the case will be presented. On taking the bench, Judge Stickler reminds the lawyers that the trial date is firm and she intends to have a panel of forty potential jurors from whom the final fourteen will be selected. She expects the trial will last about two weeks, maybe more.

The trial will be conducted Monday through Thursday from 9 a.m. to 4:30 p.m. with a break in the morning and the afternoon, plus a one-and-a-half-hour lunch. There will be days the court's calendar will be taken up with other things so there may be full-day interruptions. The lawyers inform the judge that they all intend to present their evidence electronically and have agreed on one IT person in the courtroom to assist in that process.

To this, the judge launches into explaining her rulings on the motions in limine:

> "With that housekeeping out of the way, the court will now hear argument on the three pending motions in limine, which in the court's view, could affect the length of the trial. We have four motions: the plaintiffs' motion seeking an issue sanction against defendant Family Swim Club, Family Swim Club's motion to limit the evidence of liability against it based on the concession of liability, Got You Covered's motion to preclude plaintiffs' expert, Dr. Nerdley, from testifying against it based primarily on *Sargon Enterprises, Inc. v. University of Southern California*, a 2012 case cited as 55 Cal. 4th 747. The last is Got You Covered's motion to preclude reptile arguments.
>
> "The court has considered the moving papers, the opposition briefs, and the reply briefs on all three motions. No tentative ruling has been prepared but I am ready to rule on much of this unless you all wow me with your arguments. Now, I think Family

Swim Club's motion affects whether the plaintiffs' motion is necessary, so we will take these motions together.

"Family Swim Club concedes its conduct contributed to the accident and now wants to limit or preclude certain details of its negligence. The plaintiffs oppose the motion. While accepting the concession of liability, the plaintiffs still want to put on evidence that the club's employee was, shall we say, <u>really</u> negligent, maybe grossly negligent. I am also taking from the plaintiffs' brief that they still believe the spoliation of the evidence might subject the club to punitive damages. Let me address that. I recognize the right to amend at the end of the trial if the evidence warrants it, but the club cites case law in its briefing that I think is conclusive on the issue. In Cedars-Sinai Medical Center v. Superior Court, a 1998 case, 18 Cal.4th 1, at page 17, destruction of evidence does not result in a tort remedy. Therefore, this court will not decide either of these two motions on that ground.

"Got You Covered's brief also wants the jury to hear as much detail implicating Family Swim Club as possible on the reasoning that the more the jury piles it on the club, the lower might be the percentage of negligence, if any, attributable to Got You Covered. To me, the outcome of Family Swim Club's motion turns on the court's exercise of discretion as to whether the benefit of a somewhat shorter trial outweighs any prejudice. The court is persuaded by Got You Covered's point that Got You Covered loses the chance to deflect a percentage of negligence unless Family Swim Club is called on the carpet to the extent possible. If Family Swim Club already admits fault, and the court will not allow a punitive damages claim, the situation favors allowing some evidence of Family Swim Club's negligence. The concession of liability will be accepted, but the trade is that there will be no punitive damages claim. Does that result work for Family Swim Club, Mr. Goode?"

Riley realizes his client has now escaped punitive damages that would not be covered by insurance and knows also that liability will be established anyway. He stands and says, "Yes, your honor, that will be fine."

The judge turns to Anne, "Ms. Dewey?"

Anne sees that the punitive damages attempt is doomed. She has a concession of liability, and the plaintiffs can take the club's $2 million in insurance at any time. Yet, she still wants to avoid deflecting fault away from Got You Covered. "Your honor," she says, "I believe the evidence of the club's negligence is clear anyway, so a concession of liability while allowing the evidence anyway defeats the purpose of the concession. The plaintiffs, therefore, would like to revise the relief they seek in their motion. What we'd like is for the court allow evidence about the destruction of the pool cover and to instruct the jury about it in some way. The instruction could say something like the court has found that defendant Family Swim Club was on notice to keep the pool cover as evidence in the case and was required to do so, but so mismanaged their custody of the evidence that it was accidentally discarded. And as a result, the jury should take that conduct into consideration in deciding whether the plaintiffs have carried their burden of proof as to whether the pool cover was defective.""

The judge replies, "Well, that muddies the water, doesn't it? "Mr. Havidyad, I see that you seem agitated," says the judge. "Let's hear from you on this. I am inclined to find a way to offset the harm caused by the loss of the evidence. So, keep that in mind in your comments."

"I understand, your honor," Skip says. "The problem with what Ms. Dewey proposes, as I see it, is that it seems to lessen the plaintiffs' burden of proof. That burden should not change, certainly not as to their case against my client. My client didn't discard the evidence."

"A fair point, counsel," says the judge. "Here's what the court will do. She pauses a beat to think it through. Okay, then. I think, on balance, both the plaintiffs and Got You Covered benefit by the club's admission of liability. Necessarily, though, the story of what happened, that is, how the child got access to the pool, has to be allowed. What I can do is allow the story of the destruction of evidence to come into the trial, culminating in giving jury instruction 204, entitled Willful Suppression of Evidence"; it allows a jury to consider whether a party intentionally concealed or destroyed evidence, and if so, to infer that the evidence would have been unfavorable to that party. I think this approach should be sufficient for the jury to determine a fair percentage to all sides as applicable. The effect will be to shorten the trial a bit and allow the plaintiffs to focus on their case against Got You Covered. Mr. Havidyad?"

Skip, shaking his head in disbelief, responds, "Very well, your honor."

Dewey's disappointment in how this is going also shows. "Ms. Dewey, I see by your body language you are also agitated," the judge says, smiling. All in the courtroom chuckle. "Do you want to be heard further on this?"

Anne feels her case slipping away. The plaintiffs will not get any advantage from this, and the club will get away with their conduct. Anne responds, "Thank you, your honor. I have followed along on all the court's reasoning so far, and I do understand where you are coming from. However, the end result is that the plaintiffs' case is surely and sorely harmed by defendant Family Swim Club's conduct. The plaintiffs not only get no sanction advantage at all, but actually end up the worse for it."

"How so, Ms. Dewey?" asks the judge.

"You see, your honor, by not giving the plaintiffs any advantage, which is due under these circumstances, defendant Family Swim Club not only gets away with it, but the co-defendant gets even more advantage. Allowing the jury to hear about the discarding of the pool cover was fine for the plaintiffs when there was a prospect for punitive damages. Now precluded from that claim, the only benefit of that evidence is that Got You Covered gets to emphasize the club's villainy, thereby potentially lessening Got You Covered's liability. The court should be aware that Got

You Covered is in a far better position to pay a large judgment than is Family Swim Club. This puts the plaintiffs at a strategic disadvantage."

The judge considers this for a moment and says, "I still think the jury should be told the case turns in large part on a photograph. They need to be told the reason there isn't clearer evidence is because Family Swim Club tossed the pool cover. So, I will modify Ms. Dewey's proposed order to say just that, but we will leave out the part about any problem in the plaintiffs carrying their evidentiary burden. I will simply tell them the reason they are working with the photo is the fault of Family Swim Club, not the plaintiffs or Got You Covered. I still think that feeds a bit more into Got You Covered's argument, Ms. Dewey, but it's the best I can do. I will allow some factual background about the Family Swim Club's actions in causing the accident. The parties are ordered to type up a jury instruction to this effect, agree on the language, and submit it to the court in the next two days. "That will be the order". Before we move on to Got You Covered's motions, we will take a short break."

On retaking the bench, Judge Stickler states, "Counsel, we are back in session. Moving on to Got You Covered's motion in limine to preclude the opinion testimony of the plaintiffs' expert, Dr. Nerdley. Dr. Nerdley opines that Got You Covered's pool cover was defectively manufactured because the grommet and strap connection failed, and that it would not have failed under the facts of this case if it had been properly manufactured. The motion essentially is, since all we have is a blurry photo, how can he come to that conclusion? The argument is 'Where's the beef?' Right, Mr. Havidyad?"

"Your honor, Ms. Wright, here, will be taking the laboring oar on this argument, if okay with the court."

"Of course. Ms. Wright, please proceed."

"Thank you, your honor. Got You Covered's motion falls squarely within the California Supreme Court case of *Sargon v. University of Southern California*. That's a 2012 case, cited as 55

Cal.4th 747. With the court's indulgence, I would like to discuss the details of *Sargon* to illustrate why our current motion has merit. *Sargon* establishes that the court is the gatekeeper for expert opinion. If expert opinion offered at trial is based on unreliable facts or comparisons, the court must block it from the jury. That is, the court decides first if the basis for an opinions is unreliable. Related to this, the court is also the gatekeeper for expert opinion based on questionable science.

Sargon Enterprises was a small company that developed a dental implant and contracted with the University of Southern California to test it. Sargon sued USC, alleging that the testing was not performed properly and that Sargon lost profits. At trial, Sargon obtained a verdict but for a limited amount because the court excluded the opinions of its lost profits - that Sargon would have made profits of hundreds of millions of dollars. The court found that the method used to support the opinion, by comparing a small company like Sargon's potential profits to much larger, more established companies, was too speculative."

Mary presses on, "In this present case, the plaintiffs' expert, Dr. Nerdley, testified at his deposition to two opinions, neither of which can pass the *Sargon* test. The first opinion is that there was a failure of the connection between the grommet and strap that secured the pool cover to the concrete-embedded anchors, which is based on the only piece of evidence available, a blurry photograph. The second opinion, having concluded there was a failure, is that the strap-to-grommet connection had to have been fabricated incorrectly because otherwise it could not have failed."

Moving to her conclusion, Mary continues, "The jury should not hear either of these opinions. The photograph simply does not show what Dr. Nerdley says it does. The photograph is so indistinct that suggesting there was a failure is a mere guess. The opinion that the only way the grommet or strap could fail was a manufacturing defect fails to account for other forces or wear and tear. An evidentiary burden cannot be satisfied unless all other possible causes of grommet or strap failure are eliminated. We think this situation falls squarely within the *Sargon* holding. Thank you, your honor."

"Thank you, Ms. Wright. I'll hear from the plaintiffs. Ms. Dewey?"

Anne rises to her feet and responds, "Your honor, the court has already ruled on whether the photograph is reliable enough for the jury to consider. At the hearing on Got You Covered's summary adjudication motion on June 10, the court heard the exact same argument, rejecting it on the basis that both sides have concluded the grommet area is damaged despite the quality of the photograph and, thus, the court cannot say there is no reasonable basis to know if the grommet was damaged. As to Dr. Nerdley's use of illustrations of how grommets and connections like these fail, this is reasonable and potentially persuasive. It is not for the court to simply reject the theory. Speculation is not, as Got You Covered seems to contend, a failure to eliminate all causes. Got You Covered can cross-examine him on whether there are other ways the failure could have happened."

"Thank you, Ms. Dewey. The court has considered all this and hereby denies the motion. As to the reptile theory motion, I routinely grant that, and do so here. The parties are instructed to abide by it. Now, let me ask the parties this. Have you tried to settle this case?"

Anne replies, "Your honor, we did have a private mediation a few days ago, and we are still pretty far apart."

The judge says, "All right, but getting a case settled even during a trial is not unheard of, so I encourage the parties to keep talking and to let me know, even if during the trial, if the court can be of any assistance. See you on February 10 at 8:30 a.m. Ms. Dewey, please be sure you have at least one witness ready to go, as I anticipate jury selection and opening statements will still leave us time in the afternoon session to start the evidentiary process. Thank you, everyone."

The hearing ends.

Jury Selection

CHAPTER TWENTY-FIVE

D-Day – February 10, 2025. The army of lawyers and assistants descends on Judge Stickler's courtroom. It is 8:15 a.m. The courtroom door is locked. Anne Dewey arrives to see a crowd of people milling around in front of the door. Rob Berry is plopped on a bench, drenched in sweat from pushing a hand truck piled with storage boxes from the parking lot. The boxes contain dozens of three-ring binders with all the exhibits in the case.

There are hundreds of pages of documents, including all the documents produced in discovery, voluminous medical records on Peter, and the files produced by the experts to support their testimony. The judge requires a set of numbered exhibits, in hard copy, available to the judge, the witness while on the stand, and the jurors for later deliberations. Each party's lawyers also have their own set. This is required even though, with today's technology, every exhibit will be displayed electronically during the trial on a large screen.

Paul and Patty Smithson are by themselves near the end of the corridor. Perry and Penny are with them. Anne asked for the kids to attend the first few hours so she could introduce the family to the jurors. Paul and Penny will have to be present during the trial, as painful as it is likely to be, because their absence could result in some jurors wondering if they care enough to be there, especially since the jurors are there involuntarily.

On the other side of the corridor, Riley Goode, Sasha Young-Greenhorne, Skip Havidyad, Mary Wright, and Drew Delascard are huddled together comparing notes. It appears a couple of paralegals have been brought along to help with administrative tasks during the trial. Delascard leans on the hand truck he used to wheel in all their trial material. Doug Heels is there, as is Noah Little, who obviously has flown in for the trial. Not only are these two going to be witnesses during the trial, but, like the plaintiffs, the impression on the jurors must be that the defendants care about the case, so a representative of the party should be in the courtroom.

Most of the crowd are the prospective jurors, all sporting juror badges around their necks. The lawyers know they must not smile toward or engage in any way with the jurors so as not to be accused of trying to curry favor. The jurors arrived earlier, congregating in a juror assembly room on a different floor to listen to an orientation lecture and then to be assigned to different courtrooms. Sometimes they are warned that the lawyers will intentionally ignore them, sometimes not. So, there is no way for the lawyers to know if any juror might not understand this "cold shoulder." The best the lawyers can do is to maintain composure or otherwise effect a pleasant demeanor while in the presence of jurors.

The parties have agreed to share a courtroom presentation specialist, as they informed Judge Sticklery, who will handle the electronic exhibits and display them on screen as called for at any given moment, even highlighting, magnifying, or annotating exhibits. They have selected Docker "Stamp" Bates, of Techie-Doc Trial Support, who is well-known in the area. Stamp has his equipment containers on dollies, ready to move into the courtroom when the door opens. He will connect a laptop to the court's standard equipment and will route his feed to everyone in the courtroom.

It is 8:32. At least three people in the group have nervously tried to open the courtroom door. At 8:37, the door is unlocked and opened by the court attendant who holds the door while the parties walk, wheel, and/or trudge into the courtroom. The jurors are told to wait in the corridor.

Stamp Bates immediately starts setting up his equipment, which takes about ten minutes. The lawyers, meanwhile, get themselves plugged in and booted up. Stamp then tests that all the lawyers and the judge's station are connected. The court clerk also hands to each of the lawyers a list of the jurors in the pool waiting outside.

While this is going on, Judge Stickler comes into the courtroom, stands by the clerk's station, and says, "Good morning, all. Do we have any housekeeping to discuss before asking the jurors to come in?" The lawyers, in turn, say they are ready but take the moment to introduce their respective clients to the judge, who responds in a welcoming tone. Stamp indicates everything is ready to go. The judge then retreats to her chambers to wait for the jurors to enter the room before taking the bench. The jurors are called in. The lawyers and their clients all stand up as a sign of respect to the jurors.

Once everyone is seated in the gallery, which consists of rows of chairs behind the lawyers' tables, separated by a low railing, two buzzes sound and the judge enters from her chambers, standing next to the court clerk. The clerk goes through her usual routine: "All rise and face the flag of our nation, recognizing the principles for which it stands. Department 2 of the Superior Court of the State of California for the County of Los Angeles is now in session, the Honorable Maya B. Stickler, judge presiding. Please be seated."

The judge begins:

"Good morning, ladies and gentlemen of the jury, and welcome to Department 2. If you are selected as jurors, you will hear the case of Paul, Patty and Peter Smithson versus Family Swim Club, LLC and Got You Covered Technologies, Inc. Your role is to listen attentively to the testimony of witnesses, review any exhibits presented, and ultimately reach a verdict based solely on the evidence presented in this trial, following the instructions of the court." This morning, we are going to select fourteen out of the forty of you who will be the jurors for the case, that is, twelve of you will be the main panel of jurors and two of you will be alternate jurors, to serve on the panel in case someone is forced to drop out. We are about to begin the voir dire process, which is the only time during a trial that the lawyers get to interact with you one on one. The court will ask you questions followed by the lawyers and the purpose of these questions is to determine if you will be fair and impartial in deciding the case. Before we proceed with that process, I ask the court clerk to swear you in."

The clerk stands and asks the jurors all to stand and raise their right hands.

"Do you, and each of you, understand and agree that you will accurately and truthfully answer, under penalty of perjury, all questions propounded to you concerning your qualifications and competency to serve as a trial juror in the matter pending before this court, and that failure to do so may subject you to criminal prosecution?"

A chorus of yesses occurs and the clerk signals them to be seated. All are still behind the railing. Judge Stickler continues:

"First, let me introduce the parties and their lawyers to you. The plaintiffs are Paul and Patty Smithson, and their son, Peter Smithson. They are represented by Anne Dewey and Robert Berry of the law firm of Dewey, Cheatem, and Howe. All of you may stand, smile and wave your good mornings to the jury. [chuckles around the room] There are two defendants. Defendant Family Swim Club, LLC is represented by Riley Goode and Sasha Young-Greenhorne of the law firm of Gotcha Goode, and Mr. Douglas Heels is here on behalf of the club. Is that right?"

Riley rises and booms, "Yes, your honor, Mr. Heels is present. And good morning, ladies and gentlemen."

"And last but not least, Defendant Got You Covered Technologies, Inc. is represented by Parker Havidyad, Mary Wright, and Andrew Delascard. Counsel is your client present?"

"Yes, your honor," says Skip. "Good morning, everyone, and may I introduce a representative of my client, here from New Jersey, who will be with us for the duration of the trial, Mr. Noah Little. Thank you, your honor." Skip re-takes his seat.

"Ladies and gentlemen, we will start with a series of questions I will pose to you. I will address them to all of you at once and if you have a response, please raise your hand. This will be followed by the lawyers for each party who may ask questions to the group or to each of you personally. First, I will read to you a statement agreed by the parties to the case that will provide you with a limited description of the accident, which is the subject of this case, and what the parties claim.

'On November 11, 2023, Paul and Patty Smithson
and their children, Perry, Penny, and Peter, all minors,
visited defendant Family Swim Club, LLC to decide

whether to join as members. During the visit, then five-year-old Peter, the youngest child, became trapped underwater in one of the club's pools, under a pool cover designed and manufactured by defendant Got You Covered Technologies, Inc. He was rescued by his father, Paul. The plaintiffs in this case are Peter Smithson, who claims he suffered serious injury and will never recover, and that he now needs constant medical care at substantial cost. His parents, Paul and Patty Smithson, claim serious emotional distress by witnessing the event. The plaintiffs claim defendant Family Swim Club was negligent in causing the claimed injuries and also claim that the pool cover manufactured by defendant Got You Covered Technologies was defective in causing the claimed injuries.

"Defendant Family Swim Club admits its negligence caused the accident to occur, but denies complete responsibility and claims the parents, Paul and Patty, also were negligent. Defendant Got You Covered Technologies denies its product was defective and claims the accident was caused by the negligence of the parents and defendant Family Swim Club."

"So, now that you know a bit about the case and who the witnesses will be, let me start the voir dire. By a show of hands, do any of you know any of the lawyers, their law firms, any of the individual parties, including the companies and their representatives here, or any of the witnesses? Yes, sir, please stand and give us your name first."

"My name is Jose Kanusee. I do know the Family Swim Club. I went there once about five years ago with my family. We were invited there by friends as their guests."

"Mr. Kanusee, the judge begins, was there anything about that experience, at the Swim Club, which made you feel you would be unable to be fair to all the parties to the case? That is, did you have a bad experience or a good experience that would make you biased for or against the Swim Club?"

"Oh, no, ma'am. I mean, we had fun that day, and a person from the club asked if we wanted to join, but we could not afford it. But no, I am sure I could be fair either way."

"Thank you, sir. I saw another hand, yes, please state your name."

"My name is Lois Price. About ten years ago, I was in a car accident with an employee of Family Swim Club."

The judge inquires, "Ms. Price, can you tell us a bit more about that. Do you recall the employee? Was the exchange between you at the scene difficult? Was there a lawsuit?"

"Well," begins Ms. Price, "I don't recall the person's name but he was driving a van with the name of the club on the side. That's how I know who his employer was. And I did make a claim against them. Their insurance company wouldn't pay off, so my lawyer sued them, and…"

"Ms. Price," the judge cuts her off, "let's hold up on some of the details and let the lawyers here get into it in a bit if you are called to the jury box. Thank you. Is there anyone else famil-iar with the parties, the lawyers, or the witnesses? Yes, ma'am. Please."

"Hello, my name is Barb Dwyer, and I know Dr. Proctor. He is my nephew's neurologist. My nephew has a rare condition called Rett Syndrome, and my sister found Dr. Proctor to treat him because he specializes in and is well-known for dealing with serious pediatric problems."

"Thank you, Ms. Dwyer," says the judge. "I am sure the law-yers will have a few questions about that if you are called to the jury box. Anyone else? No? Okay, the clerk will now draw four-teen names randomly from the list of all of you. As your name is called, please come up through the railing and be seated in the jury box. Each seat is numbered, one to fourteen."

The names are called and assigned numbers to match the chairs. Mr. Kanusee, Ms. Price, and Ms. Dwyer are all called in the first group of fourteen.

Judge Stickler says, "Now, to all of you in the jury box, I am directing your attention to the easel to my left and to your right. There is a list of questions there."

The questions shown to the jury are:

1. State your name and the town or city you live in.

2. Are you married?

3. Do you have children?

4. What is the highest level of education you have?

5. What do you do for a living?

6. What is your employment status, working or not working?

7. By whom are you employed?

8. Have you ever served on a jury before and, if so, did you reach a verdict?

9. If you have been on a jury before, was it a civil or criminal case?

10. Do you have any medical conditions that would prevent you from serving on a jury?

11. Are you able to commit to the full length of the trial? If not, why not?

12. Do you have any strong feelings about the legal system, including whether you think that people should be compensated for injuries they suffer?

13. Do you have any strong opinions about the issues involved in this case based on what you have heard so far?

14. Can you set aside your personal beliefs and follow the law as instructed by the court?

Giving them a chance to look over the questions, Judge Stickler says, "I'd like each of you to answer each of those questions. Let's start with Mr. Kanusee, seated in chair number one."

Mr. Kanusee looks at the list of questions and begins, "My name is Jose Kanusee, and I live in Pasadena. I am not married and have no children. I graduated from Pasadena High School. And I am now employed by the Pasadena School District. I am a maintenance technician and work at different schools within the District as needed. I have never been on a jury before. I have no medical conditions. I can stay two weeks because that's what my employer allows. I have no strong opinions about the legal system and none so far about the case. And yes, of course, I will help decide the case as best as I can."

"Thank you, sir. Ms. Price?"

"My name is Lois Price. I live in the City of Los Angeles. I am widowed, with three children, all adults. I have a master's degree in mechanical engineering that I obtained from UCLA. I am now retired from Lockheed, where I worked on a program that developed a method of securing aircraft to the decks of aircraft carriers. This included materials testing, and, yes, I have served on a jury before. It was a criminal case. I was the foreperson. We did reach a verdict. I am able to serve on the jury medically, and I have the time available. I believe the legal system is as good as we have to compensate people for injuries. As for how I feel about the case, I cannot tell for sure what happened, but if the child was caught under something in a pool, I wonder why he was not supervised at the time. I wonder where the parents were. But of course, I will listen to all the evidence before coming to any conclusion and will do so impartially."

"Thank you, Ms. Price. Ms. Dwyer, please tell us your thoughts?"

"My name is Barb Dwyer. I live in Studio City. I am married with two children, and I am a homemaker. I have a college education. I have served on a jury before, a civil jury, and we did reach a verdict. I have no medical condition that would be a problem. I would have trouble serving two weeks because my kids are in school, and I have to deal with that. I have no strong feelings about the legal system and believe compensation is due if fair. I do have the same question as the last person, that is, I am curious about why this child seems to have been unsupervised. But of course, I can be fair."

The rest of the fourteen jurors respond to the questions, one after the other. In addition to Ms. Price and Ms. Dwyer, two more people, both women, comment about parental supervision. Two others state that serving for two weeks would be a financial strain on them because of work, one of them being a small business owner. Another man attempted to fake bias by scoffing at the jury system and feigning that he already has an opinion on the outcome:

"My name is Chris P. Bacon, and I live in Hollywood. I have a high school education. I am not married. I am unemployed at the moment, but my last job was as a security guard. I have not served on a jury before, and I have no medical problems. I would be able to serve for two weeks. As for compensation for injuries, my opinion is that the amount of money people get in these trials is ridiculous. I have no problem giving fair compensation, but for heaven's sake, the amounts you see in the news are like they come here for the lottery. On the question of what I think of this case, I think I can see what happened. This kid got caught under a pool cover, and I know how these big corporations work. They probably didn't have warning signs or something like that. Trying to skimp on how much the product costs."

Judge Stickler knows from experience what is happening. She follows up, "Mr. Bacon, it is important to the trial process that jurors do not hear and decide the case with preconceived ideas. This is why we are asking these questions. You say you are concerned about verdict amounts. Let me ask you this. If the evidence shows that it will take a very large amount of money to properly compensate the plaintiffs, will you be able to award that kind of money? I mean, if the evidence convinces you."

Mr. Bacon is looking at his shoes. "Sure, yes, your honor."

"Now, you also said you have an idea of what went wrong here. But you have only heard that the boy got caught under the pool cover. You have not been told how it happened. So, my question to you is, can you put aside your opinion that big companies can skimp on the cost of their products, listen to the evidence presented to you, and make a decision about who is responsible based only on that evidence?"

Sheepishly, "Yes, your honor, I will try."

When all in the seated panel had responded, the judge said, "Ladies and gentlemen, the lawyers will now ask their questions of you. They may follow up on things you have already said, and no doubt will have other questions. Ms. Dewey, you may inquire."

Anne stands and walks to the podium, set for this purpose, centered in front of the jury box. She is a slender, attractive woman in her late forties, with dark brown hair and a winning smile. She is dressed in her most conservative suit, a tweed limestone colored, collarless jacket, and a matching skirt. Her hair is pulled back behind her ears, falling over her shoulders. She has her notepad with the outline of her intended questions and a single-page grid where she has entered the names of the jurors corresponding to seat numbers, and where she has made notes from their previous responses.

"Thank you, your honor. And a very good morning to you all. My name is Anne Dewey, and I represent the plaintiffs, Paul Smithson, his wife, Patty Smithson, and their five-year-old child, Peter. Paul and Patty are here today." She waves her hand toward them. "Those other rascals over there are Peter's siblings, Perry and Penny." (Smiles from the jurors.)

Ann continues, "I am sure I speak for all the lawyers here that we so much appreciate your being here, and we know this is an interruption in your regular lives. We all promise to work hard to be efficient and get the case to you as quickly as possible, but there are a lot of witnesses, as you will see. Let me ask some questions first, addressed to all of you, and then I will ask some things of each of you separately. You are going to hear that little Peter Smithson was seriously, catastrophically injured. He was nearly drowned and seconds from death, he was rescued by his father, with his mother and siblings screaming and whimpering nearby, and revived by heroic EMTs, but he is now in a care facility, on a breathing apparatus, fed through a tube, and has little if any ability to understand what is happening around him; he is barely responsive, and you will hear evidence that he does not have much longer to live."

"Objection, your honor."

This comes as a chorus from both Riley Goode and Skip Havidyad. "May we approach for a side bar?" The judge waves them all up to a spot next to her bench, away from the jury's hearing. The court reporter brings her stenotype machine to the area. When she is situated, the judge indicates to Goode and Havidyad to make a record of their objection.

"Your honor," says Riley, "Ms. Dewey is arguing her case. I don't know if it's an opening statement, a closing argument, or what. But right out of the box, she is attempting to precondition the jurors." Skip chimes in, "And further, she's already trying to elicit sympathy and turn this into a wrongful death case."

The judge responds, "I agree. Ms. Dewey, I understand you are about to ask the jurors if they are comfortable dealing with a tragedy and whether they can award significant amounts. But I think you should tone it down. The objection is sustained, but I will allow you to finish this question area after you've cleaned it up."

The lawyers and the court reporter return to their positions. Anne is back at the podium.

"Ladies and gentlemen, as I said, Peter suffered a severe injury, and his parents saw what happened, something they will have to live with forever. You will hear evidence that caring for Peter has cost a lot of money, and more will be needed. My question, therefore, is whether any of you may feel there are limits to what you can award if the evidence persuades you? And before you respond, let me remind you of something you have already been told. One of the defendants here, Family Swim Club, has already admitted they were at fault for what happened. So, you will have to consider an amount of damages in this case. I see no one is raising their hands. Mr. Bacon, you mentioned you have concerns about the size of verdicts in recent times. Having now heard a little about the effect of the injury and its cost, do you still have reservations?"

Mr. Bacon replies, "No, I'm fine. I will certainly hear it all out."

"Thank you, sir. Now, ladies and gentlemen, you are going to hear opinions from experts, on the subject of who is at fault and on the medical side, including an opinion about how long Peter has to live. On the issue of fault, you will hear from experts on the subject of mechanical engineering, that is, how defendant Got You Covered Technologies' pool cover was designed, how it was fabricated, how it is attached and fastened down when used for its intended purpose of keeping an unused swimming pool safe and also free of debris. And you will hear how the pool cover failed.

"Objection, your honor, counsel is arguing," says Skip Havidyad.

"Overruled," replies the judge.

Anne continues, "Do any of you have any concerns about understanding this technical area, including the engineering jargon you may hear?" Yes, ma'am? Ms. Turner?"

"Yes, my name is Paige Turner. I can tell you that I am not a handy person. My husband would probably understand all of this. He fixes all kinds of stuff around the house, and we have a swimming pool too, but we don't have a cover. I am just nervous that I won't be able to follow, literally, the nuts and bolts of the story."

This gets a bit of a chuckle around the room. Anne presses on, "Ms. Turner," says Anne, "I am hopeful this will not be too complicated, and all the parties here have experts whose job it is to make their opinions clear. So, can you hang in there? I think the court will allow you, all of you, to submit written questions if you need something clarified, and we can respond to that by having the witnesses add to their explanations."

Ms. Turner nods affirmatively.

Anne continues her voir dire after a mid-morning break. She covers a range of topics aimed largely at finding out if anyone is squeamish about the injury or the amount of damages she will ask for, trying to determine if these are open, sympathetic type people, and trying to determine from their backgrounds whether they will have a problem with technical or medical evidence. She, of course, is also very concerned about the several comments to the effect that the parents may have been neglectful and moves on to that subject. She continues:

"Some of you expressed, maybe, a predisposition about the role of the parents in what happened. You all understand you have not heard exactly how this happened, but as I said, you have heard that Family Swim Club admitted responsibility already. Just hypothetically, if the evidence persuades you that the parents, Peter, and Patty, properly relied on the fact that entry to the pool area was supposed to be blocked off, could you put aside your concerns about the parents?"

The question was a clear suggestion of how to interpret the evidence, and Anne is glad it didn't draw an objection. Most of the jurors nodded yes to the question.

When Anne finally concludes, Riley Goode stands and goes to the podium. Riley is a large man, tall and overweight; he is unable to button his suit jacket, exposing a mass of white shirt and a bright red tie, not quite pulled tight at his neck. His hair is a bit long in the back. He has a boisterous, friendly personality, sort of a John Candy look to him.

"Good morning, ladies and gentlemen. My name is Riley Goode, and I represent defendant Family Swim Club, LLC in this case. You will hear a shorthand for my client during the trial, just using the words 'the club.' Later in the case, the judge will instruct you that a business, whether an LLC, like my client, or a corporation, like Mr. Havidyad's client, should be treated as fairly and impartially as if it is a person. Some people think of businesses as some big, unfeeling, greedy machine. But the club is made up of people, employees, managers, owners – people with families making a living. My question to you all, then, is even though my client is a limited liability company – an 'LLC,' can you set aside any notion that the club is to be treated any differently or more coldly just because it is a business?"

Various affirmative nods from the jury.

Riley continues, "Now, my client has stepped up here. The club has accepted responsibility for this accident, but not all of it. But we did the right thing. In the proof process that you will hear, everyone in this case will point the finger at each other. You have already heard that the defendants think Mr. and Mrs. Smithson are responsible. And the plaintiffs think defendant Got You Covered is responsible, and so on. But each party has what is called a 'burden of proof'. Riley shows air quotes.

"The burden of proof in this case is what is called 'preponderance of the evidence.' More air quotes.

"You all may be more familiar with the criminal case burden of 'beyond a reasonable doubt,' but that does not apply here. You will be instructed on what preponderance means later in the case, but my question to you is whether you all feel comfortable with following the judge's instructions about what preponderance of the evidence means, that it is different and has a lower threshold of proof than in a criminal case." Shrugs and nods. "Now, a few of you commented on your initial impressions of the case by saying you had concerns about what role the parents played in this accident. And you will hear evidence and argument about their contribution. My question to you all is whether you can put aside any sympathy you may feel toward the parents, given the terrible injury that young Peter suffered. This is really important, so please be honest in responding to this."

Some of the jurors nod affirmatively, others look down or away.

"And finally, you will hear evidence from medical professionals about Peter's condition. The evidence will be conflicting on two important things: the total cost of care and how long Peter will survive. I would like to ask if any of you have any medical training, and secondly, whether that medical training has anything to do with drowning injuries, comas, or injuries that limit one's life span. I see two hands. Yes, ma'am, please tell us about that."

"Hello, my name is Tish Hughes. I am a surgical nurse, and I also used to work in an emergency room. To respond to your question, I have seen patients in a coma, both induced because of head trauma and because of strokes. But that is just because of how long I have been doing this. I can't say that I particularly treated people in a coma, never a child, and I have no idea about how you tell if someone's life is shortened."

"Ms. Hughes, thank you for telling us that," says Riley. "What I think we need to know is whether your familiarity with the medical profession and your frequent interaction with doctors might make you feel like you should take over any discussion of the medical side of the case when you are deliberating with your fellow jurors, or, more importantly, whether you will substitute something you know about a medical issue over what you hear from medical professionals on the witness stand."

Ms. Hughes gives a look showing she now understands the issue, and responds, "I would like to think I can try to be a blank slate when the medical evidence is presented, but I am not sure I can put it aside if they say something I know to be incorrect."

Riley then asks, "Ms. Hughes, you heard earlier that you will be able to submit questions for us to take up with witnesses. Before deciding something is incorrect, will you please just make us respond to your concern?"

"Yes, that's fair. Thank you," says Ms. Hughes.

"Thank you, Ms. Hughes." says Riley.

Riley turns to Ms. Price. "Ms. Price, you had a lawsuit against my client. We need to know if, as a result of that experience, you now harbor any ill will against Family Swim Club. Can you please expand on that experience?"

Ms. Price responds, "Mr. Goode, it was no fun to get into an accident, and it took time and treatment to heal up, but the real frustration was how long the lawsuit took. We finally settled without going to trial, and I think both sides were not happy with the amount, but my lawyer said sometimes that's the key to knowing each side made the right compromise. As for how I feel about Family Swim Club, you know, it was an accident. No one was mean or impolite. Just an accident. And from the sounds of this case, it is a far cry from a car accident. Of course, I can be fair."

"Thank you for that, Ms. Price," says Riley.

Riley continues, moving in front of Ms. Dwyer. "Ms. Dwyer, you say your nephew was treated by Dr. Proctor and that was a positive experience."

"Yes, it was," responds Ms. Dwyer.

Riley makes this point, "Ms. Dwyer, you are going to hear from medical experts on both sides of this case. There will be an expert opinion from a doctor in the same field as Dr. Proctor. Now, you will be the judge of which opinion from which expert to accept. And I believe you will see that the qualifications of the medical experts on both sides are at least equal. My question is this: Will the fact that you know Dr. Proctor successfully treated your nephew give his opinion, in your mind, extra weight? Think about this and be straight with us, ma'am."

Ms. Dwyer thinks about this for a moment and responds, "I guess I understand your concern, Mr. Goode. While I know Dr. Proctor did really well for my family, I certainly don't want that to influence the outcome of this case for everyone here."

"And thank you, Ms. Dwyer. Thank you, your honor, that's all I have." Riley returns to his seat.

Skip Havidyad methodically gathers his notes and walks deliberately to the podium. He is a fit-looking man in his mid-fifties, graying at the temples, and he is a very sharp dresser. His button-down collar is crisp, and his tie is meticulously knotted, a lawyer from central casting. There is no hair out of place. He begins, in his modest mid-Atlantic accent.

"Ladies and gentlemen, just a few questions about some concerns my client has. The case against Got You Covered Technologies will come down to two important things: first, you will be shown a photograph of a portion of the pool cover where, it seems, the boy fell in, and that photograph shows an attachment mechanism is missing, something to do with the parts, called grommets, d-rings, and the like. And the second important thing is what you will hear about how the competing experts in the case interpret that photograph. Do any of you think you will have any trouble understanding what grommets and d-rings are? Seeing no hands, I assume this is not a problem. How about whether you will feel overwhelmed or intimidated listening to an explanation about how polyethylene material is fitted with grommets and d-rings along the edges so that strapping can be secured to the outside of a swimming pool?" He deliberately made this sound complicated to see if he could figure out who might have more familiarity with technical things. Again, no hands.

"Doesn't sound that complicated, does it? You will also hear expert testimony about how a pool cover is supposed to be maintained once put to use, and how and why certain kinds of material can break or tear. Do any of you believe you will have difficulty with that kind of technical information? No?

"Okay, I know this was asked, but is there anyone who feels that just because my client is a corporation, a manufacturer of a product, it deserves less consideration and less fairness than the Smithson family, who we know have suffered greatly from this accident? No hands? Ok, thank you for that."

Skip takes a deep breath, looks seriously back and forth at all the seated jurors, smiles, pauses, and then allows his face to return to a contemplative expression.

"Ladies and gentlemen, this is a case about a devastating, life-shortening injury to a child. There is no question about it. This little boy, Peter Smithson, will never be the same. You will hear that he nearly drowned and is now in a kind of coma called a permanent vegetative state, where he really does not know he is alive. Heartbreaking. This voir dire process is intended to find out if, despite that, you will be able to come to a fair and impartial decision about who was at fault and how much you might award for the injury suffered. Now, in my business, you see cases like this quite a bit, and I can tell you it's still hard to remain objective when you see something like this. But my client, indeed all the parties in this case, are entitled to a fair trial, a trial free of sympathy, passion, or prejudice."

Skip draws out these last few words.

"You have been sworn to be truthful in answering our questions here in the voir dire process, and once the jury is finally empaneled, you will take another oath where you will promise to listen carefully to the evidence and decide the case fairly. So, if there is any doubt in your mind about whether you can approach this case with the scales evenly balanced, now is the time you need to tell us. And you need to be honest and candid with us. So, I am now going to ask you each the same question.

"Mr. Kanusee, can you promise me, and the court, and the other lawyers, and the parties, that you can and will decide this case free of sympathy, passion, or prejudice?" He slows down to deliver the end of this line, carefully and dramatically enunciating each word.

"Yes, sir," says Mr. Kanusee.

Ms. Dwyer, if you are selected as part of the final panel of jurors for this case, can you promise me you can and will decide this case free of sympathy, passion, or prejudice?"

Now, Skip moves from behind the podium and stands a respectful distance from, but in front of Lois Price. "Ms. Price, can you promise me you can and will decide this case free of sympathy, passion, or prejudice?"

Ms. Price responds resolutely, "Yes, I can."

Skip moves in front of the next person and the next person, and so on, delivering the repeated line purposefully. All fourteen people, in turn, grant him their promise.

"Thank you, ladies and gentlemen. And thank you, your honor, I have completed my questions."

"All right, everyone," says the judge. "It is time for our lunch break. Ladies and gentlemen, please come back at 1:30, and you are admonished, as you will be every day of the trial, you are not to discuss the case with each other at all. Please follow that rule. If you do not, and it comes to our attention, it will be considered a violation of your oath and could have a devastating impact on the fairness of the trial, which is a concept these fine lawyers have made very clear to you. So, we'll see you later." The jurors file out of the courtroom, with counsel standing in respect.

"Counsel," says the judge. "I have to say I am amazed at how few of the prospective jurors tried to get out of serving based on the length of the trial or for other personal reasons. I don't think I have ever had a trial, as a lawyer or as a judge, where there weren't a lot of people trying to run away. Maybe that bodes well for the case. So, let me ask you, will there be any challenges for cause? If so, please let me know now."

Anne Dewey says, "Your honor, the plaintiffs move to excuse Mr. Bacon for cause. He clearly expressed that he has a distaste for damages, a clear bias."

The judge replies, "I agree, Ms. Dewey, that he started with a bias, but he then said he could listen to the evidence and be fair. I don't think what he said rises to the level of cause to excuse him. I'm afraid you will have to use a peremptory challenge on him if you are that concerned. Anything else? Okay, see you after lunch."

Anne is satisfied that she was able to do some preconditioning of the jurors. While you are not supposed to do that, it is common practice to push that envelope. She remains concerned about the comments suggesting this jury will be looking for parental negligence. Unless those people who said something about it seem better suited to be jurors than others, she will exercise peremptory challenges on them. She found Riley Goode's voir dire to be a little thin, but it covered the kinds of things defense lawyers need to. He was able to highlight that the parents' negligence is part of the case and introduced that there will be a fight over life expectancy.

Skip Havidyad's approach was obviously a well-practiced pitch to make sure the jurors would not decide the case on sympathy. Her feeling is that the effect of that will only go so far when the jury sees the day-in-the-life video showing Peter's condition. She also noted that Skip Havidyad's questions, intending to force the jurors to an impartial mindset, also could have the positive effect of reminding them that this is a serious and big case.

She intends to have Doug Heels as her first witness. She can ask him leading questions as an adverse witness, and this way she can have someone other than her own clients set the scene, including the dramatic events that unfolded. She wants to close her presentation with the emotional testimony of the parents.

She now also thinks it might be best to settle with the club. The jury has heard the club admits responsibility, and their witnesses, Heels and Gonzalez, will testify regardless. Settling will also eliminate the two against one aspect of the trial and will eliminate the club's expert, who opinions at deposition added nothing about whether the pool cover was defective.

Further, her investigation of the club shows there is a lot of debt, and so it may be difficult to get any money out of the property. This is too bad, because, unless she is able to win against Got You Covered, the two million is all her clients will get. She explains all this to the Smithsons during the lunch break. The children have been picked up by their grandparents and will not be in the courtroom again. They have served their purpose. She will approach Goode or maybe call the mediator, Judge Ismael, after the day's session is over.

At 1:30, the crowd re-enters the courtroom, and the judge takes the bench a few minutes later after the now familiar double buzzer, and begins:

"All right, welcome back, ladies and gentlemen. We will resume the jury selection process. The first challenge is with the plaintiffs. Ms. Dewey?"

Anne rises and says, "The plaintiffs would like to thank and excuse Mr. Bacon."

The judge turns to Mr. Bacon and says, "Mr. Bacon, you are excused. Please return to the jury assembly department where you started your day. Thank you."

The defense side, that is, both defendants together, has a total of six peremptory challenges and so must work together. Each side goes through the process of excusing jurors. Along the way, the defense lawyers excuse Ms. Dwyer, not wanting to take a chance on her positive feelings about with the plaintiffs' doctor, Dr. Proctor. They excuse Ms. Price because she was, herself, a plaintiff in an accident case in the past, and it happened to be against Family Swim Club; they do not want to take a chance, even though she said she could be fair.

As each juror is excused, another prospective juror is selected out of the hat and is called up to sit in the vacated chair. The judge and the lawyers then repeat the voir dire process, though more limited because it is directed only to the new juror. Once the questions are concluded, the peremptory challenges resume until each party states they will accept the jury as constituted. By 2:30 p.m., they have a jury. The jury consists of six women and six men, four of whom are African American, one Hispanic, and one Asian. Five have college educations.

They are listed as follows:

Al Beback - postal worker

Mack Burger – Amazon delivery person

Jed Dye – truck driver (alternate 1)

Freida M. Fider – elementary school teacher

Joanna Behere – postal worker (alternate 2)

Tish Hughes – registered nurse

Jose Kanusee – maintenance worker

Anita Job – bartender and part time lounge singer

Sam Manila – postal worker

Chip Monk – professional comedian

Duane Pipe - plumber

Jean Poole – homemaker

Ken Reade – staff lawyer for the California State Bar

Paige Turner – independent journalist

The rest of the jury pool, not called to the jury box, are excused to return to the jury assembly room.

After the mid-afternoon break, the judge says, "Ladies and Gentlemen, the clerk will now administer the oath to you. I will give you some preliminary instructions, the lawyers will give their opening statements, and then we will hear our first witness. Before we do that, I want to inform you that we will not be in session tomorrow due to court business that came up just this afternoon. We will reconvene on Wednesday morning at 9 a.m. The judge nods at the court clerk to proceed.

The clerk asks the jurors to rise, raise their right hands, and says, "Do you, and each of you, understand and agree that you will well and truly try the cause now pending before this court, and a true verdict render according only to the evidence present-ed to you and to the instructions of the court?"

All say "yes" or" I do," and the clerk signals them to be seat-ed. The judge takes over again:

"Ladies and gentlemen, the plaintiffs have the burden of proof in this trial and will present their case first. Once the plain-tiffs are finished with their witnesses, that is, they will 'rest,' the defendants will proceed with their case. First, I will give you some instructions advising about your role and other things intended to assist you in following along with the evidence.

"You are not to talk about the case or your deliberations with anyone outside of the jury room. Do not contact the parties, law-yers, or witnesses. If someone tries to talk to you about the case, tell them you can't discuss it and report that contact to me. You are not to discuss the case with each other until all the evidence has been received and you begin your deliberations.

"You are not to use the internet or other sources of informa-tion during the trial or during your deliberations.

"Keep in mind that the arguments, statements, and questions by the lawyers are not evidence. The only evidence you are to consider is the sworn testimony of a witness, the exhibits admitted into evidence, and any facts to which the lawyers have agreed.

"In this case, there are two facts that have been agreed to. First, defendant Family Swim Club has admitted that its negligence is at least partially responsible for what happened.

"Second, Family Swim Club has admitted that, even though they knew the pool cover was to be held as evidence in the case, its employees nevertheless discarded the pool cover as part of an upgrade to the pool area after the case started, and the lawyers and experts in the case did not have an opportunity to examine it. What remains, as you will see, is a photograph taken by a Family Swim Club employee on the date of the accident. You are instructed to give your best effort to consider what this photograph shows and listen carefully to the expert witnesses, each of whom will give you their opinions as to what happened based on that evidence.

"In addition, I am instructing you not to be influenced by objections. If I overrule an objection, you are not to hold it against the objecting lawyer. If I sustain an objection, you are not to hold it against the asking lawyer. If I order that something said by a witness is to be stricken, you are required not to consider it in any way, even though you heard it."

The judge goes on to explain what preponderance of the evidence is, the distinction between circumstantial evidence and direct evidence, what discovery is, including the different discovery methods they will hear about, and the kinds of things that affect witness credibility. She concludes with an instruction that the jurors are to listen carefully, submit written questions if they feel the need to, and keep an open mind until all the evidence is in.

Opening Statements

CHAPTER TWENTY-SIX

"It is now 2:55, and we will go to 4:30 today," announces the judge. "Ms. Dewey, please give your opening statement."

Anne returns to the podium, takes a deep breath, smiles, changes her expression to one of intensity, and proceeds:

"Ladies and gentlemen, I am now going to tell you what happened, and I assure you the evidence you will hear will, in this case, reveal the events and their aftermath exactly as I am telling it to you. My esteemed opposing counsel, Mr. Havidyad, said it during the voir dire process. The story of what happened in this case is heartbreaking. Petey Smithson, five years old, drowned. He fell into a swimming pool owned and operated by Family Swim Club. Petey only got near the pool because the club's employee, Mr. Gonzalez, left the door to the outside pool area not just unlocked, but propped open, and left it that way to retrieve a tool.

"You will hear evidence that if only Mr. Gonzalez had pulled the door closed, and even if he had left it unlocked, little Petey probably was not strong enough to open it. He could only get out there if the door were open. Mr. Gonzalez made a clear path to the danger. You have been told that the club admitted responsibility for this horrible accident, and that is the reason they did so.

"But the accident still does not happen if the pool cover was not broken. The evidence will prove to you that the club's installation of the pool cover some three years earlier was not the reason the pool cover was broken. The evidence will prove to you that the club's maintenance of the pool cover was not the reason the pool cover was broken.

"Rather, what the evidence will show you is that a piece of hardware, called an eyelet, fabricated into the pool cover by Got You Covered Technologies, Incorporated, failed when it should not have. We will present you with the testimony of a mechanical engineer, whose job it is to figure out how failed products cause accidents to happen, Dr. Max Nerdley. Dr. Nerdley will explain to you that a very small part, an eyelet used to pull the cover taught to its anchors surrounding the pool, did not serve its useful and intended lifespan. It corroded and pulled out under the force of the connection. This allowed the pool cover to come loose, leaving a space at the corner of the pool, just large enough for a five-year-old to slip through.

"This accident, caused by the premature failure of a part, affected another lifespan, Petey's. You will hear from physicians and specialists who will explain to you that Petey suffered from hypoxia, lack of oxygen, resulting from drowning. This affected his brain, heart, and other tissues. As a result of the brain hypoxia, Petey suffered cerebral edema and permanent neurologic damage. In short, he is in a kind of coma, called a permanent vegetative state. This means he might react to light or a voice, but this is not necessarily because he has any cognition, any ability to think or understand he is even alive, but it might.

"You will hear from an expert that Petey will die before he reaches adulthood. You will hear competing opinions about how long Petey will live, but no one associated with this case disagrees about one thing. Petey will die before adulthood. The plaintiffs' expert gives him about ten years with today's available medical care, though during that time, Petey will be essentially unconscious and kept alive by being fed through tubes and will need drugs, at a cost of over $1 million per year.

"The evidence will show it was not just Petey who was injured. Paul and Penny Smith, mom and dad, saw all this happen. Unimaginable terror. You will be asked to compensate Paul and Penny for the emotional upheaval that they went through.

"That's it, ladies and gentlemen. A pretty straightforward case, and an awful situation. We certainly hope you will make sure to focus on the key evidence about the eyelet, and then about the damages, and come to sensible and fair decisions. Thank you."

"Ladies and gentlemen!" shouts Riley Goode as he hurries past Anne on his way to the podium. He continues in a friendly and reasonable tone, "No one associated with my client, and I am sure none of you, feels anything but sympathy for what happened. As Mr. Havidyad pointed out this morning, though, sympathy is not the measure of how to decide the issues in this case. What you already know is that my client, Family Swim Club, stepped up here. They have owned the fact that the door to the outside pool should not have been left open. They did the right thing by admitting this.

"What we can't agree on is who else might have been a contributor to what happened, and, as Ms. Dewey said, there will be disagreement as to the medical evidence. I am about to describe what you will hear, and, frankly, I need your understanding about two difficult things I am going to tell you and that you will hear from the witnesses. Here they are.

"First, as much as the Smithsons went through watching their little boy, drowned and taken away in an ambulance, the question must be asked. Why were these children, three of them, ages ten, eight, and five, left alone, unsupervised in a building that was unfamiliar to them? Ms. Dewey said the evidence will show that if the door had been closed, the accident would not have happened. I am here to tell you that if the parents had kept the children near them, the accident would not have happened. If that is hard to hear, I understand, but the evidence will show that my client was not the only cause of this accident. We selected you not because you are unfeeling robots, but because you promised us you would hear and consider both sides equally and fairly.

"Second, if that wasn't hard enough to hear, the evidence will show a terrible truth. Petey likely will not survive a year, based on his condition, maybe even as little as a few months. I see by some of your expressions that this is troubling to you. It should be. But it is the truth, and it is the correct medical diagnosis, which will be given to you and explained by the defense experts. The evidence will show you a clear reason why it is important to understand that young Peter might not make it very long. You will hear evidence that it will cost millions of dollars per year to keep Petey alive in his unfortunate state. Expert testimony will show you that if the boy in fact succumbs sooner rather than later, the money the plaintiffs will ask for will not be in play in your final decision. Again, I know it's hard to hear, and frankly, it's hard to talk about, but I ask you to view that reality in the evidence and give it fair consideration.

So, thank you in advance for being tough-minded as all this comes at you, and I am confident you will make the right calls. Thank you."

"Mr. Havidyad, you may proceed," says the judge.

"Thank you, your honor," Skip says as he approaches the podium. "Let me explain first what our purpose is in talking to you at this point, since this is the last time we will have an opportunity to address you until the evidence is all in and we deliver closing arguments to you. An opening statement is like a program you get for an event or at the theater. It gives you the cast of characters and a little bit about what you will see, about the plot of the play, and things like that. Another way to describe an opening statement is that it is a roadmap. What we are telling you this afternoon is like setting the navigation in your car, which will display how you will get to your destination and what you will see along the way. So, let me explain my client's case and what evidence we will show you as we move down that road.

"Ms. Dewey and Mr. Goode have introduced you to the evidence about who is at fault and what the medical experts will say to you. For sure, we share with Family Swim Club the medical points that Mr. Goode told you about. In fact, both defendants are using the same medical experts. After all, you don't want to hear all this twice. But as to fault, my client's case is a little different than Family Swim Club's, which has already told you the accident was their fault.

"The fact is that we do not have a lot of evidence to examine. It turns out that Family Swim Club threw the pool cover away before any of us got a chance to look at it. All we have is a photograph taken by the club's maintenance person, Javier Gonzalez. That photograph, that blurry photograph, shows a part, maybe two parts, that have been torn off the pool cover. Ms. Dewey, as she said, will offer you evidence through an expert that a brass part, called an eyelet or a grommet, pulled out when it was not supposed to. Yet, you will hear evidence that Mr. Paul Smithson, Peter's dad, in a frankly heroic show of strength, ripped the pool cover off at that corner of the pool. That's what damaged the grommet.

"Now, we do not have the grommet; it was lost or thrown away. The importance of this is that the plaintiff has the burden of proof. What you will see in the presentation of evidence is a showdown between me and Dr. Nerdley, where I will challenge him about how he drew his conclusions about corrosion and why he concludes Mr. Smithson's tug at the cover supposedly was not the cause of the missing grommet. Ladies and gentlemen, the evidence will show you that the pool cover was properly designed and fabricated, and I am sure you will wait for all the evidence to come in so that my client gets fair consideration of their version of what happened.

"Thank you, and I look forward to speaking with you at the close of the case."

The First Witness – Douglas N. Heels, Manager of Defendant Family Swim Club, LLC

CHAPTER TWENTY-SEVEN

Judge Stickler looks at the clock. "It is 3:50 p.m., so we still have time to start the testimony, even if it finishes on Wednesday. So, Ms. Dewey, you may call your first witness."

Anne stands and announces, "Your honor, the plaintiffs call Douglas N. Heels."

Heels walks to the witness stand located between the judge and the jury. He is sworn in by the court clerk.

"Good afternoon, Mr. Heels. It is nice to see you again," says Anne.

"Yes, hello, Ms. Dewey. Same here."

"Mr. Heels, you are the manager of Family Swim Club LLC, the highest-ranking person working at the facility. Is that correct?"

"Yes."

"All operations are under your control; the buck stops with you?"

"That's correct."

Anne leads the witness through basic facts in the complaint, including the location, ownership, and history of the club, the length of his employment, the number and roles of the employees, the size of the membership, and the cost of joining. She has him lay out the location of the several areas of the facility. She uses an overhead map of the property from the club's brochure and photographs, which Stamp Bates puts on the screen and enlarges for easy visibility.

There is an indoor pool, so members can enjoy the club year-round. There are two outdoor pools, one for adults and a general one for all. There are indoor and outdoor hot whirlpools. There are lifeguards or similar supervision present at all times, or the doors to the pools are locked.

The kitchen has access to the indoor recreation room and a walk-up window to the outdoor general pool. Snacks and light lunches are available. The recreation room has a large screen television and a ping pong table. There are indoor and outdoor areas for fitness and yoga classes, and a workout room.

She offers the brochure and the photographs into evidence; there is no objection, and the judge admits them. She then establishes that the pool was installed by Knight Pool Company.

"Now, Mr. Heels, let's get to the heart of the matter. Your company, Family Swim Club, is responsible for causing little Petey Smithson to nearly drown and ending up in a permanent vegetative state, kept alive by tubes, isn't that true?"

"Not exactly, Ms. Dewey. We know that our maintenance guy, Javier, had been out there working on the retractor mechanism for the pool cover and went to find a tool. We know that the Smithson kids were left unsupervised in the recreation room while the parents met with me to discuss joining the club, but we also know there was something wrong with the pool cover."

Anne follows up, "Mr. Heels, you know your company has already told the court, and the court has told the jury it is an established fact that your company's negligence is at least part of what caused this accident. You know that don't you?"

"Well, yes, but…"

"And the reason your company has agreed, stipulated, to being negligent is because of the negligence of your employee, Mr. Javier Gonzalez, correct?"

Heels juts his chin out and responds, "Not for everything. I mean Javier was doing his job and just went to get a tool; he was working on the retractor."

"Mr. Gonzalez, that is, Javier, will testify tomorrow, as he did under oath in his deposition, that he had been out there working on the retractor mechanism and left the area unsupervised when he went to get a tool, right?"

Objection, your honor," interjects Riley Goode. "May we have a sidebar?"

When the lawyers get to the side of the judge's bench and the reporter is in place, Riley begins,

"Your honor, this is improper. The court has ruled that once liability is admitted, the jury does not have to hear the details of what my client did wrong. I mean, the court did say some of this evidence will come in, and we all worked on the special jury instruction about that. But I think Ms. Dewey now intends to go too far."

The judge responds, "Mr. Goode, she hasn't gotten there yet, but there is another problem. All Ms. Dewey asked was for your witness to confirm the concession of liability. He balked at it, so I think he's opened the door for cross-examination on what we previously thought was agreed to."

Anne adds, "And, your honor, we intend to show the employee was not only working on the retractor. He was working on the pool cover that they knew was defective, and they were trying to fix it.

"The objection is overruled, says the judge.

All return to their position, and Anne continues.

"Mr. Heels, Javier was negligent, and the club is responsible for that negligence, because the door to the outside pool, which was out of use for the season, was supposed to be locked. Isn't that right?

"Yes."

"But he propped the door open because he was working out there, intending to go back and forth as needed, and he left the area to retrieve a tool, but left the door not only unlocked, but propped open, so that anyone could get access to the outside pool. Please admit all that to be true, sir."

"Yes, I can agree to that."

"Now, you also were present at Javier's deposition when he said he needed to get a tool to work on a problem with the retractor mechanism."

"Yes," says Heels, "I believe that to be correct.

Anne says, "Let's look at a picture of the outside pool area. Mr. Bates, please put up on the screen Exhibit 10."

"Mr. Heels, the retractor is that blue cylinder at the back of the pool area we see in the picture, in a recessed area where we see the ivy, correct?"

"Yes."

Anne continues, "The purpose of the cylinder, the retractor, is that it winds up and stores the cover when not in use and unfurls it to pull over the pool. Correct?"

"Yes."

"And you would agree that the mechanism cannot be used to pull the cover in if the cover is secured to the concrete deck. The connections fabricated into the pool cover have to first be disconnected manually from the anchors drilled into the concrete deck."

"That's correct," Heels testifies.

"After the accident happened, you saw that the corner of the pool where Petey Smithson fell in was not secured, right? I mean, you were there when it happened, and you investigated it afterward?"

Heels focuses on the picture and responds, "That appears to be correct. The area where Mr. Smithson was able to grab the boy was at the corner of the pool on the lower center or bottom part of the Exhibit 10 photograph."

"And that was far from the retractor," Anne asks.

"Right, that's correct."

"Mr. Heels, you investigated how this accident happened, and you saw that one of the attachment spots near where Petey was pulled out was disconnected from one of the D-rings."

"I saw that."

"And as part of your investigation, you spoke with Javier Gonzalez and satisfied yourself that the reason why the spot was disconnected was not that he had engaged the retractor while the pool cover was secured to the deck."

Heels looks a bit confused and then gets it, "Well, right. Once the cover comes off the roller, it has to be all the way off to then pull the cover over the pool and secure it all the way around. Besides, if it were attached, which is silly, it would have broken a bunch of connections."

"Did you find anything wrong with the retractor, Mr. Heels?"

"No, and I tested it myself."

"You also concluded that the D-ring spot that was broken was not caused by Mr. Smithson pulling at the cover, isn't that right?"

"I don't think I can agree to that," says Heels. "I mean, I saw him take a mighty rip at that thing and even wondered how he had the strength to do it."

"Mr. Heels, at your deposition, you commented that you couldn't understand why Mr. Smithson was able to pull that cover up the way he did, but you agreed that, after investigating it later, Mr. Smithson's pulling at it was not the cause of the D-ring failure. Isn't that right? That is what you told us."

Heels stiffens up a bit defiantly, "I don't remember saying that. I stand by my answer today."

Anne turns to the judge. "Your honor, I would like to read to the jury Mr. Heels' response under oath on this at his deposition. This is on page 74, lines 6-12.:

"Proceed, counsel," says the judge.

"I will now read from the transcript, your honor. 'Question: Mr. Heels, please tell us what you observed once you had a chance to conduct an investigation of where the pool cover was pulled up. Answer: I saw that the eyelet, which is the grommet where the D-ring would go and attach to the strap, was kind of decomposed, a little rusted, and had kind of popped out. It left a little torn area on the underside of the cover.'

Anne turns back to face the witness. "Mr. Heels, will you confirm that you were indeed asked that question and you gave that answer under oath?"

"Yes, I now see what you were getting at. I guess I wasn't sure where your question was coming from. Yes, that was my observation."

The judge then intervenes, "On that note, ladies and gentlemen, we will conclude for the day. See you at 9 a.m. Wednesday morning, tomorrow is off. Remember the admonitions. You are not to discuss this case with anyone, even at home and do not conduct any of your own research about any of this. Have a good evening."

Further Negotiations with Family Swim Club

CHAPTER TWENTY-EIGHT

As soon as Anne gets to her car, she calls Judge Ismael, the mediator. She leaves a message. Next, she calls Rob Berry to be sure he arranged for Max Nerdley and Dr. Ben Proctor, the pediatric neurologist, to be ready to testify the following afternoon. She already confirmed with Riley Goode that Javier Gonzalez will go after Doug Heels. She heads to her office to work on her outlines for upcoming testimony and await a return call from Judge Ismael.

At about 6 p.m., Anne's phone rings, and it is the mediator.

Judge Ismail asks, "Ms. Dewey, how are you? Did the trial start?"

Anne responds: "Yes, it's going fine so far. We opened today, Family Swim Club has conceded its negligence, at least in part, and the manager is halfway through his testimony."

Judge Ismail says, "Well, I'm glad it's moving along. I assume you didn't call me just to give me the trial status."

"Right," says Anne, "Now that fault is admitted by the club, I don't think I need them in the trial any longer. We've done our due diligence, and the property is heavily encumbered, so getting anything out of that seems problematic. But I still want to see if the club will pay anything over the $2 million policy limit and thought you might be able to help."

Judge Ismail replies, "Of course, I'll try. I have everyone's phone number. Do you have a deal in mind?

Anne adds, "I thought maybe they could pay $25,000 per month for a certain period, maybe until Peter passes away? So that would be 5-10 years. If so, that would add another $1.5 million."

"I think, Ms. Dewey, that might be wishful thinking, and then there is the uncertainty about how much longer the boy will survive. I think a payment plan might work, but I would advise asking for a specific period, like two to four years."

Anne runs some numbers on a calculator and agrees that her first thought was unrealistic. "Judge, I'd like to see if we can get another million dollars. So, if they paid $25,000 for 40 months, that would do it."

Judge Ismail says, "Let me make a call and see what I can do."

Judge Ismael reaches Riley Goode to say that the plaintiffs are still willing to settle with the club, but they really need something over the policy limit. He gives him the proposed payout over time and says that whatever they work out for progress payments, the plaintiffs are looking for a total of $3 million, which would include the insurance proceeds. Riley anticipated this might occur during the trial and has discussed the possibility already with Doug Heels and the club's Board of Directors. The club is a thriving and established business, but it competes with sports and fitness clubs and runs at a thin profit margin.

"Judge," Riley responds, we will never get that far, but if we can work out a one- or two-year payout, my client is willing to pay $50,000 in cash and $5,000 per month for 24 months, for a total of $170,000 over the insurance limit. But that's all they'll do."

The negotiations go on through the evening, Anne in constant touch with the Smithsons and Riley, calling the Board Chairperson as needed. The Smithsons recognize that anything they get now from the club should probably be considered found money, and they still believe in the case against Got You Covered, as does Anne. The calls continue the next morning so the plaintiffs can try to make a deal on the medical liens, and approval can be obtained from Lottie Cash at KMA Insurance Company. By 1 p.m., the deal is made.

Family Swim Club agrees to pay $2 million from its insurance, $100,000 immediately from the club's own money, and $10,000 per month for twenty-five months. The total settlement is $2,350,000. The medical lien of approximately $1.5 million is cut down to $600,000. This took a lot of arm-twisting of the medical insurers. But they can only recover if the case is won. Given the reality that the club does not have enough insurance and the case against Got You Covered is uncertain, they capitulate.

The entire amount will be considered for Peter and will be deposited into a special trust account for his care.[1] This also means the attorney's fee calculation is at 25%, but the Smithsons agree the fee will come off the top, not contingent on the two years of payments. After all is said and done, the Dewey, Cheatem and Howe fee is $585,500, and $75,000 in costs are reimbursed to the firm. Peter Smithson will net $1,089,500. This is still far from what it will take to care for him if he survives more than a year, but fingers are crossed. A settlement agreement will be circulated. A motion to approve the settlement will be filed promptly.

The last detail they consider is whether to make any portion of the payout a "structured settlement." In situations involving a minor or someone who cannot take care of themselves, an amount can be put into a life insurance policy, also called an annuity; in fact, this consideration occurs in almost all such settlements, especially when a minor is involved. Not all will be structured, but the option should be discussed. When minors are involved, the payout can be delayed until the age of majority, and that results in substantially higher payments. As for Peter Smithson's situation, they elect not to structure any amount at this time because it will all be needed for medical care soon. If they get a good verdict against Got You Covered, they will reconsider "structuring" the payments from that payout.

All this will be told to the judge, the jury, and the Got You Covered people the next morning in court.

That same day, Skip Havidyad and Mary Wright are feverishly preparing for upcoming witnesses. They anticipate the plaintiffs' case against Got You Covered will mostly come from their expert, Max Nerdley. To this point, they have a lot of information on Nerdley's prior trials, and clearly, he sells himself as a jack of all trades; he tries to qualify as an expert in almost any kind of engineering

---

1 The law protects the interests of the child. Mentioned earlier, a minor must be represented by a guardian ad litem. So too, the law requires the judge to approve the amount, and the order will call for the special account to be set up and can be accessed only with court approval.

situation. Mary asks Drew Delascard to see if he can dig up anything else, which he does and provides them with a written summary by about 4 p.m.

On arrival at court on day two, Anne and Riley ask the clerk if they could have the judge take the bench for a brief conference before resuming the testimony. The jury is asked to remain in the hallway at the clerk's request.

Judge Stickler: "All parties are present. Counsel, you wanted to discuss something?"

Riley replies, "Good morning, your honor. We are pleased to inform the court that the plaintiffs have settled with my client, Family Swim Club. We have agreed our two eyewitnesses, Mr. Heels and Mr. Gonzalez, will complete their testimony today, but we will no longer attend the trial after that."

The judge replies, "If I understand correctly, then, the plaintiffs will be filing a dismissal of the case once the funds have been paid, and after I approve the settlement. Is that correct?"

Anne responds to this, "Yes, your honor, and we'd like co-defendant Got You Covered to agree that the settlement is in good faith. Though the deal came together quickly, and we have not had the chance to discuss it with Mr. Havidyad."[2]

Skip Havidyad is leaning back in his chair with his hands clasped behind his head. He is not overly surprised since he knew Family Swim Club has a limited amount of insurance, but wonders why it took so long. He knows trying to block a seven-figure settlement would be fruitless.

---

2 In a multi-party case, if one defendant settles, there still may be a cross-complaint by the remaining defendant(s) also blaming the settling party, or it may still be possible that such a cross-complaint might be filed. The settling defendant, under California law, can bring a motion to have the court approve the settlement, called a "Motion for Good Faith Determination of Settlement." The court decides if the amount of the settlement is "in the ballpark" of what that defendant should pay. The amount does not have to match or be equivalent to what actually could be awarded against them at trial. The state encourages settlement and so will allow a settling defendant to save something off what might be a full verdict amount. The opposition by a remaining defendant will try to show the settling defendant has much more culpability and is not paying enough; the motive is to get as much credit as possible so the remaining defendant is not left holding a larger bag. Once a "good faith motion" is granted, cross-complaints are barred (as always, with exceptions).

Skip stands and says to the judge, "Your honor, I will confer with counsel later in the day, but I am presuming an amount of about $2 million at least. If so, I am sure my client will allow me to stipulate to good faith."

"Thank you, counsel," says the judge. "Ms. Dewey, will the settlement be structured?"

Anne replies, "No, your honor. This will be explained when we file our motion asking the court to approve the settlement, but the short version is that the amount does not fully cover everything, so it all needs to be earmarked for medical care."

Judge Stickler comments, "I see. Then please check with my clerk later in the day, and we'll give you a hearing date within a month or so. The next issue is what to tell the jury. I have to tell them the case has changed, and Family Swim Club is no longer in the case. I think it is fair to tell them there has been a settlement, but we will have to instruct them that they should not speculate about it. I will give them a modified version of Instruction number 217."

The parties consult their jury instruction materials and agree.

Judge Stickler turns to the clerk, "Madame clerk, please bring in the jury, and let's get started. Mr. Heels, please resume your place on the witness stand. Thank you."

Once all are seated, the judge begins, "Good morning, ladies and gentlemen, and thank you for being patient while I discussed a development with the lawyers. I am going to tell you about that now, and I will be giving you a jury instruction now, not at the end of the case, because of that development.

"You see, the plaintiffs, Mr. and Mrs. Smithson, and their son, Peter, have settled this case with defendant Family Swim Club. This means the case will be a bit shorter, maybe by a few days, because we will no longer hear from all the witnesses that Family Swim Club would have brought us. Mr. Heels and their employee, Mr. Gonzalez, will complete their testimony today, and then we will bid goodbye to Mr. Goode, Ms. Young-Greenhorne, and Mr. Little.

The judge continues, "Here is the instruction which you must follow: You have heard that there was a settlement between the plaintiffs and Family Swim Club. You must not consider this settlement to determine responsibility for any harm or in your consideration of whether, or in what amount, to award damages. However, you may consider that there was a settlement only to decide whether Mr. Heels or Mr. Gonzalez is biased or prejudiced and whether their testimony is believable.

Testimony of Douglas N. Heels - Continued

CHAPTER TWENTY-NINE

Judge Stickler: "Okay, that's it. Ms. Dewey, you may resume your examination of Mr. Heels."

Anne heads to the podium, "Mr. Heels, when we ended yesterday, you had just commented on your observation of the pool cover, including that the grommet was rusted and had popped out, leaving a tear on the underside of the cover. You recall that testimony?"

"Yes, I do," responds Heels.

"It would be nice if we had the cover to look at, wouldn't it?" Anne's question is delivered in a deadpan, but the sarcasm is unmistakable.

Heels looks down at his lap, sheepishly. "Yes, and I need to say something here. I have to apologize to the jury, to you, to the judge, to Got You Covered. I knew I was supposed to keep that cover once the lawsuit started, and then we upgraded the system; however, I simply forgot to inform the workers about it. I feel awful that happened."

"Mr. Heels, we are now in a situation where, for my client to prove their case, we are dependent on what you saw and what you say here about the condition of that pool cover. You understand that and recognize that we need you to be detailed and clear. Will you do that?"

"Yes, Ms. Dewey, I certainly will. Look, I just heard what the judge said to the jury about whether I would say something to help you or hurt Got You Covered just because we settled. Let me put that to rest. I am here to help the process by providing everyone with whatever I can. I would have done that with or without a settlement."

"Very well, sir," says Anne. "I want to focus on two things you said. First, you said, and I quote you, 'the grommet was a little rusted.' You saw it that day, so the rust could not have formed after the accident, do you agree? It was already rusted."

"Yes, that appears to be correct."

Anne keeps going on this, "You also said it had, and again, this is your testimony, 'popped out.' Please explain that further."

"From my observation," says Heels, "the grommet was shaped like a spool, circular with two outside round sides and a circular, indented middle section. To put it in, you would push it somehow so that one side would push through a hole in the cover fabric. I am not sure, of course, but it probably is crimped in once it's through the hole."

"Mr. Heels, I am going to show you a picture of a brass grommet fitted into a polyethylene surface, and it shows stitches where the surface, or fabric, is folded at an edge."

No one objects, and Stamp Bates puts up Exhibit 27.

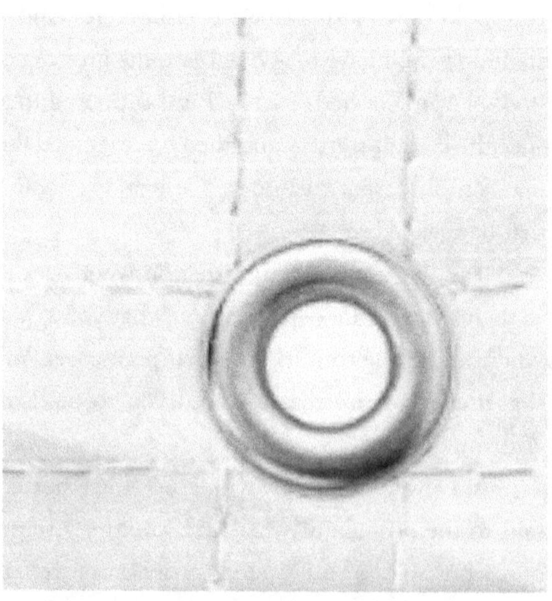

Heels makes a gesture of acceptance with his hands and then points at the picture, saying, "Oh, my goodness, yes, yes, that's exactly what it looked like. I mean, the cover was blue, of course, but that's what the other grommets in the cover looked like, and yes, they were brass." He then pauses contemplatively and adds, "If it were brass, I wonder why it was rusted."

Anne comments, "We'll get to the rust issue later in the case, Mr. Heels. But thank you. Now, you recall that even though everyone connected to this case thought all was lost when the cover was thrown out, but good old Mr. Gonzalez had taken a picture of one corner of the pool that day, after the accident?"

Heels nods in agreement, and Anne continues, "I am going to have Mr. Bates put that picture on the screen now, as Exhibit 6."

"Okay, Mr. Heels, Exhibit 6 is on the screen. I have asked Mr. Bates here to put three arrows on the picture, in different colors. First, please look at what the arrow labeled number 1 is pointing to. There is a white strap and a circular-looking thing of a different color at the end. Can you tell us what that is?"

"Yes, that's the strap threaded through one of the brass grommets – eyelets, if you will."

Anne follows up, "Now, look at the arrow labeled number 2. That's a D-ring, correct?"

"Yes."

"Lastly, look at what the arrow labeled as number 3 is pointing to. From your observation at the time, what happened there?"

Heels takes a moment to be sure he is seeing it clearly, and says: "Right, so that's the spot where a grommet pulled out, and it left that little rip in the fabric, showing as white."

"Did you see a D-ring lying around or in the pool that seemed to come from that spot, Mr. Heels?"

"No, and frankly, I can't say why one spot or another would or would not have a D-ring. That would be either for Javier or the maintenance people before him."

"Mr. Heels, when you arrived at the poolside during the emergency, you were behind Mr. and Mrs. Smithson and the other two children, is that correct?"

Mr. Heels: "Yes."

"Did you see Mr. Smithson working to get Petey out?"

"I saw that he was at the corner of the pool and struggling somehow, but I was a few feet back and I was dialing 911."

"At your deposition, Mr. Heels, you testified Mr. Smithson summoned some kind of extra strength and – this is exactly what you said – 'he yanked the strap right off. You could hear it rip.' But you didn't actually see the strap coming off, did you?"

"No, not exactly, but I recall seeing a piece of strap in the area."

"So you assumed he was able to pull the strap off, because you didn't actually see it happen, right?"

"Yes, but I heard what sounded like a rip."

Anne presses her point, "So, based on seeing the strap off after the accident and hearing, as you say, what sounded like a rip," Anne employs air quotes as she is framing the question.

"You thought Mr. Smithson had yanked the cover from its attachments, is that correct?"

Heels seems confused. "Yes, I guess that's so. I didn't see him actually pull the cover back, but I heard it."

"Okay, Mr. Heels, I want to cover a couple more things."

Anne draws out testimony from Mr. Heels, illustrating a step-by-step sequence of events, focusing on how much time was passing. She needed that for her expert to use in support of his opinions.

"And finally, Mr. Heels, I would like you to describe everyone's state while the rescue was happening, what was the behavior, what was said?"

Heels gives an expression of sincerity and says, "Goodness, let me think. First, the kids were yelling in the hallway for their parents, and then the running happened. I think Mrs. Smithson was saying something like 'show me where,' something like that. At the poolside, a lot of shouting happened all at once. Mr. Smithson bent down, and the mom held both of the other kids close to her. She was kind of whimpering. The kids were very upset."

"Mr. Heels, what were the kids saying?"

Heels takes a deep breath, lowers his eyes, and says, "This is what I heard after the boy was pulled from the water, CPR was happening, the EMTs got there." He is now choked up and stops.

"Mr. Heels, Doug? Do you need a glass of water?"

"No, I'm okay"

"What did you hear?"

"The kids were murmuring, crying, over and over, 'Don't die, don't die.'"

"Thank you, Mr. Heels," says Anne in a low, serious tone. "Your honor, those are all my questions of this witness."

Judge Stickler says, "All right, we'll take our morning break. When we come back, will you, Mr. Goode, have any questions?"

"I will not, your honor."

"Then, when we come back, Mr. Havidyad, you may begin your cross-examination."

After the break and all are back in their seats, the judge instructs Skip Havidyad to proceed.

"Mr. Heels, you have no idea if there was something wrong with the pool cover, do you?"

"Not really, I saw and will leave it up to you folks to sort it out."

"You are not an engineer, are you, Mr. Heels?"

"No."

"You are not a pool cover designer, are you, Mr. Heels?"

"No."

"You are not a mechanic."

"That's correct."

Skip keeps going on this point, "The only thing you know about grommets, how they're designed, how they're made, how they're used, or what they're made of, comes from this case, isn't that right?"

"Well, I guess so. But, goodness, I think most people understand what they're used for."

"And, you have no expertise about how grommets fail, right?"

"I suppose that's true," Heels agrees.

"And finally, sir, when you arrived at the poolside, behind other people, you didn't see if the pool cover at the corner was pulled like in the picture, did you?"

"I did not."

"Thank you, sir. That's all I have, your honor."

Judge Stickler turns to Anne and says, "Ms. Dewey, do you have any redirect examination?"

"No, your honor."

"All right, Mr. Heels, you may step down. Ms. Dewey, you may call your next witness."

Testimony of Javier Gonzalez – Family Swim Club's Maintenance Employee

CHAPTER THIRTY

With a nod from the judge, Anne says, "The plaintiffs call Javier Gonzalez." Riley Goode goes to the hallway to bring in the witness. "And, your honor," says Anne, "We have arranged for an interpreter.

Gonzalez is sworn in and Anne begins her examination.

"Mr. Gonzalez, let's establish some background facts quickly. On the date of the accident, you were an employee of Family Swim Club, you had been hired about a year earlier, and your job was as a handyman, the maintenance guy for the club, correct?"

"Yes," answers Gonzalez through the interpreter.

"Sir, you testified in your deposition that you were working on fixing the reel, or retractor, at the back end of the outside pool, you left the pool area to get a tool from your truck and left the door to the pool propped open. Will you please confirm those facts?"

"Yes, true"

"The fact is that the reel mechanism wasn't the only thing you were working on that day, was it?"

"I don't understand. I am sorry."

Anne rephrases, "Mr. Gonzalez, isn't it true that at the corner of the pool where the boy fell in, a section of the pool cover had come loose, one of the connections had broken?"

Gonzalez nods affirmatively and responds, "I was going to fix that area, yes, but much later in the day."

"So, the pool cover in fact was broken on the day of the accident and before the accident happened, correct?"

"Yes, I went outside to the pool to work on whatever needed to be fixed. We had closed the pool for the winter, and it was time to work on it."

"Sir, did you do anything to or with the pool cover before you went to the work where the reel was located?"

"Yes, there was one connection that needed to be fixed, so I released the straps near it. But then, I decided to come back later after I fixed the winder mechanism on the spool."

"Was the corner of the pool pulled up at all when you left it to go work on the spool's winder mechanism, the reel?"

"No, I had disconnected it. It was not fastened down. But I pulled it back down over the edge because while I was not working on it, leaves could get into the water."

Skip was concerned with where this was going. This testimony was unexpected. That added detail, that the witness had disconnected the cover over the corner of the pool where Peter fell in, was not in the deposition. He quickly scribbled a note to Mary asking her to check the deposition transcript to see if anything the witness was now saying was inconsistent with what he'd say before under oath.

At the same time, Anne was thinking that she'd suspected all along that more was going on that day than just the repair of the retractor mechanism, and that the corner of the pool was already disconnected, either by someone intentionally doing it or because it had broken. She recalls thinking maybe that Mr. Gonzalez was covering something up. But he hadn't been. In his deposition, he did say at page 47, "I had other things to do in the meantime, but that day I wanted to repair the mechanism." Neither she nor any of the others at the deposition thought to follow up on the question of what the "other things" were. And he would not have volunteered that information because his lawyer would have appropriately coached him not to give more information than precisely what the question called for. She mentally kicked herself for missing a chance to go into that at the deposition, but at least she got it out now.

Anne forges on, "Mr. Gonzalez, at your deposition, we talked about how the cover was supposed to be attached, including what the grommets were for. Right now, I'd like to ask you to point out some things we see in this photograph, Exhibit 6. Mr. Bates, please display that again, thank you."

"Now sir, please tell us what part of the pool cover we see in this picture was broken that day, before the accident happened."

Gonzalez responds: "It was where the arrow labeled number 3 is pointing. Do you see the grommet where the arrow labeled number1 is? Well, there was no grommet at the red arrow. It had been that way since I installed the cover much earlier, and I needed to fix it. But because the cover it was connected down at the corner, I had not been in a hurry about it. But this was the day I decided to repair it."

"Let me see if I understand," says Anne, "When the day started, on the day of the accident and before you did anything, the pool cover was secured, flat to the pool deck except for this one connection at the green arrow, but there was no space underneath, that is, the cover at that spot was still flat to the ground?"

"Yes, but I opened it up at the corner and removed the grommet and the strap at that corner location. They were there on the ground, but not in this picture."

"Thank you, Mr. Gonzalez, for that, but I have one more question area. Do you see what the arrow labeled number 2 is pointing at? What is that?"

"That is a metal ring, used to connect the straps."

"Mr. Gonzalez, why are there rings in a couple of places in this picture but not on the one where the green arrow is pointing?"

"Well, those rings were not original. I had only put this cover on two times, once just after I started working there, and then not long before this accident. But the original way the straps were connected between the anchors and the cover was to pass them through the grommets, like you see where the green arrow is. When the grommets would fail, the straps would also tear, so the rings are what I used to replace them."

"Had some of the rings been replaced before you started to work there?"

"Yes, and I copied what they did before."

"Thank you, sir, that's all I have."

Skip stepped up to the podium. With this new factual development, he had to think on his feet quickly about how to approach this. His instinct was to try to magnify the club's negligence, which would deflect away from his own client's liability. He thought Got You Covered was not necessarily affected by this. It was an old cover that was breaking down, not necessarily that there was a problem with how the cover was made.

Skip begins, "Mr. Gonzalez, you've been employed by the club for nearly two years? correct?"

"Yes."

"In that time, you've installed the pool cover two times, and each time, you have had to repair one or more of the connections, using the metal rings. Is that right?"

"Correct."

"And you noticed that even before you were employed at the club, other people had the same problem and needed to repair connections using the metal ring. Is that also true?"

"That seemed to be what happened, yes."

"Then, months ago, when you returned from your vacation, the pool cover had been replaced by a brand-new cover, the one we see in Exhibit 10. Yes?"

"Yes, that's correct."

Best practice is to not ask a question at trial unless you know the answer already from discovery. But Skip was blindsided by this witness's testimony, so he took a chance.

"Mr. Gonzalez, the old pool cover was replaced because it was old and breaking down. Isn't that true?"

"Well, I don't know, sir. No one ever told me the reason. The new one was just there when I returned."

"But the old cover was worn out, don't you agree?"

"I suppose so."

Skip was hoping the witness would admit the cover was just old and mis-used. Misuse is a defense to a product liability case. If the product is not used as intended or is not cared for properly, then a defect by the manufacturer may be excused. The witness's answer did not establish for certain that the reason for replacing the cover was because it was old and in disrepair, but the question itself may have planted the idea with some of the jurors.

"Those are all my questions, your honor," says Skip.

Judge Stickler asks, "Counsel, may the witness be excused?" Seeing nods from the lawyers, she tells Mr. Gonzalez to step down. "All right, ladies and gentlemen, we will take our lunch break, and we will see you at 1:30. Counsel, please stay behind."

When the jury had filed out, the judge says, "I understand there are no further Family Swim Club witnesses, so, Mr. Riley and Ms. Greenhorne, sorry to see you go, but you may be excused from the trial at this time."

Testimony of Maxwell S. Nerdley, II, Ph.D. – Plaintiffs' Mechanical Engineering Expert

CHAPTER THIRTY-ONE

At 1:30, everyone comes back into the courtroom. Drew Delascard takes his seat in the gallery, behind Skip and Mary. As Skip walks by, he taps Drew on the shoulder and says, "Hey, Drew, that was good stuff you got me on their expert yesterday. I think it will be useful. Thank you." Drew says, "Oh, good, I'm glad." He did not realize Skip even knew his name.

When all are seated, the judge says, "Ms. Dewey, please call your next witness."

"Plaintiffs call Dr. Maxwell S. Nerdley II."

Nerdley enters the courtroom and takes his seat on the witness stand. He is about 5'7" with a slight build. His hair is balding, with thin strips swept back on his head. He has thick black glasses and wears a bow tie. He is sworn in.

Anne dives in, "Good afternoon, Dr. Nerdley, please tell the jury what you do for a living."

"Yes, of course. I am a forensic engineer. What I do is analyze evidence from accidents and resolve who was at fault."

"Please tell the jury what 'forensic' means in a court of law."

Nerdley turns and speaks directly the jury, smiling, and begins, "Forensic is a term used to describe the process of using engineering concepts, and scientific tests and techniques to determine how something happened." "I'm sure everyone here has seen a TV show like CSI. Solving the crime is done by analyzing things like using DNA evidence or using geometry to figure out the direction of a bullet, things like that. In a civil case, we figure out what happened by looking at the accident scene, testing materials, and so forth. As in this case, we used those techniques to determine the lifespan of a grommet by relying on engineering data about how they are made, the material used to make them, and how they are used."

Anne continues, "Doctor, let's take a few minutes to tell the jury why you are qualified to conduct the kind of forensic inquiry you made in this case. Please tell us your education and career background."

Nerdley recites his qualifications in a practiced way, having done it many times before, "I received a Bachelor of Science degree in Mechatronics Engineering, a 'BME', from the Monterrey Institute of Technology, in Monterrey, Mexico. The other "MIT." This gets some laughs around the room.

Nerdley continues, "Mechatronics combines different disciplines, transforming graduates from this program into experts in the design and creation of products and processes in a wide range of areas. It is the equivalent of mechanical engineering but has a broader base of subjects that it covers. I received my master's in engineering from Hiram Rogers Institute in Coeur d'Alene, Idaho, also in mechanical engineering, and I received my doctorate from the same institution. Since graduation, I have, for the last twenty years, worked as a forensic investigator for Forensic Research Laboratories, also in Coeur d'Alene. I have been solving these mysteries in civil accident cases ever since."

Anne waits a beat to let all that sink in, and changes the subject, "Dr. Nerdley, please tell the jury what you have done in connection with this case."

"I attended a site inspection at Family Swim Club and saw the layout of the facility, and especially the subject outside pool area. I located and obtained a sample Got You Covered pool cover of the same estimated vintage. I examined Got You Covered's website to compare the old design to newer designs and read the relevant depositions in the case. Oh, and of course, I examined the one key photograph, the one from Mr. Gonzalez, as best I could."

"And based on that work, Doctor, have you formed opinions about the cause of the accident to Peter Smithson?"

"Yes, I have."

"What are those opinions and the bases for them, sir?"

Nerdley turns again to address his answer directly to the jury, "In my opinion, this accident was caused in part by Family Swim Club and in substantial part by Got You Covered Technologies, Inc. As to the club, it's very simple. Mr. Gonzalez was going about his business in a normal way. The pool cover had been stretched over the pool and secured to the outside anchors, as it had been time and again in the past. Noticing a problem with the retractor mechanism and that yet another grommet had failed, he planned to make repairs. In my opinion, the fact that he forgot a tool or the fact that he elected to work on the retractor before the cover itself has nothing to do with it.

Nerdley continues, "In my opinion, a cause of this accident was because Mr. Gonzalez left the door propped open. Very simple; if the door is closed, even unlocked, the boy cannot gain access to the outside pool area. I personally tested the door, and it takes quite a push to open it. I then tested the force it would take to open the door using a device called a 'door force gauge', also called a door pressure gauge, and pushed the gauge against the door, applying steady force until the door opened. I then read the gauge for the required force. This kind of gauge is often used because there are ADA rules about how much force should be required. There is no ADA standard for how much force is needed to open an exterior door. But this door took close to twenty pounds of force to open. I just can't see that a little five-year-old could have opened that door. So, if Mr. Gonzalez had closed the door when going to his truck, Peter would not have been able to access the outside pool area."

Anne prompts him on, "And what is your opinion of Got You Covered's involvement in causing the accident?"

"In my opinion,' Nerdley says, "the use of a small brass grommet, through which a strap is pulled, is an inferior design. A defective design. The strap they supplied was fine; that kind of stitching should last a very long time. But the pulling force on the cover, both static when in place and in the process of installing the cover each time, can definitely wear out materials like this brass grommet inserted into the material. In my opinion, the small brass grommet is the weakest link in the system, the system consisting of the polyethylene cover, the grommet, the stitched strapping, and the buckle and anchor at the other end of the strap."

"Why is the grommet the weakest link?" asks Anne.

"Well, it's just the basic strength of each material element. The one place most likely to pull out or fail is that grommet. And it is important to note that Got You Covered does not use that system anymore. The newer product uses only stitching. I have pictures of it."

Anne turns to Stamp Bates and asks for Exhibits 30, 31, and 32.

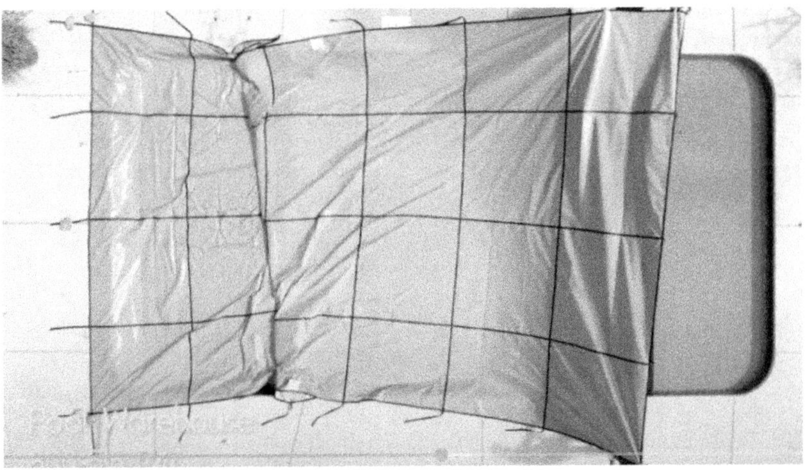

Once the picture, Exhibit 30, is on the screen, Nerdley continues, "This is a still picture taken from Got You Covered's most recent installation video. You will see that the entire cover is cross-hatched with sewn-in straps. Those straps are also at the edges and extend out to be pulled through a buckle and attached to the anchor. There is no grommet. Let's go to the next one."

"As you can see in Exhibit 31, there is no grommet," continues Nerdley. "A closer shot from elsewhere in Got You Covered's internet catalog is in the next photo, Exhibit 32.

"As shown here, it's all stitched together. Very strong."

Anne follows up, "Do you also have an opinion that, in addition to the ill-advised use of grommets instead of stitching, the cover was defective in any other way?"

"Yes, I believe Got You Covered takes the position that the grommet failed, but failed because of age. I disagree. We know the cover was purchased and installed not too long before this accident. So, if so many grommets needed replacement in that time, the assembly of the product more probably than not was performed poorly. So, we have both a design flaw and a manufacturing defect."

Anne further inquires, "Dr. Nerdley, what happened to the grommet in our situation?"

"Ms. Dewey, as you know, the grommet itself was not retained. All we have is Mr. Heels' description that it had 'popped out'." Nerdley uses air quotes to get his point across. "Grommets like the ones used in this cover are round and have an indentation along the outer, circular edge. The material gets embedded into, and snaps into, that recess. Well, that recess can give way, or the material can give way. Eventually, with a soft brass grommet of this small circumference, it's going to pull out. And Mr. Gonzalez's testimony, that it had happened over and over, proves it."

"Doctor, what do you make of Mr. Heels' testimony that what he observed was that the grommet was rusted?"

"This was a brass piece. It probably looked tarnished, that's all, but rusted or tarnished, it had nothing to do with the failure anyway. The failure was in the small, weak amount of brass material the grommet consisted of. This product was inferior, and if it had been designed with stitching like they do now, it would have taken an extraordinary amount of abuse before it would have failed. In my opinion, we would not be here today."

"Thank you, Dr. Nerdley. I pass the witness to Mr. Havidyad, your honor."

"Good afternoon, Mr. Nerdley," says Skip.

"It's Dr. Nerdley, and good afternoon to you."

Skip smiles and says, "Ah, yes. Sorry. So, Dr. Nerdley, your opinion is that the grommet connection does not hold long enough before it breaks down, and another design would have lasted longer. That's the sum and substance of your opinions, right?"

"I'd say yes to that summary of the first part of my opinion, but it's more complicated than that."

"Coming to your conclusions requires education and training in materials science and materials testing, as well as education and experience in scientific analytical methods, wouldn't you say?"

"Yes, I would."

"And applying scientific methods properly means to do so evenhandedly. You shouldn't be trying to help the side that hired you unless you really believe it, right, Dr. Nerdley?"

"I agree with you, and I will add that I always conduct my investigations according to the science, regardless of the outcome.

Skip keeps going on this theme, "And in conducting your investigation fairly, this is why you have never, not once, testified that a product was designed or manufactured properly. Do you think that's a good indication that you have no bias in your investigations, Dr. Nerdley?"

Nerdley gets this question a lot and responds, "This comes up from time to time, counsel. The fact is that even though I tend to be hired by plaintiffs' lawyers, if I find they have no case, they don't proceed with it."

"But the fact remains, sir, that you have never been hired by a defense lawyer. Why is that?"

"I don't know. It just developed that way."

Skip is holding papers in his hand, casually waving them around, and says, "Now, Dr. Nerdley, let's talk about your education. You went to college in Mexico but you did your post-graduate work in Idaho, at the, let me see here, the Hiram Rogers Institute. Then you went to work for Forensic Research Laboratories. Is the Hiram Rogers Institute a good school?"

"Yes, sir. It is very focused on teaching students to do exactly what I do."

"So, for a master's degree and a PhD.," says Skip, "the main focus is on investigating the cause of accidents and using those findings to help lawyers prove their cases in lawsuits?"

"That would be a substantial focus, yes."

"Dr. Nerdley, do you know Hiram Rogers, the person whom the entire university is named after?"

"Yes, I do, or did. He's passed now."

"Please tell the jury who Hiram Rogers was --- to you."

"Hiram Rogers was my grandfather."

Skip pauses as there is silence in the room. He lets the moment sink in, as all eyes are on Nerdley.

"Was Hiram Rogers working and teaching there when you attended?"

"Yes."

"Was the Hiram Rogers Institute a big school? How many students were there?"

"I don't recall how many students," responds Nerdley, "but it was a technical school, so it was not huge."

"Now, sir, let's talk about Forensic Research Laboratories, where you have been employed for twenty years in the same Idaho town. Are you the owner, and did you start the company?"

"Yes, I am a partner, but no, the company already existed."

"Who is or are your partners?"

"My cousin is my partner."

"And what is your cousin's name?"

"Hiram Rogers III."

"Wait a sec, Doctor. Let me ask this. Who founded Forensic Research Laboratories?"

Nerdley responds, "Hiram Rogers."

"Your grandfather? And your cousin's grandfather?"

"That's correct."

Again, Skip lets this all register with the jurors. "Sir, let me get into one more thing. Your opinion is that Family Swim Club and my client are responsible for the accident, but do you have an opinion about whether Mr. and Mrs. Smithson contributed to the situation?"

"My opinion is they had nothing to do with it."

"Let's see," says Skip, his hand on his chin, "the Smithsons arrive at this facility with their three minor children, a place they'd never been before, walk around a little bit with the manager, and then go into a closed room with him, leaving the kids, including a five-year-old, completely unsupervised to wander around the place. And that's okay with you?" The question is phrased to make a point. Skip intends to set the witness up for the next point.

"Counsel, they were indoors, in a recreation room, playing ping pong. I hardly think that means they were abandoned in a zone of danger. The only reason the accident happened was because the very thing that kept them safe from the pool was a propped-open door. The parents certainly didn't do that and had every right to assume that area would be closed off."

"How many indoor pools were there, sir? How many free weights were strewn about in the fitness room? Was it foreseeable, do you think, that someone else could come into the building from the outside, leaving the door open for them to find their way to the parking lot?"

"I think there were two other pools, but again, behind doors. I can't answer as to the rest of what you raise."

"Your honor, that completes my cross-examination of Mr. Nerdley." Nerdley rolls his eyes on the witness stand.

Anne and Rob are seated at counsel table, stunned. During the cross-examination of Max Nerdley, Anne was frozen, arms crossed with one hand over her mouth. The attack on Max's credentials seemed to score points with the jurors. The opinions, nevertheless, were solid and supported, but credibility means a lot. Maybe she can regain ground when cross-examining the defense expert, Marc Mewords. But she needs to rehabilitate the situation a little.

Anne heads to the podium and asks, "Dr. Nerdley, have your education and other credentials been recognized by other institutions?"

"Yes. I have been a regular speaker at the engineering school at UCLA, and I have taught a course in forensic studies at the University of Southern California. In addition, I have sat on Committee E30 of the American Society of Testing and Materials, or ASTM. That committee, on forensic sciences, has jurisdiction over seven standards that provide general guidance on conducting investigations and handling evidence."

Anne follows up this point, "And no court, in any state, or whether state or federal, has refused to let you testify based on your qualifications, education, training, and experience?

"No, never."

"Thank you, sir. No further questions."

Seeing that there is nothing further, the judge excuses Max Nerdley. "It is 3:45 counsel, what's next?" She is told that doctors are planned for the next day to accommodate their calendar. "All right, we will end a little early today. See you all at 9 a.m. tomorrow."

Got You Covered's Settlement Offer

CHAPTER THIRTY-TWO

Mary Wright's daily report to the client and their insurance carriers, which she was compiling in real time during each trial day, explained the new factual development that the pool cover had been jury-rigged over time to be able to resecure the attachment points because the grommets were failing. She emails the report promptly, and she is able to discuss it before leaving the courthouse with Noah Little, who had been present. Noah suggests they try to set up a Zoom conference at 7 a.m. the following morning, before they need to head to court.

Skip, Mary, Noah, Sue Dembach, Sharon Little, Holden De Monet (from CAGI), and Luke Askance (from Bumbershoot) all participate in the call the next morning. The trial evidence is summarized during the call, culminating in the fact that the maintenance person, Gonzalez, who at first was thought would be a questionable witness, would probably now be seen as credible, and that his testimony about the failing grommets was not positive for Got You Covered's case.

They discussed Marc Mewords' anticipated testimony will focus on the fact that a grommet component to the attachment system was complied with all applicable standards at the time. Mewords also will say that any product has a certain expected life span, and it should not be considered defective because the cover did not last forever; the club should have replaced it sooner. There was concern that the jury heard that the design had been changed recently, away from the use of grommets. Noah Little will testify that the design change was in keeping with the industry trend, not because of any evidence that grommets were failing sooner than expected.

Sue and Sharon let the group know that one of the other pool cover cases was dropped and two more settled inexpensively, so the need to be careful settling the Smithson case to avoid an effect on other negotiations is now less important. Hearing all of this, Holden sternly advised the Got You Covered people to make an offer up to their SIR limit. He is told that was done at the mediation and there is about $1.3 million left. He tells Skip that CAGI will contribute another $700,000, making a total offer of $2 million.

The group discusses that the witnesses for the day will be Dr. Proctor, the neurologist, the certified life care planning expert, Crystal Ball, LVN, and the economist, Robin Do. This will be followed on the next Monday morning by the Smithsons since the court conducts other business on Fridays. The plaintiffs will then rest. The lawyers have kept each other informed of what witnesses will appear each day as a courtesy to allow them to prepare overnight.

Before the door is opened at 8:30, Mary approaches Anne in the hallway and asks if they can speak away from where the jurors are standing. They walk to the end of the hallway and down the stairs to the next floor. "Anne, we are all impressed by the case you are putting on though we are still convinced the jury will find the club and parents substantially at fault and that, unfortunately, Peter is not likely to survive long, thereby limiting the verdict. But I am authorized to make the plaintiffs a settlement offer because a previous impediment to doing so has become less important."

Anne has no idea what the so-called "impediment" is or was. This could simply be Mary just trying to steer her away from the idea that the settlement offer coming now is the result of how well the plaintiffs' case is going. She looks expectantly at Mary, who says, "The offer is $2 million." Anne thinks this is barely an offer but she is ethically required to advise her clients about it. She thanks Mary and promises to get back to her as soon as possible, but probably not before Friday.

Testimony of Benjamin Proctor, M.D. – Plaintiff's Pediatric Neurologist

CHAPTER THIRTY-THREE

When the trial resumes at 9 a.m., Dr. Benjamin Proctor takes the witness stand. Dr. Proctor is a marvelous-looking witness. He is the poster child of what juries expect doctors to be: well-tended salt and pepper hair, wire rim glasses, with a professorial countenance. He has a baritone voice and speaks calmly but assertively. Dr. Proctor is indeed a professor of pediatric neurology in the Cedars-Sinai Health system. He is the doctor who treated Peter Smithson at the special care facility after he was moved from the hospital. He also agreed to serve as a retained expert for the plaintiffs due to his extensive knowledge of how long children in a permanent vegetative state will survive. He knows to look at the jurors when he provides his opinion and does so with aplomb.

On direct examination, Dr. Proctor describes Peter's injury, going into detail about how the lack of oxygen in a drowning accident affects the body. Drowning quickly progresses from respiratory arrest (breathing stops) to cardiac arrest (heart stops beating) due to lack of oxygen, requiring immediate CPR with rescue breaths and chest compressions. Peter is in what is called a permanent vegetative state, not exactly a coma, because he does respond to stimuli and seems to track things happening in the room, particularly when attended to. He describes the treatment and care provided to Peter, who is dependent on staying alive on a ventilator with tracheostomy, has chest tubes on both sides, and receives nutrition through a percutaneous endoscopic gastrostomy. In lay terms, he cannot breathe or eat but instead has tubes surgically implanted into his body.

His opinions about survival stem from the timing information shown in the medical records, and EMT reports that Peter was deprived of oxygen for up to eight minutes, and his clinical course for the last fifteen months. The eight-minute oxygen deprivation means the chances are very high that Peter will not recover. Dr. Proctor has treated hundreds of children in permanent vegetative states, whether from drowning, blunt trauma brain injury, disease conditions, or other problems. In that time, he notes there have been maybe one or two patients who came out of the vegetative state after eight or nine months. The vast majority of the patients do not survive past five to seven years, but Dr. Proctor opines that Peter Smithson could survive up to ten years with the excellent care he is getting and because, from daily observation, he is resting comfortably, and more recently, he does exhibit some seemingly cognitive behaviors.

The jury hears that the cost of caring for Peter will be about $1.5 million per year, consisting of the cost of the care center, the medical care, treatment, and monitoring, and the cost of medicine.

On cross-examination, Dr. Proctor agrees that patients who wake up from a permanent vegetative state are those who are not so far gone that they need mechanical help to breathe and need to be fed through a tube. He also concedes that under those circumstances, the chances of survival may not be as long as the ten years . But he adds that his patients have sometimes lasted longer, and there have been a few miracle cases, where the patient wakes up. Dr. Proctor also testifies that the prognosis for recovery is a bit difficult to assess because the timing information is also uncertain; it could have been four minutes or as long as eight minutes. He agrees it is more likely than not that Peter is not in the "miracle" category, and lasting ten years is an estimated maximum time, the average being five to seven years.

Dr. Proctor is also cross-examined on his comment that Peter had exhibited seemingly cognitive behaviors. The doctor concedes that these behaviors, like responding to his parents' voices and grunting when being moved around by nurses, might be just physical, not mental responses. However, Dr. Proctor explains that some thinking processes could be intact and cites neuroimaging studies (like fMRI or EEG) that have shown that some patients respond to spoken language with brain activity patterns similar to healthy individuals. He concedes the imaging he has seen on Peter's brain is not conclusive either way, but the possibility of cognition is recognized in his field.

Testimony of Crystal Ball, LVN, CLCP, CNLCP – Plaintiffs' Life Care Expert

CHAPTER THIRTY-FOUR

Crystal Ball then testifies for the plaintiffs as their life care planner. Crystal is very much in demand for her expert witness services and testifies constantly. She has given more than a thousand depositions and has testified in court hundreds of times. She is known as a plaintiff-side expert whose opinions, despite any perceived bias, tend to generate very large verdicts; that is, she tends to be trusted by juries. Her opinions in the Smithson case are based on Dr. Proctor's cost figures and additional costs she foresees, which come to about $2 million per year.

On cross-examination, Crystal, as is her tendency, fights any attempt to show her numbers are too high, that any item could possibly cost less, or that the additional costs she throws in might not be necessary. She dismisses articles and studies suggesting her numbers are inflated by discounting the credibility of the authors.

Got You Covered's
Increased Settlement Offer

CHAPTER THIRTY-FIVE

During the lunch hour, Anne goes over the Got You Covered offer with the Smithsons. Anne explains that the offer now includes insurer money over and above Got You Covered's SIR, and in her opinion, the insurer was waiting to see how the trial started before deciding if the case had the kind of high value shown in the original $50 million demand.

To Anne, this means they should be patient and see if the number goes up. Since it is unusual in a settlement negotiation for a party to bid against themselves, that is, without a counteroffer, she suggests to the Smithsons that they make a substantial counter-proposal but remain in the many millions of dollars. The strategy is agreed.

Anne texts to Mary that the $2 million offer is rejected but the plaintiffs will accept $22.5 million, a number that is now under the combined insurance policy limit. Mary reports this to her clients, and to Holden De Monet and Luke Askantz, and awaits instructions.

Testimony of Robin Do, MBA, CPA, CFF – Plaintiffs' Economist Expert

CHAPTER THIRTY-SIX

Resuming the trial after lunch, Anne calls economist expert Robin Do. Do's job is to take the opinions of the doctor and the life care planner and show the total cost of the out-of-pocket dollars claimed. Then, she will reduce that number to "present value." The amount a plaintiff may claim is not the sum of the annual costs multiplied by the number of years involved, in this case, by the life expectancy. Rather, since the amount awarded must be paid with the judgment, the amount payable is what, if placed into an interest-bearing account, would add up to the total cost years later, the so-called present value.

There are variables that go in to economist experts' opinions that can maximize or minimize the amount of the judgment; chief among them is the amount of interest predicted to exist over time. Based on Do's estimate of the interest, assuming a ten-year maximum life expectancy, and adding that to Crystal Ball's total cost estimate, Do calculates the total costs to be $20 million. Her opinion is that the present value of that amount is $11,167,895.54.

Testimony of Plaintiff Paul Smithson

CHAPTER THIRTY-SEVEN

It is now 2:30. The jury is excused for the afternoon recess. Anne asks the judge if they can end the day, and she will have her last two witnesses on Monday. The judge refuses this, seeing that she has almost two hours left and the case is moving along efficiently. She tells Anne to start with her next witness, even if not finished.

Anne was hoping for the weekend to prepare with the Smithsons. This will be an emotional event for each of them, and she wants to have a full-fledged rehearsal. She decides to put Paul on now, who will testify a little more calmly than she expects that Patty will, and he will establish basic facts important to the story.

"Plaintiffs call Paul Smithson." Paul heads to the witness stand, is sworn in, and takes his seat. Anne will use Paul to go through the events of the accident methodically. This will be a bookended repeat of the story that came out with the first witness, Doug Heels. This telling will be more personal but will remind the jurors of the details and also establish the parents' claim of emotional distress.

Paul explains his background, job, family, and life aspirations, culminating in the ill-fated decision to investigate joining Family Swim Club. He describes his kids' activities and how they were doing in school, with emphasis on the fun-loving, impish personality of Peter. Anne then turns to the accident sequence. After a few of these questions, Anne gets to the heart of it.

"Paul, tell us your thoughts as you followed Penny and Perry to the pool area and realized Peter was in the pool and trapped under the cover."

Paul starts his testimony, "I have been trying to retrace my actions and feelings for about this for some time. To answer your question, I felt panic, yet a kind of wild sense of needing to find Petey and grab him, all the while hoping he had not been in there too long. I could see his shadow a little under the cover, not far from the corner. I couldn't get my arm in there far enough, so I pulled at the cover, and it flapped over, at the corner there, to where I could get my arm in far enough by lying flat on the pool deck. I think I was immersed up to my shoulder. I got hold of his arm and pulled him out."

"Was he conscious?"

"No, his eyes were closed and he was not breathing." At this point, Paul was starting to lose it on the stand.

"Okay, Paul, just hold on so we can get through this." She waits a beat until he looks up and nods. "What were your next thoughts?"

"My first thought was to start CPR, though I had never really done it before. I alternately did chest compressions and blew air into his mouth. I remember pinching his nose. But I didn't do it very long when someone pulled me aside and started doing it. I'm not sure who it was, but that woman seemed to know what to do. The paramedics got there after that, and all I could do was stand there. I was very tense and worried. I don't know how else to describe it."

Paul's testimony gets into further detail about the ride to the hospital, the frustrating wait for word from the doctors, and dealing with the family. He tells the jury what it's like to see Petey now every day with tubes coming from everywhere. When the direct examination is finished, the session ends for the day, to resume with Skip Havidyad's cross-examination on Tuesday, since Monday, February 17, the court is closed for Presidents' Day.

Further Settlement Deliberations

CHAPTER THIRTY-EIGHT

As the parties file out of the courtroom following Paul Smithson's direct examination, Anne tells Skip and Mary that the plaintiffs may rest their case on Monday, so he should arrange for his first witnesses. She also thanks them for the $2 million offer earlier in the day, but the plaintiffs reject it. She repeats that the plaintiffs' settlement demand has been lowered to $22.5 million but invites an increased offer.

On Friday, another Zoom conference occurs with the Got You Covered team to discuss the rejection of their offer and the counteroffer they received. Hearing that the case can be settled for less than his full policy limit, Luke Askantz becomes more assertive, suggesting he thinks the case now has more risk based on how the evidence has come out, but remains somewhat defensible. He offers his opinion that the case can settle between $8 million and $10 million (which just happens to be below Bumbershoot's attachment point).

Holden De Monet has heard this tired pitch before from excess insurers who are pleased to let him pay millions and not a dime themselves. Yet, the plaintiffs do seem, though unexpectedly, to have made a case that will capture at least some jurors. His job is to minimize risk so he now thinks the effort to settle should be pursued further. While disagreeing with Luke's comments, he authorizes the Kaniver team to negotiate up to $5 million.

Mary calls Judge Ismael for his help in trying to bring the plaintiffs' number down. Judge Ismael reaches Ann Dewey after the lunch hour. "Anne, you have their attention. And I understand the plaintiff's number has dropped from the original $50 million to the $25 million global policy limit, and now to $22.5 million. Your case ends Monday with probably your most sympathetic testimony, from the mother, and you will play the day in the life video. That will be your peak moment. When the defense starts, they will pick at your life care plan and, frankly, from what the defense tells me, Peter is not likely to survive very long, despite Dr. Proctor's opinions about the maximum survival time. That will cut millions out of your medical cost numbers. I also heard your engineering expert faltered a bit. So, with all that to chew on, can you tell me your bottom line?"

Mary listens carefully. This mediator knows what he's talking about. She replies, "Judge, in today's verdict climate of very high jury awards, I am reluctant to recommend to my clients much less than where we are. I will tell you, without authorizing you to make a demand, that I would consider recommending a $15 million settlement, but I can't see going any less."

"All right, let's leave it at that for now. However, I am authorized to tell you Got You Covered is now offering $3.5 million."

After the call, Anne confers again with Paul and Patty. Once again, they break down how much would be available after costs and fees based on a global settlement of $5,850,000, when the club's settlement is added in. The rough number amounts to a little over $3 million to be divided between the parents and Peter. The Smithsons are realistic that Petey will not survive the entire time Dr. Proctor gave as the maximum. But even if it is five years, they will need about $5 million after all fees and costs are paid. To achieve that, they will need a settlement of no less than about $9 million. After further discussion, Anne is authorized to lower the demand to $18.5 million to see how the defense will respond.

Anne emails Judge Ismail with the number. No further offers or demands occur on Friday, but the Got You Covered team now suspects the case can be settled under the $18.5 million demand, perhaps $15 million. They stand pat for now.

Testimony of Paul Smithson – Continued

CHAPTER THIRTY-NINE

It is Tuesday, February 18, and the parties, counsel, and jurors are in their places. Skip Havidyad then gets up to cross-examine Paul Smithson. He needs to
explore the parents' negligence, but he has to be careful not to seem rude after
their previous emotional testimony.

"Good morning, Mr. Smithson. May I say on behalf of my
clients and everyone on our side of this case, how badly we all
feel for what happened to Peter. I hope and trust you will understand that lawsuits like this are needed to resolve who was at
fault, among other things, and this case is not being contested by
my client based on any lack of empathy or sympathy toward you
and your family."

"You are kind to say that. Thank you."

"I want to focus this morning, Mr. Smithson, on two details,
one about how the accident sequence started, and the other
about how you were able to pull back the pool cover. So, you
know right where I'm going this morning. Okay?"

"Okay."

"Good. Now, Mr. Smithson, when you all arrived at Family
Swim Club, Mr. Heels walked you around and showed you all
the facilities, right?"

"Yes."

"During that walk around, your children were with you, or
at least they were in your field of vision, weren't they?"

"Yes, they were very excited. I remember they were a little
loud, running around by one of the indoor pools. We were right

there when they were putting their hands in the water. Then, we went into the rec room, and they immediately went for the ping pong table. We were fully indoors at that point, and you have to open doors to access most other areas."

"Once your group was inside, sir, how did Mr. Heels get you into his office to try to sign you up?"

"Oh, he didn't have to try. The only issue was the cost, and we needed to find out about that and maybe a payment plan. So, we followed him down the hall to his office."

"The kids were left in the recreation room?"

"Yes, they were occupied, and there was a TV there."

"Was anyone else around in that room, Mr. Smithson?"

"No one was in the rec room at that time."

"And you were positive none of the kids would go wandering around?"

"We had no reason to believe there were any dangers," replied Smithson.

"Mr. Smithson, have you ever lost sight of one of your kids? In a store, in a mall?"

"No, but I know that happens, and I'm sure it's frightening until you figure out where they went."

"Now let's turn to a harder part. You are at the pool where Peter has fallen in, there is commotion and yelling around you, and you placed your arm into the water trying to grab Peter, is that right?"

"Yes, that's what happened."

"When you couldn't get hold of him immediately, you pulled back the cover more and then grabbed him, true?"

"Yes."

"Did you rip the cover from its attachments?"

"No, I don't think so. I mean, I don't remember doing that."

"You are aware, sir, we have heard testimony that you summoned extra strength in the emergency and may even have pulled the cover right out of an anchor embedded in the concrete. Someone said they heard a rip. Is that what you recall happened?"

"I'm not sure I remember. I know someone said that. I think it was Doug Heels who said that. I am sure I must have made some big move to yank the rest of the cover further open. I was panicked and trying to move fast. But nothing gave way as far as I know. The sound could have been just the noise of the cover flapping on itself. I don't know."

"So, in conclusion on this point, Mr. Smithson, when you approached the pool, you saw Peter under the cover, the corner of the cover was in place, but when you pulled him out, the cover was flapped open as we saw in the photograph. Can you confirm this all was the case?"

"Yes, I believe that's what happened."

"Thank you, sir. I have no further questions."

Testimony of Plaintiff Patty Smithson and the Plaintiffs Rest Their Case

CHAPTER FORTY

Shortly after Paul is excused from the stand, the morning recess is taken, and he is replaced on the stand by Patty. Patty is a nervous wreck. She is trembling. Anne makes a show of pouring her a cup of water and handing it to her on the witness stand. She waits at the podium a few moments to allow the jurors to take in Patty's demeanor, sitting alone, waiting to talk about this terrible accident in front of a crowd.

"Patty, I will try to be…"

"Thank you," Patty interrupts.

Anne starts up again, "I was going to say I will try to keep it short." Anne smiles, as does Patty, a little. Some of the jurors also smile a bit,

"Let's jump right in. Patty, tell the jury about the terror you felt from when Paul was trying to fish Peter out of the pool until he was taken away in the ambulance."

Patty looks down and begins, "My first instinct was to grab Penny and Perry and turn them away from what was happening. I had them both, one in each arm, a few feet away. But I couldn't turn away myself. I was staring at Paul as the seconds ticked by. It seemed like forever until he got Petey out. And there was my baby, lifeless on the ground."

Patty weeps uncontrollably at this point. The judge orders a five-minute break for her to compose herself.

They resume, "Patty, you rode to the hospital with Peter. What happened in the ambulance?"

"Petey was unconscious, but I think they had gotten oxygen into him. I couldn't hug him up or anything. I just put my hand on his face and in his hair and left it there the whole trip. At that point, I was fearing the worst. I was praying."

"Tell us what happened at the hospital."

"There was a lot of commotion and people running. When Paul got there, we had to sign a bunch of papers, but they took Petey into a closed room and worked on him. We were not allowed to see him at first, but we went in later."

Patty lays out the ordeal of being with Peter at the hospital after he was admitted to the pediatric intensive care unit, and just watching him in the bed with tubes. She talks about how she and Paul slept on the floor in Peter's room.

"The nurses and the rest of the staff at the PICU were amazing and very accommodating to us."

"Patty, who gave you the diagnosis that Peter might not wake up and, in fact could pass away while still a child?"

At this question, Patty is again fighting to hold back tears, dabbing a tissue to her eyes, "It was Dr. Proctor. What an amazing guy he is. He was so nice. So understanding. But he didn't shy away from giving it to us straight. He said Petey probably would not survive more than five to seven years with proper care, ten tops. He explained what a permanent vegetative state is, as compared to a coma. I asked him why Petey seemed to respond when we spoke to him and when the nurses would attend to him. The doctor said sometimes this is sort of automatic behavior. Maybe he said autonomic. But he could not discount the possibility that Petey is in there aware of what's happening."

"Objection, your honor," says Skip, "What the doctor said on this subject is hearsay, and what was brought out in his examination here was not conclusive."

"Objection overruled," says Judge Stickler, "I think Dr. Proctor said that studies reveal that cognition can occur. I will leave whether it is happening to Peter Smithson for the jury to solve as part of the plaintiffs' burden of proof."

At this point, Anne introduces the day in the life video, using Patty to support what is seen, since she was there the entire time the video was taken. After a pre-trial discussion between counsel, objectionable matter was taken out, so there is no objection to playing the video at the trial. The video shows the three children at different ages, playing and interacting, at parties, and at special occasions. One section shows them splashing in the surf at the beach. The scenes then switch to show Peter in the pediatric intensive care unit with his mother reading to him, his siblings talking to him, and the nurses attending to him. The video ends with a shot of Peter, alone in the bed, with tubes attached to his face and abdomen.

"All right," says Anne, "I will stop there."

Skip elects not to cross-examine Patty. If he is seen to be tormenting her, it will not look good. He got what he needed from Paul, who volunteered information he should not have about how the children were allowed to run around. Patty is excused from the witness stand.

Anne stands and says, "Plaintiffs rest, your honor."

Judge Stickler responds, then we will be in recess until 1:30, when the defense will call their first witness.

The Last Offer?

CHAPTER FORTY-ONE

During the lunch break, Mary approaches Anne and offers a settlement of five million dollars, adding, "I think this may be our best offer, Anne. The plaintiffs' case is at its peak, but the defense case will make some points and possibly decrease the settlement value". No deadline was put on the offer. Anne responds with the analysis she and her clients had gone through earlier. The cost to care for Peter, even for a short time, plus the parents' emotional injuries, plus attorney's fees, can't be evaluated for less than ten million dollars, but the case has a much greater value in any event. Anne tells Mary that if the case is to be settled, Got You Covered and their insurers need to start the bidding at no less than ten million dollars, and it better be soon.

Anne advises the Smithsons of the latest offer and what she told Mary. They quickly agree and decide not to engage again immediately on the subject of settlement.

Testimony of Ivana Brainsby, Ph.D. – Defendant's Human Factors Expert

CHAPTER FORTY-TWO

When the trial resumes after lunch, Skip begins the defense case by calling Ivana Brainsby, PhD. to the witness stand. Dr. Brainsby explains that human factors is the study of how human beings react to their environment in almost any context. Practitioners in the field consider, for example, how best to organize a dashboard and manual controls in a vehicle based on human physical characteristics and tendencies, and how they react to certain things. Is it better to have a turn signal on one side of the wheel or the other, or how far should you have to reach to adjust the radio before it is an unacceptable distraction from the road?

She explains that the subject of human factors also crosses over into psychology and studies the tendencies of how, in this instance, a parent will react in a situation such as the Smithsons faced when they went to the club. In essence, her opinion is that most parents would be expected to, at least, issue some instruction to the children to stay where they were, in the recreation room, and not go around this unfamiliar building without them, particularly because of the presence of swimming pools in different places on the property.

On cross-examination, Anne gets Brainsby to admit that there were doors between the rec room and any pool area. However, Brainsby refuses to concede it was reasonable to expect the door to the outside pool area not to be propped open. She adds that it is the kind of thing that happens all the time and is why parents should be more diligent in unfamiliar settings. In a final effort to get the witness to say something helpful to the plaintiffs, Anne gets Brainsby to acknowledge that club personnel certainly know children are often running around the premises.

Testimony of Cameron Payne, M.D. J.D. M.S. MPH – Defendant's Life Expectancy Expert

CHAPTER FORTY-THREE

Skip next calls his life expectancy expert, Dr. Cam Payne. Dr. Payne sets out his impressive credentials. He is a medical doctor, has a law license, a master's in statistics, and a master's in public health. His career has involved primarily studying the life expectancy of children born with cerebral palsy, persons in the vegetative state, and those who have sustained spinal cord injury or traumatic brain injury. He has testified as an expert more than two thousand times. He reviewed the medical records and the opinions of Dr. Proctor and opines that, based on the amount of time Peter was deprived of oxygen and the number of months that have elapsed with minimal improvement means he will not survive more than a year.

On cross-examination, Anne can only spar a bit on the exceptions to the rule that Dr. Proctor pointed out, that Peter could survive up to ten years.

Testimony of Noah Little – Defendant's Chief Staff Engineer

CHAPTER FORTY-FOUR

Following the afternoon recess, the testimony of Noah Little begins, to be followed the next morning by Marc Mewords. The defense will then rest. Noah is straightforward and likable in his demeanor. He is an engineer and tells the jury, somewhat jokingly, that engineers tend to think in black and white terms. He relates his favorite engineering joke: The optimist says, "The glass is half full." The pessimist says, "The glass is half empty." The engineer says, "The glass is twice as big as it needs to be." Not everyone in the room gets the joke immediately.

Nevertheless, Noah does a good job of selling the merits of his company and the success they've had with their products. He adds that pool covers are not their only products, but in fact, they stumbled into the military defense business in the early nineties, during Desert Storm. The army needed to cover tanks to protect them while parked in the heat of the Iraqi desert, and his company was able to develop such covers using some of the same materials used for pool covers.

He talks about changes in design over the years. When asked about why they no longer use grommets, he explains that the industry has not necessarily moved away from the use of grommets. In their experience, grommets actually prevent tearing. His company moved away from grommets because they were able to be more efficient in the manufacturing process with the use of modern stitching machinery.

On cross-examination, Anne Dewey forces him to say he couldn't explain why multiple grommets failed on this particular pool cover. He is unable to say just from the photograph of the portion of the cover how old the cover was, but speculates it could have been more than ten to fifteen years old.

Little's testimony does not go as long as anticipated because of the short cross-examination. The day then ends, to be resumed on Tuesday. The judge advises the jury they are close to the finish line. She expects the testimony to end on Tuesday or no later than Wednesday morning, with closing arguments and deliberations to start mid-week.

Anne instructs Rob Berry to make sure Phil Knight is available on Wednesday afternoon.

Testimony of Marc Mewords – Defendant's Mechanical Engineering Expert

CHAPTER FORTY-FIVE

It is Wednesday morning, and Got You Covered's engineering expert, Marc Mewords, takes the stand and is sworn in. Skip Havidyad brings out Mewords' credentials, specifically that he, like Nerdley, is in the business of figuring out if products were defective in some way so as to cause accidents. Unlike Nerdley, his work is devoted solely to product defect cases.

He explains he has worked on several swimming pool cases, and one of them was very similar to the Smithson case. In that other case, the child also got caught under the cover because an attachment point failed, and was also at a corner of a rectangular pool. This happened at a private residence. His opinion in that case was that the failure was caused by poor maintenance; specifically, a piece of equipment accidentally fell on the strap area, partially cutting through the stitching. The problem was that the homeowner did not take steps to repair the damaged strap, and it got worse; essentially, the problem was neglected.

With respect to the Smithson accident, Mewords gives the opinion that there was no defect in Got You Covered's product. First, it was not a poor choice to use an attachment system dependent on a grommet. That kind of system remains in use throughout the industry, as is a stitched strap connection. There are no industry guidelines or standards saying a grommet connection should not be used.

Second, though he agrees the grommet in question here probably popped off as Dr. Nerdley thought, the only way that happens is simply age or abuse. This had to be a very old cover, and this seems to be proven by the evidence that several grommets had failed, and someone at, or on behalf of, Family Swim Club set about to fix it. He suggested another possibility was that the club was too cheap to replace it, and it looks suspicious that it was replaced only after this accident. In his opinion, for a facility like a commercial Swim Club not to be careful to update and maintain equipment is improper, and a pool cover is considered safety equipment.

On cross-examination, Anne Dewey has a plan. She will not make a direct attack on the witness since she believes Mewords has not effectively refuted Nerdley's opinions, so she will just make a small show demonstrating how Got You Covered brags about the strength and durability of their products.

Ms. Dewey: "Mr. Mewords, you realize, do you not, that Got You Covered Technologies advertises the strength of its covers?"

Mr. Mewords: "I had not looked at that."

Ms. Dewey: "I will ask Mr. Bates to put Exhibit 34 on the screen. Sir, this is a photograph taken from Got You Covered's website."

Mewords, seeing the exhibit on the screen, says, "Yes, I can see they believe when properly secured, the cover can hold the weight of a child and a family dog."

Ms. Dewey: "They are also advertising that children can play soccer on it, supervised only by the dog, don't they?"

This gets a laugh from the jurors.

"So you say, counsel," responds Mewords.

Ms. Dewey: "The same would be true of Exhibit 35, yes?" It goes up on the screen.

Mr. Mewords: "I understand the argument you are trying to illustrate, counsel. Is there a substantive engineering question I can answer?"

Ms. Dewey: "How about this one, sir? Exhibit 36"

Mewords tires of this game and says, "Well, counsel, if anything is relevant about these pictures, you can see the attachment points in the last two pictures do not have straps. The cover is secured by a different kind of mechanism. There are several different kinds of approved systems, and Got You Covered seems to make different kinds of covers."

Ms. Dewey: "Is it your opinion that a strap system, like the one Family Swim Club used to replace the grommet cover can take a lot of abuse?"

Mr. Mewords: "I would say so."

Ms. Dewey: "How about this one? Exhibit 36"

Everyone in the room, including the judge, laughs. Anne hopes the jurors get the point that even though Got You Covered markets their products as sturdy, that message may be false. The examination ends there, and the defense rests its case.

Testimony of Phillip B. Knight – As Plaintiffs' Rebuttal Witness

CHAPTER FORTY-SIX

Judge Stickler asks Anne if the plaintiffs have any rebuttal witnesses.[1] "Yes, one, your honor, and he is here now."

Phil Knight enters the courtroom, is sworn in, and takes the witness stand.

Anne moves to stand in front of the witness and opens, "Mr. Knight, I will be brief." Did your company, Knight Pool Company, ever provide pool maintenance services to Family Swim Club?"

Knight says, "Yes, we did that for three years."

"As part of that service, Mr. Knight, did you install the pool cover that was involved in our accident?"

Knight replies almost exactly as he had on the phone with her months earlier, "Our employees installed the pool cover, and I personally worked on the cover installation. I recall following the manufacturer's instructions to the letter; we even carefully followed their installation video."

Mr. Knight, "I know you no longer worked for the club, maybe for a year or so before the accident, but are you aware of when the accident happened?"

"Yes."

"How long before the accident did you install the cover?"

"About three years."

---

1 Because plaintiffs have the burden of proof, they are allowed to put on witnesses after both their case and the defense case is closed to counter or challenge evidence or testimony presented by the opposing party. Rebuttal witnesses often address new issues raised during the trial that could not have been anticipated earlier. In this case, Noah Little testified, for the first time at trial and not at his deposition, that the pool cover had to be very old for it to break down as it did.

"So, you are saying, Mr. Knight, that the cover was three years old and therefore it was set in place once a year, meaning it was used only three times?"

"If your math works out, then I suppose so."

"Those are all my questions. Thank you, sir."

Hearing this, Skip senses something is off. His client said the cover appeared old and his expert, Mr. Mewords, assumed it in his analysis. If the cover installed by Knight was only three years old, it should not have broken down, which is Dewey's point. But witness Gonzalez also said other grommet spots had seemed to fail over the years, and he copied how someone before him re-rigged the connectors. The three-year thing does not make sense.

"Mr. Knight," says Skip, "just a couple of questions. "Was the cover new or used when installed?"

"I don't remember."

"Can you tell us, Mr. Knight, if there is a market for used as well as new pool covers?"

"Yes, there is."

"Do you recall having to open a new box and its packing at the time you installed this cover?"

Knight looks up, thinking about this for a moment, then says, "I wouldn't know that. I had a foreman who would have been in charge of obtaining the cover, pricing it out to the club, and he and his crew would have done most of the work, including unpackaging it."

"I thought you said you personally worked on this. Let me ask this. Do you recall that some of the connectors had metal rings as connectors and some didn't?"

"Counsel, I did say I worked on it, but actually, what I recall is that I helped the day they did it. I arrived to see how it was going, and it was getting dark. I remember that, so I pitched in. But I have no recollection of how all the connectors worked. I only did a few of them."

"Thank you, sir. I have nothing else."

"Ladies and gentlemen," says the judge, "the evidentiary portion of the trial is now concluded. Tomorrow at 9 a.m., you will hear closing arguments and jury instructions, and then you will set about to decide the outcome of this case. All have a very good evening."

Closing Arguments

CHAPTER FORTY-SEVEN

It is Thursday, February 20, 2025. The parties and their lawyers are assembled. Paul and Patty are now seated at the table with Anne. Patty's parents have Perry and Penny in the gallery behind the rail. Rob Berry is back in the gallery with them. Noah Little is at the table with Skip Havidyad, along with Mary Wright. Drew Delascard is in the gallery. Riley Goode has shown up to hear the closings out of curiosity. The jurors are in their places. No further communication has occurred as to settlement. Judge Stickler enters the courtroom, takes her place on the bench, and begins.

"Okay. The record will reflect that all the members of the jury are in their respective seats in the jury box. Ladies and gentlemen, we have come to that point where you have all the evidence that you need now to determine the facts of the case. We can't give you any more, we can't take anything away, you've got it all now.

"The next phase of the trial is that the attorneys will have an opportunity to argue the case to you. Again, what they say is not evidence; it's their interpretation of the evidence. It's to help guide you in your deliberations. If something they say differs from the way you remember it, it's your memory that controls. If there is some difference there, it's not that they are trying to mislead you; many times, people will see or hear something differently. It's your memory that controls.

"The plaintiffs will go first, and then the defendant will go second, and then the plaintiffs will have a rebuttal at the very end, because they've got the burden of proof. After they are through arguing the case, I'll read the instructions that you are to use to determine how to apply the law to the facts of the case, and we'll send you back to deliberate. Ready to go, counsel?"

Anne steps to the podium, notes in hand. She looks back and forth to all the seated jurors, smiles, takes a deep breath, and begins.

"Good morning to all of you. All of us, I'm sure all of you included, have had a range of experiences in this trial that's lasted nearly two weeks. We laughed a little. We heard experts pontificate. We saw tears. But it's all serious time now. It is time to focus on the facts and come to a decision about what happened to little Petey Smithson, and also to his parents, Paul and Patty." She waves a hand in their direction. "The rest of the family is here too, to find out what you good folks decide. So, I first want to thank all of you on behalf of my clients and their family. We have seen during these two weeks that you all have been very attentive, and we appreciate you taking time out of your busy lives to come here. We know you have made sacrifices to be here.

"Let's start with some of the mechanics of what you will do in deliberations. You will first appoint a foreperson who will hopefully lead you through an organized review of the case and allow each one of you to voice your thoughts and opinions. The goal is for you to work as a team to come to that decision, and in doing so, you will follow the instructions the court gives you, some of which I will talk about this morning.

"There may be facts or issues on which some of you cannot agree, but in the end, we are all hopeful that nine of the twelve of you do agree and we can get a verdict. My goal now is to provide you with a guide back through the facts, pointing out which of them I think are important for you to consider in deciding this case. Remember in Mr. Havidyad's opening statement that he talked about how you use your navigation in the car? Now, I am going to walk you along that directional line that you'd see on the nav screen, the path you follow to get to your destination.

"The Smithsons. The All-American family. Wife, husband, three kids. Live in a suburb of a major metropolitan city in a house with a fence, with grandma and grandpa nearby. Both Mom and Dad have good jobs and are successful at them. The kids enjoy outdoor activities, but they don't have a pool, and the beach is way across town in L.A. traffic. I don't have to convince any of you about that, right? They hear about a local, private Swim Club and drive over to see it. It's wonderful. There are classes, indoor and outdoor activities, a swim camp in the summer, food, you name it. You can do your fitness workouts there. One terrific package for the whole family. This is great. The kids are into it. Let's sign up.

Anne leans forward for effect and says, "This fun setting suddenly turns into one of the worst nightmares anyone can conceive of. Life-altering. Earth-shattering. There is no place to put this kind of thing and make sense of it, given how your world has changed - in minutes.

"Here is what happened. A five-year-old, a little guy weighing about forty-five pounds, finds his way to a swimming pool not open to the public or the club members. Literally any area of that club that led to a pool required that you pass through a doorway, a doorway that could be closed and locked. And when it is unlocked, there are lifeguards. That's their company policy.

"Why was there no lifeguard where Petey fell in? Because the outdoor pool was closed for the winter, covered by a special device designed and manufactured by defendant Got You Covered Technologies, Inc., from New Jersey. So, why wasn't the door locked? Because an adult not only left the door unlocked, but it was also propped open. Not only was the door wide open, but the pool cover was also disconnected at a corner because the cover was broken and needed to be fixed.

"So, that corner of the cover was pulled up, leaving enough space for a forty-five-pound little boy to put his hand in the water and tumble in. The negligence of Family Swim Club was that they left two barriers open, in a way. The door to the outside was propped open, and the pool cover was pulled up and left unsecured, so Mr. Gonzalez could go work on the retractor mechanism. There can be no doubt about the club's negligence. And, of course, they admitted it.

"When Mr. Havidyad stands up, you will hear energetic finger-pointing at Paul and Patty. 'Where were the parents in all this?' He'll say, 'Don't let them off the hook!'

"But I'll tell you where they were. They were in a facility especially operated so that there is supervision, in the form of lifeguards, in areas that can be considered dangerous. They were in a facility laid out so that passages to those areas are locked if there is no supervision. It was company policy. Got You Covered Technologies wants you to blame the parents for Family Swim Club's breach of their own safety policy. But the real question is this: Why should the parents not be allowed to rely on the club properly carrying out that policy? Please, please don't buy what they're selling on that point.

"What we need you to do is focus on why the pool cover broke down. When you think back through the evidence, you will recall that what Mr. Gonzalez was doing was fixing the cover. A repair he had done before on other areas of the cover, and a repair that others before him had to do. Why?

"We start with what facts everyone agrees on. The cover needed repair. The needed repair was because a grommet had come off. The fabric of the cover was torn." She puts the Gonzalez photo on the screen and uses a laser pointer to show the area. "The evidence is that the brass grommet was in some way corroded or tarnished. Either way, it gave way and needed replacement. That's what we know.

"Mr. Little, from Got You Covered, told you, in essence, this had to be an old cover, and the use of grommets is an acceptable choice of materials in a pool cover attachment system in the industry. And you are supposed to believe they changed their design away from the use of grommets. Why? Because stitching is easier to manufacture? Their expert, Mr. Mewords, said no industry standards prohibit the use of grommets. He also said, in contrast to Mr. Little, that grommets are still in use in the industry.

"Mr. Little could not explain why so many of their grommets failed, over and over again, so his story is that the cover must have been old. What Got You Covered is up to here is to deflect blame away from their product and onto how Family Swim Club maintained it. The only evidence you have, evidence you must rely on, is that the cover was properly installed originally, properly reinstalled to close the pool for this particular season, and that they had to do repairs on the grommets, which kept failing despite proper use, installation, and maintenance. Remember, there is no evidence of misuse of the cover.

"And when Mr. Little speculated, and I mean guessed, that the cover had to be ten or fifteen years old, we brought you the guy who installed it. It was purchased by Family Swim Club only three years earlier, yet it had all those breakdowns.

"Here's something else I expect you will hear from Mr. Havidyad. And this is crucially important considering the rules of how you are to view the evidence. When he asked Mr. Knight if the cover was purchased new or used, Mr. Knight said, and I quote exactly, 'I don't remember.' What does that mean here? It means two things. First, Mr. Havidyad's question is not evidence." She emphasizes the word 'not' as she delivers the line. "He wanted to plant that seed, but, again, it is not evidence. The judge has already told you a few times, and you will hear it again in the instructions, that you are not to consider a lawyer's question or comment to be evidence. You have to ignore that point.

"The evidence you can and must use is that the cover was first put to use three years before the accident and needed multiple repairs during its three uses, and at least one repair was needed by Mr. Gonzalez at the time of the accident. The fact is, ladies and gentlemen, this Got You Covered product failed either because of the use of grommets or simply because the assemblers at Got You Covered did a poor job of manufacturing it. There is no other reason in the evidence that this cover was in that condition. I know Mr. Knight said there is a market for used pool covers, but that is not enough to actually prove to you that this cover was more than three years old.

"What has this done to little Petey Smithson? I will say this to you, something that is an unpleasant reality. There are times when life is an unwelcome alternative to death." Anne's voice cracks a little while making this comment. She pauses. "Wow, that was really hard to say. But we can't change the reality that Peter Smithson has no five-year-old life, he will have no teenage life, he will never marry, he will never – well, you get the idea.

"Peter will be attended to for the rest of his life by doctors, nurses, and attending staff, at a cost of millions of dollars. Tubes will be replaced from time to time.

"No one here disagrees that Peter's life has been stolen, but there has been a debate in this case about how much of his life has been stolen. Peter's doctor says at least five years, maybe longer. Got You Covered's expert, Dr. Payne, says it could be any minute. There is a reason why the defense expert would say that. With little variation, it will cost close to a million dollars a year to care for Peter. We say more, they say less. You decide, but if you believe his survival will be shorter, they say, money is saved. Not a good look."

Anne goes through her expert's numbers, putting on the screen a summary of Robin Do's total, $11,167,895.54. She also displays a few jury instructions to familiarize the jurors with them and to explain some key concepts, like the burden of proof is by a preponderance of the evidence. She tells them that "to preponderate" means just barely tipping the scale in favor of the existence of one fact over its alternative. She provides a brief tutorial on several of the key instructions, using the opportunity to repeat a few important facts, and how they fit into the instructions.

She then displays the verdict form, which is essentially a questionnaire. The verdict form asks first if the product is found to be defective either in design, in manufacture, or both. If yes, it also has to be the cause of the accident – the causation phrasing is that it has to be a "substantial factor" in causing the event.

The form goes on to ask the jurors to assign a number for both past and future medical and other economic loss, and both past and future pain and suffering, that is, non-economic loss. For the parents, their version of pain and suffering is called emotional distress. Anne runs through the form quickly, stopping to show where Robin Do's figure would go.

The form goes on to ask if the parents were negligent and if that negligence was a "substantial factor in causing the accident." Finally, the jurors are asked to assign a percentage of fault, out of a total of one hundred percent, to any party they think contributed; the form has separate lines for each party asking the jurors to decide what part of that one hundred percent may apply to each.

Anne continues:

> "Ladies and gentlemen, I have not yet offered a suggestion on the non-economic damages. For Petey Smithson, there is a very key thing I'd ask you to think about. Remember, there was testimony from Dr. Proctor that Petey's mind may be working, at least somewhat, and it certainly is the mind of a five-year-old. If that is true, how frightening would that be to live through this in that condition? How terrifying?

At this point, Skip Havidyad half rises, looks at the judge, and says, "Your honor, I'm sorry, quick sidebar please?"

The group assembles near the judge.

> "Your honor," says Skip, "it is not my practice to interrupt an opponent's closing, but I think counsel just crossed the line into improper reptile argument." The judge responds, "I understand you wanting to preserve your record, counsel. I think it was close, but I will overrule the objection." The group returns to their places, and Anne resumes:

> "Petey has been in his present condition now for close to a year. You will decide based on the evidence you have heard how many more years this will go on. I am suggesting you need to

account for his suffering, especially to the extent you are persuaded he has some consciousness, his discomfort with inserted tubes and being manhandled every day in bed, with occasional infections around the insertion sites.

"Consider the medical care costs, which you have to award based on the amount it has cost to care for him. You could even round the annual medical cost down to $1 million, assume he will survive no more than five years, though you have evidence it could be longer, and award a pain and suffering figure using his age at the time of the accident as a multiplier. With that formula, the minimum pain and suffering award would be $25 million, and the maximum is up to you. But if you believe Dr. Proctor, it would be $50 million. Add to that no less than the $11,167,895.59 for the life care plan.

"And finally, I turn to the parents, Patty and Paul. Let me say that I am concerned about what I am not supposed to say to you. I know that may sound weird, but I will explain it. This is not a wrongful death case, so I can't make this case sound like it's a wrongful death case because you would be instructed about damages in such a case a little differently than what you will hear in the instructions later today."

Anne continues, "Regardless, someone who suffers emotional distress by witnessing an accident to a loved one is entitled to compensation for witnessing the event. I will leave it at that. I will read that part of the jury instruction that I think you should carefully consider. The instruction says, 'Emotional distress includes suffering, anguish, fright, horror, nervousness, grief, anxiety, worry, shock, humiliation, and shame. Serious emotional distress exists if an ordinary, reasonable person would be unable to cope with it.'

"Go through any of those words and, with the evidence you have heard, every one of those words applies. Think of Paul's panic at trying to save his boy. Think of the horror Patty is feeling watching this happen in real time while at the same time trying to shield her other children from the anguish and shock she told you about. The trip to the hospital, not knowing what will happen. Getting the bad news from the doctors. Both of them suffered through this experience. It is almost unimaginable. My suggestion is an award to each of them of ten percent of what you award for Petey."

She adds all this up and writes it on a whiteboard in large numerals. The total is a range depending on how long the jury decides Peter will survive, from five to ten years: $48,167,895.54 as the minimum, and $73,167,595,69 as the maximum.

Anne puts down the marker and heads back to her seat, stops and turns and says,

"Ladies and gentlemen, I thank you for your attention to me in laying all this out. I know you will follow the instructions, you will use your common sense, but you will be human here. You will figure this case out like so many juries before you have done. I will speak to you again when Mr. Havidyad is done with his argument, but I just want to say that you should view the arguments of both counsel skeptically. Make sure what is said is consistent with your view of the evidence, and I will see you again in a short while. Thank you."

She turns and sits.

The court takes its morning recess. On return, Skip Havidyad approaches the podium.

"Good morning, ladies and gentlemen. This is a closing argument. This is my opportunity to tell you what I think you've seen here and what I think you should do about it. The case is done. The evidence is all in. The Court will instruct you on the law shortly. Very soon, the case will be yours to decide the outcome.

"Why do we have juries? The thinking is that you gather together twelve people, men and women, of different backgrounds, ages, and experiences, and working together as a team, they will be able to spot the truth. We believe that you've now seen what you need to see to do the job of finding that truth.

"But before we get into that, let's talk about what this case is not about. This case is not about the death of anyone. It is not about the distress of the parents for having to care for Peter or the change in their lives that requires them to go to the care facility all the time, or the change to their family dynamic. None of that is recoverable here. Emotional distress for the parents in this case is limited to distress arising from perceiving the accident. You may not award any amount based on anything that happened afterward. The jury instructions you are sworn to follow explain that to you.

"There is a reason why the jury instructions charge you, compel you, demand that you figure out what happened free of sympathy, passion, or prejudice. The reason is that feelings steal the ability to look at facts objectively. The law directs you to look at the facts objectively. That is, you will use your common sense for sure, but you are to view the facts like they are specimens in a laboratory, because that way no one is favored, there is no pre-determined outcome.

"Remember, we all told you that the jury selection process, the voir dire, when we asked you questions before you were selected as jurors, focused on whether you had biases. Were you going to favor one side or another? Did you come here already wired against lawyers, businesses - the legal system itself? In the end, I think we ended up with a really good group. You seemed to understand the medical issues, and the engineering issues; you have been very attentive, day after day. Based on that observation, we are all expecting a reasoned, carefully considered verdict. So, thank you in advance for that.

"You may recall there were some people concerned about the role of the parents. Some of you who said that are here on this jury, some were excused. You all said, though, you would listen to the facts and not make a decision about the parents' involvement until you heard the entire situation. That is as it should be.

"Now that you have those facts, I think it should be clear that this accident would not have happened if the parents had done a very simple thing that, in my view, most parents would do. They should have had the children with them in Mr. Heels' office. This was a strange place, with dangers we all recognize. By their own admission, Mr. and Mrs. Smithson said the kids were amped up, running around because everything was so inviting. They had been to one of the indoor swimming pools, and what did the kids do? They couldn't resist putting their hands in the water. My friends, I think that is exactly what Peter did when he found his way to the outdoor pool. There was a corner of the cover flapped open or in a way where the water was partially visible, and Peter most likely put his hand in that water. Somehow, he leaned over too far and fell in.

"All of us who have had kids know that feeling. You're in a department store and stop for just a second to look at a price tag. You turn your head for a moment. And they're gone. Your heart is in your throat until you catch sight of where they went. Happens all the time, unfortunately. We know that can have terrible results, what with kids being taken in malls and all. Vigilance about your kids in public places is crucial.

"I think the evidence in this case is enough for you to conclude that the parents were a little excited themselves and wanted to get the deal done. They mistakenly thought they could leave their kids where they were, and they would stay in that spot. That mistake was devastating. Ladies and gentlemen, the evidence compels you, in my opinion, to award a substantial percentage of negligence to Mr. and Mrs. Smithson for that mistake. If you are not looking at the case objectively, that statement is hard to hear. I know. But you are supposed to be objective, and objectively, the parents are at fault.

"Who else is responsible? It has already been established, by their own admission, that Family Swim Club is responsible for this accident. They said it themselves. And what else could they say? They left the door open. They left the pool open. They might as well have had a trail of cookies leading to the corner of the pool!

On top of that, they threw the evidence away, and I'll talk about the consequences of that in a moment. But folks, even if you want to discount the role of the parents in this, you can't let Family Swim Club off, frankly, with most of the fault. If you're not inclined to blame the parents, then the club gets all of it.

"So why is Got You Covered Technologies in this suit? They are here on a flyer. On the word of an expert in all things engineering, with no particular engineering specialty. Dr. Nerdley (Skip mockingly emphasizes the word doctor) does have one specialty. He knows how to formulate an argument for people who make claims, and for those people only. Trained, initially, not under this country's educational system, but then trained in a course of study specifically designed to help lawyers.

"And he was trained not by a known, accredited university. No. He was trained by his grandfather. His grandfather created a school, which apparently has as its star graduates his two grandsons, whom he can then employ in his own separate business helping plaintiffs' lawyers. Folks, he could have saved a little by just hiring people and training them on the job. But isn't it better for business if your employees have doctorates? Doctorates that you, yourself, bestow on them?

"You will be given an instruction that tells you it is up to you to decide whether you believe the expert's testimony and choose to use it as a basis for your decision. One of the things the jury instruction about experts says you should consider, and it uses that language 'you should consider,' is the expert's training. It is therefore abundantly fair for you to reject those opinions you think are biased or if the expert's credentials do not measure up to other experts.

"You heard from Marc Mewords, a properly trained mechanical engineer. I don't want to sound inconsistent here, since Marc was trained in another country, but that was Germany, where priority is placed on engineering. But he got his advanced education at Florida State, one of the top schools for engineering. And you heard that Marc, and not Max, has experience with pool covers.

"Before I get to the core of my comments about my client's product, let's talk about what evidence the experts on both sides had to work with. The cover involved in the accident is gone. Ideally, the experts get a chance to look at it, to test it, to measure it, to see, perhaps, if there are signs of other stresses on it that could have affected those attachment points that are central to the analysis of this case. But Family Swim Club threw it away, even though the lawsuit was going on at the time. Even though they were told to hang on to it. And they get to settle? You don't think there was a bias in what they testified to?

"I am going to remind you of what Judge Stickler told you just as the case started. It was an advance instruction that explained to you that Family Swim Club had discarded the pool cover and asked you to do your best to figure out what happened as best you could from the infamous photograph taken by Mr. Gonzalez. And as you also heard during the trial, we don't even have the infamous grommet, that dastardly little villain supposedly at fault for all this. There was a reason for that instruction. It was an acknowledgment that the parties here were hampered in their attempt to find the truth, and I think it was an acknowledgment that the evidence we do have is tenuous, and that affects whether the plaintiffs have met their burden of proof.

"Where does that leave us? Maybe they could have made a case against the installer or whoever might have owned the cover before. But that cannot occur without more evidence. Without 'the' evidence.

"We have talked a bit about the burden of proof. The plaintiffs must prove their case by a preponderance of the evidence. Ms. Dewey likened preponderance to mean just that much past even to weigh more, even the smallest possible amount. If you win a game by a single point, you win, is their argument.

"That is not what preponderance means. In fact, you will see in the instructions that scale-weighing is not mentioned at all. Winning by a point is not mentioned. What it says is that the burden of proof requires that something is more likely to be true than not true. I know we've all grown up with the image of the scales of justice. It's something you see even on lawyers' business cards and websites. And that's because, as a concept, we do 'weigh' the evidence, a common figure of speech. But the fact is that deciding whether a fact exists or does not exist is done with words, not scales. The phrase is what is 'more likely.' That means something that persuades you enough.

"So, what have the plaintiffs offered you to persuade you that my clients cover, seen in a grainy picture, my client's infamous grommet, not seen anywhere, was so poorly designed or manufactured that it caused this accident. There are two points.

"First, Max Nerdley says they should have used stitching like they use now and not grommets because grommets are the weakest part of the attachment components. What is unrefuted is that the use of grommets remains in the industry, and the strength of the attachments in that system is fine. That enough pressure or use might cause one part to fail before other parts does not mean it lacks strength, only that it is not as strong as the other parts. That's all. Nothing more. This argument Max Nerdley made, frankly, is smoke and mirrors and amounts to nothing. It does not establish a design defect.

"Second, Max Nerdley says that because there had been grommet failures on this cover, the failure of the grommet in question, therefore, must mean several grommets were installed incorrectly at the factory. What a leap in logic that is. Recall that it was never clearly established how old this cover was. Mr. Knight was not sure if it was a used cover at the time it was installed, but did say you can buy used covers. And that's the problem with not having the cover. We might have been able to figure that out.

"And I put it to you, the plaintiffs have the burden of proof here. I am arguing to you that proving their case means they must, repeat must, prove the age of the cover. They have to eliminate other causes. Otherwise, concluding that the only reason the grommets were failing was due to a factory assembly error becomes mere speculation. Logic, folks. If something happens, then something else must be the result. But if more than one thing can cause the same result, you need more information to make a conclusion, and that's what we have here. The plaintiff's case cannot be proven based on the facts available.

"I cannot stop there, though. There is another proof problem. It is one thing if the grommet should have lasted longer. If so, the cover was in disrepair and needed to be fixed. When that was recognized, Mr. Gonzalez planned a repair project. If he had not started that project that day, if he had not started that project and left the corner of the pool cover disconnected to work on the retractor, we would not be here today. Family Swim Club created an unreasonable risk of harm for Peter that did not exist that morning before Mr. Gonzalez got to work, even if the cover needed repair.

"At the start of the day, the cover was still tight and flat to the ground. I urge you to consider another instruction you will hear concerning what is called a superseding cause. That instruction will tell you that negligent conduct occurring after previous negligence, and that a reasonable person would consider a highly unusual or extraordinary response to the situation, cancels out the previous negligence. Propping the door open to a known danger, with kids around, then releasing the corner connection and leaving it open, and then walking away – that is, walking away from a product they knew needed repair – I submit to you, was extraordinary. On that basis as well, you should bring back a defense verdict because that cause superseded any perceived problem with the product."

Skip pauses to take a breath. He shrugs his shoulders for effect. He looks back up to the jurors.

"At the beginning of this case, I asked each one of you separately if you could decide this case free of sympathy, passion, or prejudice. In fact, I didn't just ask, I asked you to promise to do so. And each of you agreed. I am now calling in that promise. We all know this was an awful thing to happen. And you may be tempted to lean in the plaintiffs' favor on any given fact, most particularly the question of whether my client's product was defective in some way. Though we all feel bad, finding a fact in the plaintiffs' favor is not to be decided that way.

"I will now wrap up by saying this is the last time I will get to talk to you. Ms. Dewey will have a chance to tell you how wrong I am." He smiles. So for my part, I can only leave you with this.

You know, there is the closing argument I wrote down, there is the one I rehearsed in front of my wife last night, and there is the one that came out of me today. I will tell you that doing this is something that evolves in your mind continuously until you finally do it. There may be things I wanted to say and forgot. I have no way to come back to you and say, 'Oh, and one more thing.' So I have to count on you to consider what I've said and consider the evidence you heard carefully, and then fill in those blanks. Those things that could be left blank, the 'oh just one more thing" I forget to say here, are just not intentional, so I hope you understand.

"I thank you for your attention and your service. I know you will do the right thing, even if it's the hard thing. My best to you."

Skip takes his seat.

The plaintiff has the last word, having the burden of proof. Anne moves toward the podium. She has no notes.

"Ladies and gentlemen, my role at this point is to comment on what Mr. Havidyad just talked about. Since the plaintiffs have the burden of proof to show Got You Covered is at fault and how much the damages are, the plaintiffs are given this last opportunity to discuss the case. Let's start with what the defense did not say, because I think that is very revealing. Mr. Havidyad did not say a single word about the injuries or the damages that I spent a lot of time on. Therefore, what I said about it is all you have to consider."

"Objection, your honor, improper rebuttal," Skip calls out.

"Objection sustained," says the judge. "Counsel, you may rebut only what the defense did argue."

"Thank you, your honor, says Anne. "Well, it seems Got You Covered only wants to deny its responsibility for what happened. Okay, then let's talk about that. Got You Covered does not deny that it designed and manufactured the pool cover. Fact proven. Got You Covered does not deny that it used grommets as a component of the attachment system. Fact proven. Got You Covered does not deny the grommet failed and ripped the fabric of the cover. Fact proven. Got You Covered changed its design – away from using grommets. Fact established.

"We have a pool cover that suffered multiple grommet failures. That's established by the testimony of Mr. Gonzalez and both experts. The pool cover was only in use at Family Swim

Club for three years. That's the testimony of Mr. Heels, Mr. Gonzalez, and Mr. Knight. Fact proven.

"The only reliable evidence you have is that Knight Pool Company purchased and installed the cover three years ago. There is no evidence that there were any added D-rings to the system before or at the time of installation. Therefore, the clear inference is that it occurred later, after the club obtained it. Ask yourself this. Why would an established business like this buy a used cover? It's not as if there was a shortage of new covers. There is no evidence that the club was just cheap about it. There is no evidence that Mr. Knight somehow slipped them a used cover and didn't tell them.

"Got You Covered advertises that its covers can fit any pool. Knight followed Got You Covered's installation instructions. I submit to you that there was something simply wrong with the cover. Once the stresses of stretching the attachments were engaged a few times, that cover couldn't take it. At least this cover couldn't take it. You have an explanation from Dr. Nerdley. He said the only logical explanation, the circumstantial evidence, is that the cover was made wrong at the factory. I sincerely believe that is the only conclusion available to you since all other explanations are inconsistent with what we know, what the established evidence is.

"I will leave you with this thought. There was an anthropologist and cultural commentator named Margaret Mead. She was one of the most famous and outspoken women of the twentieth century, on subjects like morality, race relations, and the environment. She was a kind of philosopher. Her most famous quote is this, 'Never doubt that a small group of thoughtful, committed citizens can change the world; indeed, it's the only thing that ever has.'

"When this case started, we spent time with you trying to make sure you all could be fair jurors using your common sense. You are now a small group of citizens who we hope will now be thoughtful about the evidence. Who we hope will be committed to getting it right. The right thing to do once you have carried out your role as thoughtful, committed citizens is to provide the Smithson family with the compensation they request because their lives are now and forever will be devastated because a product, something advertised as a safety device, did that to them. Thank you, and my clients and I look forward to your decision."

With that, the judge launches into reading the jury instructions, which takes nearly an hour. She tells the jurors they can have a copy of the instructions with them, that they may ask questions by submitting them to the bailiff, and that they will have each issue decided once nine of the twelve of them agree on each, including the ultimate verdict. She tells them that when they have a verdict, they are to hit the buzzer inside the jury room twice.

The Jury is Out

CHAPTER FORTY-EIGHT

There is a reason why the phrase "the jury is out" is part of our cultural lexicon. It is a time of suspense and uncertainty, and thus naturally could lend itself to broader, metaphorical use. Everyone knows the phrase. Everyone uses it.

The first order of business for the jurors is to select a foreperson, something they are instructed to do. There are many ways, depending on the makeup of the group, a foreperson (sometimes called the presiding juror) may be selected. Sometimes one of the jurors will volunteer for the task. There may be debates among the jurors selling themselves as the proper candidates. A vote can be taken. The foreperson then presides over the deliberations, hopefully to ensure an orderly discussion, will communicate with the court through the bailiff, will sign the verdict form, and, in some jurisdictions, will read the verdict.

Earlier, we learned about the alternate jurors. They do not go into the jury room for deliberations. It can happen that a juror will become sick or have an emergency and thus not be able to continue. If that happens after deliberations begin, one of the alternates takes that place, and the discussion must start over. In theory, the twelve-person group is entirely different, even with one person's addition and another's subtraction, because the dynamic among the individuals and influences can change.

You have heard that juries sometimes are sequestered, meaning they may be separated from the outside world, their work, their families, and the news; they often will be put up in a hotel. Sequestration happens because there is a perceived danger that they will be hounded by the press or, in some other way, they may be influenced by outside information. Sequestration is most often used for criminal trials, but it is also possible, but rarer, in civil trials.

Each side in a litigation thinks their case is persuasive. Even if you feel your case is not solid, you can hope that at least some jurors are persuaded by your case, or maybe one forceful juror will take your side and influence the outcome in your client's favor. Waiting for a jury often becomes a kind of sport, where you try to read the tea leaves from facial expressions and body language you observed during the trial, or from assumptions you made about a juror's possible predisposition during voir dire. Guessing can happened as to which juror will become the foreperson and thus who could have potentially more influence on the outcome. The identity of which juror is the foreperson tends to come out early; the court bailiff communicates with the jurors during deliberations and usually figures it out.

There are general rules of thought, like the shorter the deliberation, the more likely a defense verdict because the jury never got to the damages discussion. A longer deliberation could mean the opposite, but you never know, they could be hotly debating for days about the first issue presented to them.

The lawyers usually have to just sit around, maybe do some work on a laptop or make phone calls. In a situation where the law offices are not far, they may be permitted to leave the courthouse as long as they can get back in a short period of time. The waiting period is both boring and tense. When the two buzzes happen, many hearts leap to throats.

The clock's ticking. Let's see what's happening in Judge Stickler's courtroom.

A Means to an End

CHAPTER FORTY-NINE

It is now 2:40 p.m. A single buzz is heard in the courtroom. Anne and Rob are in the room. The bailiff collects Skip and Mary from the hallway. The judge takes the bench, and the court clerk informs everyone that the jurors have a question. They would like the court reporter to re-read to them the testimony of Doug Heels and Dr. Nerdley about corrosion on the brass grommet. The jurors are called into the courtroom and are seated in their usual places. The lawyers are at counsel table. The reporter reads back the testimony, and the jurors return to the jury room.

In their separate groups, the lawyers speculate on why the jurors wanted that section read back. Sometimes, a single juror is confused about one point and refuses to believe the others' recollections. Sometimes, they are all confused about what could be a pivotal issue. Focusing on whether the grommet broke down because it was corroded could mean anything, or it could be something that, when heard again, showed it meant nothing.

At about 4 p.m., the jurors buzz again. While they have a color copy of the Gonzalez photo, Exhibit 6, they would like to see it enlarged, as it was on the screen in the courtroom. Fortunately, Stamp Bates has stuck around and can do that for them.

The two juror requests in the afternoon clearly mean the jury is still working out the issue of fault.

At 4:30, the judge excuses the jurors for the day.

The next morning, all assemble in the courtroom. The Smithsons are present and chatting with Rob Berry as Anne arrives. The jury has gone directly into their room to resume deliberations. The Smithsons ask Anne and Rob if there is any reason they should now consider accepting Got You Covered's settlement offer of $5 million. Anne suggests they now make an official demand of $15 million. This is relayed to Mary and Skip, who are in the corridor. Skip says he will call the insurer right away to see what they say, but telephone reception in the courthouse is notoriously bad, so he walks to the far end of the hall and down the stairs to be nearer to the outside exit. He comes back soon after saying he is so far unable to reach the carrier in Boston but will try again later.

During the morning, the Smithsons are in the corridor. Anne and Rob are seated in the courtroom gallery, working on emails on their phones. Time wears on, and they all go to lunch in the courthouse cafeteria. They return to the courtroom at 1:30; again, the Smithsons wait outside while Anne and Rob resume their seats in the gallery. Skip Havidyad has now reached the insurer, who is unwilling to make any further offer.

At about 2 p.m. Rob hears a commotion in the hallway and gets up to see what happened. He comes back in and whispers to Anne that he just saw their clients run out of the courthouse. Anne tells him to try them on their phones to see what happened. He is unable to reach them. This is very unsettling, and Anne is not sure what to do. She worries about what will happen if they are not there to take the verdict. Worse, she worries that Peter has succumbed.

A half hour later, Rob is still on the main floor of the courthouse, trying to get better reception, trying to reach Paul. Paul's phone has to be blowing up. Rob does not understand what is going on. Anne is in the courtroom, as are Skip and Mary, who are oblivious to Anne's predicament with her missing clients.

At 2:40 p.m., two buzzes go off. The judge walks out, and Anne asks her to wait until she can find Rob Berry and her clients, who were called away for a reason she is not yet clear about. The jurors remain in the jury room.

Anne goes into the hallway and sees Rob running toward her. "Come on, Rob, we have a verdict!"

"Anne!" Rob says breathlessly, "Petey Smithson just woke up!"

Epilogue

I wanted a happy ending to the Smithson story. Though the goal was to give you a real-life look at how a lawsuit starts and progresses, and what happens at trial. Some of you may view the evidence in the Smithson suit in favor of the plaintiffs, and some may see it as a defense verdict. But the least I could do was have the little boy come out of his vegetative state and have a chance at life. So many cases, just like this story, are based on terrible, permanent injuries and loss of life, so at least the Smithson family may be okay. But let's play out the ending to the trial.

You are the jury. Picture yourself in that jury room with the evidence presented during the Smithson trial. Is it a multi-million-dollar verdict for the plaintiffs? Is it a defense verdict? How did you apply the burden of proof, that is, did the plaintiffs persuade you by a preponderance of the evidence that the pool cover was designed or manufactured defectively because the grommet failed when it should not have? Did the plaintiffs' expert, Nerdley, convince you by talking about how the cover required so many repairs that something must have gone wrong at the factory?

And did you care that Max Nerdley's grandfather essentially manufactured his credentials? After all, he did get an undergraduate engineering degree. Was it a cheap shot to criticize his undergraduate degree because he got it at a Mexican university? Maybe Grandpa trained him better than a more legitimate doctoral program would on how to conduct forensic investigations into accidents. The criterion to qualify as an expert is that the expert has more knowledge than a layperson does about a subject, which assists the jury in understanding complex issues and evidence about that subject. That's it, just more knowledge. Some experts have more education, training, and experience than others, but ultimately, the soundness of the opinion is what matters.

Who do you think would have been the jury foreperson? We had two postal workers, a truck driver, a maintenance worker, a plumber, a nurse, a journalist, a comedian, a teacher, a homemaker, a lounge singer, and a lawyer. If you think it might have been the lawyer, that's a reasonable guess, but you never know. That lawyer, Ken Reade, does not necessarily have litigation experience; while working for the California State Bar, his job could have been to process cases about lawyers who were improperly handling their clients' money, having nothing to do with lawsuits or accidents. Sometimes the selection of a jury foreperson is just a function of personality, that is, who the others found worthy after spending a week or two at lunch with them. My vote is for the comedian (Chip Monk) or the lounge singer (Anita Job). Whatever.

Maybe after hearing all the evidence, you think the plaintiffs did not carry their burden of proof. If so, there would be a defense verdict. But for the sake of argument, let's assume fault was established. Based on the injury to Peter, where the evidence was that essentially his life was over – it may take five or ten years for him to succumb – and that he might actually have some cognition in the vegetative state, would you have awarded the kind of money for pain and suffering that Anne Dewey argued for? Did her formula help you get there? Did you reject it? And how much would you have given to the parents? Remember, the award is supposed to be for the trauma of what they witnessed, not for the suffering of dealing with watching Peter slowly slip away. It would be easy to combine those two things.

Given the evidence and the possibility that the trial could result in a defense verdict, the decision to turn down a $5 million settlement offer had to be a brave one. That kind of thing happens all the time. In some cases, the negotiation process and the settlement decision-making evolve with the pre-trial evidence. When the case does not settle and goes to trial, the settlement evaluation continues, and negotiations are still open, as occurred here.

Let's think about what should have happened when word came back to Anne Dewey that Peter might be okay, and that the news came while the verdict was pending. Did Anne have an obligation to tell anyone else about it? Maybe, maybe not. I imagine there may be strong opinions in both directions.

If she announced it, the judge might have been inclined to declare a mistrial, that is, render the entire two-week trial they just went through null and void. But what would be re-tried? A lesser injury? Peter came out of the persistent vegetative state, but maybe he will be severely brain-damaged and live like that for the rest of his natural life, say seventy-five years, and have to be cared for at a cost of hundreds of thousands of dollars per year. Would it end up as yet a bigger case? And even then, how can you declare a mistrial on the parents' case? The value of the parents' emotional distress at witnessing the accident to their five-year-old son would not have changed.

By the way, notwithstanding anything about the change in Peter's condition, the settlement with Family Swim Club was contractual and would stand no matter what. Any retrial would only be with Got You Covered.

I think they would have taken the verdict, and the matter would be addressed on post-trial motions (where the judge can cut down a verdict for various reasons) or on appeal. If there was a defense verdict, then it would be over no matter what, regardless of whether another kind of injury really was at issue, subject, of course, to a possible plaintiffs' appeal.

I can tell you that after the verdict, the Kaniver firm submitted an invoice to CAGI for $321,000, consisting of the last few months of pre-trial work and the two-week trial. The firm and experts had already charged and had been paid, $200,000 up to that point. The experts charged quite a bit for the deposition phase and trial, adding another $100,000 or so. CAGI sent the Kaniver invoice to its billing auditors, who cut it by $180,000, more than half of the bill, citing the fact that there was no justification for having three lawyers in court for two weeks. In addition, they refused to pay for any time entries, all the communications about scheduling things. They also cut a lot of time for the intra-office meetings among the Kaniver lawyers and for the constant editing that Mary Wright did of Drew Delascard's work.

Skip Havidyad hit the ceiling. He had not handled a case for CAGI in the past and was confused as to why the insurer was auditing the bills since the defense costs were still within the self-insured retention. The firm challenged the cuts to the invoice with both CAGI and Got You Covered Technologies. In the end, Sue Dembach, of Got You Covered, agreed to pay all but about $50,000 of the bill, but the process took nine months. During the entire time, until the deal was made, the firm was not paid a dime. Had it been CAGI's money, Holden the Monet would have fought harder. Skip vowed never to accept another case involving this insurer.

Here is a true story about an insurance company that challenged a law firm's charges, a case in which I was involved. A company was insured by multiple insurers covering a series of losses across time. One of the insurers, Lloyd's of London, hired a law firm to defend all related litigation about those losses, and the other insurers agreed to share in the cost of defense using that same firm.

When the litigation was over, the law firm sent out invoices, and one of the sharing insurers, let's call it ABC Insurance Company, refused to pay the bill because it had so many violations of their rules, including block billing, intra-office conferences, you name it. The firm sued ABC to get paid, and ABC sued them back for legal malpractice.

At the trial, I had the chance to cross-examine the insurance person who had refused to pay based on his own company's billing rules. First, I pointed out that the billing rules were never sent to the firm and so were not part of the retainer contract. Then, I went through some of the rules with the witness. I asked him why his company refused to pay for intra-office conferences since it was a big case and he knew multiple lawyers in the firm were working on it. He did not really know the reason for the rule, but guessed that such a conference was to train a younger lawyer, and the insurer should not have to pay for that. He agreed the younger lawyer often would be less efficient than a more experienced lawyer, and he understood he was charged less per hour for the younger lawyer to account for that inefficiency.

I asked him about a hypothetical situation. I asked him to assume the senior lawyer in the meeting charged $200 per hour and the junior lawyer charged $100 per hour. I asked him also to assume that what the senior lawyer did in the intra-office conference with the junior lawyer included showing the junior lawyer which book or resource to use to write a motion. I asked the witness to assume as well that the advice resulted in the junior lawyer preparing the motion in three hours instead of the eight hours the junior lawyer would have taken spinning his wheels to figure out the project. The meeting took twelve minutes, or .2 hours for each lawyer, for a total of $60 (.2 times $200 plus .2 times $100). Without the senior lawyer's guidance, the junior lawyer would have taken eight hours and billed $800. By finishing the motion in three hours instead of eight, the total charged would have been $60 for the training meeting and $300 for the motion, for a total of $360. This would have saved the client $440. The witness followed along as I put these numbers on a blackboard in front of the jury, and he agreed it was all correct.

I then asked, "Sir, if I understand your company's rules correctly, since intra-office conferences will not be paid, your company would prefer to pay $800 for the junior lawyer's time rather than the $360 combined amount because it included the senior lawyer's instruction time, is that correct?" He answered, "Yes, that's right." Go figure. And we got a unanimous verdict against the insurance company.

Three months after the trial, Drew Delascard resigned from the Kaniver firm, taking a job with a similar firm in Santa Barbara. You see, he lied that he was in an accident as the reason he could not make it back to help Mary with the summary judgment motion. What actually happened was that he reconnected with an old girlfriend at the Santa Barbara wedding, someone he dated while going to college there. He was moving to Santa Barbara because that's where the girlfriend was. In doing so, he left a job at a prestigious firm in Los Angeles, where he was paid $160,000 per year as a first-year associate, for a job that paid him $125,000 per year. Two years later, the relationship ended because she thought Drew was not ambitious enough.

The Dewey Cheatem & Howe firm underwent a change within the next year. Anne Dewey and Howie Cheatem were unhappy with Oscar Howe's poor productivity and had been imploring him to turn it around, as the firm could not afford the losses. Alternatively, they suggested Oscar should draw less compensation. This problem was solved when Oscar was disciplined by the State Bar for failing to properly report that he had completed his continuing education, a requirement which he had neglected, it turned out, for years. His license was suspended until he demonstrated that he had gone through continuing training to catch up for all those years. The firm used this to ask him to resign. The firm became simply Dewey Cheatem.

Juror number 4, Paige Turner, who was a journalist, wrote a book about the trial. She called it "Juror Under Cover."

Glossary

<u>Admissibility</u>: The determination of whether the judge or jury is allowed to consider certain *evidence* to decide the outcome of an issue or trial. If the evidence is admissible, it becomes part of the *record*. If it is inadmissible, the judge or jury may not rely on it in deciding an issue or a trial.

<u>Affidavit</u>: A written statement made under oath. Also called a *declaration*.

<u>Answer</u>: A formal written p*leading* filed in court by a *defendant* that admits or denies the allegations of the *complaint* and sets out expected defenses to the case. Typically, the *defendant* has 30 days to respond.

<u>Authority</u>: A legal source, like a *statute*, case *precedent* [see also, *case law*], or regulation, cited to support an argument and is considered to have the power to influence or bind a court in making a decision for a case.

<u>Bailiff</u>: A court official, often a deputy sheriff, who keeps order in the courtroom and handles various errands for the judge and clerk.

<u>Bias</u>: A predisposition in favor of, or against, a side or an issue. For example, bias can take the form of:

- Being prejudiced against a class or race;
- Having the opinion that corporations should not be treated as fairly as individuals in a trial;
- Having the opinion that accident case verdicts are too high or too low; or
- Embracing stereotypes, such as assuming that all nurses are female. (See, *Challenge for Cause.*)

Brief [also, "legal brief"]: A written legal argument supported by facts and *authority* submitted to persuade the court how to decide a particular issue.

Burden of proof: The obligation to produce sufficient proof to establish facts sufficient to win a case. In civil cases, the burden is to prove something by a preponderance of the evidence (more likely true and not true). Some civil issues require proof by clear and convincing evidence, a higher standard. In criminal cases, the burden is to prove a case beyond a reasonable doubt. The standard California jury instruction, number 220, defines "beyond a reasonable doubt" as "proof that leaves you with an abiding conviction that the charge is true. The evidence need not eliminate all possible doubt because everything in life is open to some possible or imaginary doubt."

Case law: Court decisions decided by appellate courts that established what the law is on a given subject.

Cause or Causation: The causal relationship between a party's conduct and the end result. In a personal injury case, the plaintiff must prove that the defendant's negligence directly caused their injuries, that is, it is a separate concept from the negligence itself, which is unreasonable conduct. Causation, also known as proximate causation, refers to whether there is sufficient connection between a party's unreasonable conduct and the harm; whether the conduct is or is not too remote or attenuated to impose liability. Example: A person shows up to the hospital with symptoms of poisoning, but they don't get to him before the person dies, though they should have examined the person sooner. A later autopsy shows he could not have been saved anyway. The hospital was negligent but did not cause the death.

Cause of action: The legal theory contained in a *complaint* alleging the facts of the claim and the legal grounds recognized in the law as the basis for suing on those facts. A *complaint* may consist of one or more causes of action. For example, a case on one set of facts may be based on negligence and product liability, which are similar but derive from different elements of law and so are contained in separate causes of action.

Challenge for Cause: If a prospective juror expresses a *bias* suggesting an inability to listen to the evidence fairly, a lawyer may move to excuse that juror and the judge will rule on that *motion*. There is no limit to challenges for cause. (See, *Peremptory Challenge*. See also, *Bias*.)

Complaint: A formal document *filed* with the court by a *plaintiff* containing all legal theories (*causes of action*), factual allegations, and damages claimed against a *defendant*.

Continuance: Decision by a judge to postpone a hearing or trial until a later date.

Court reporter: A licensed professional who makes a written account of acts and proceedings in a lawsuit, usually in the form of a *transcript*.

Cross-complaint: After a *complaint* is filed against a *defendant*, the defendant may file a written complaint, called a cross-complaint, against the party suing him/her or against a third party as long as the subject matter is related to the original *complaint*. Depending on the court system, a cross-complaint back against the *plaintiff* may also be called a "counterclaim," and a complaint bringing into the case a new party (third party) may be called a "third party complaint." (Don't worry, you get used to all this pleading jargon.)

Cross-examination: Questioning of a witness by the attorney for the other side.

Declaration: See *Affidavit*.

Defendant: A *party* that is sued, for wrongdoing and harm, or where other things are asked for, like prohibiting or requiring certain actions.

Default: Failure to respond to a *summons* and *complaint*, the result of which could be forfeiture of the right to defend a suit and have a judgment entered involuntarily against a *defendant*.

Deposition: Testimony under oath by a party or witness during the course of *discovery*.

Discovery: The process used by litigants to obtain information and evidence to evaluate a case and prepare it for trial. The process includes statutorily prescribed methods, such as *depositions, interrogatories, document production requests, requests for admissions, medical examinations*, and *inspection demands*.

<u>Document Production</u>: A discovery method requesting a party to produce/provide copies of documents falling into categories described in a *notice* to produce. The party served with the document production request then must gather and provide the responsive documents.

<u>Evidence</u>: *Testimony*, writings, material objects, or other things presented to the senses that are offered to prove the existence or nonexistence of a fact. (This definition is directly from Section 140 of the California Evidence Code.

<u>Exhibit</u>: Physical evidence or documents that are presented in a court proceeding. If *admissible*, they are evidence and may be considered in deciding the case.

<u>Ex Parte</u>: This Latin phrase, meaning "for one party", has two applications: (1) It refers to a communication by a party to the court without the other party knowing about it. Such communications are considered unethical; (2) When used in connection with a motion (sometimes called an application), the party seeks emergency help from the court on very short notice, requiring the other party to respond also on short notice, and the motion must explain the urgency. The court will read the papers on the day of the hearing and may or may not permit oral argument before deciding the issue.

<u>File or filing</u>: The act of placing a paper (*pleadings*, *briefs*, etc.) in the official custody of the clerk of court to enter into the files or records of a case.

<u>Hearsay</u>: Evidence learned second-hand, without personal knowledge.

<u>Inspection Demand</u>: A discovery method requiring a party to allow the requesting party to inspect, test, photograph, etc. some evidence in the responding party's possession, like a damaged vehicle. The request also can require the responding party to permit entry onto land to inspect, test, or photograph.

<u>Interrogatories</u>: A discovery method consisting of written questions asked to one party by an opposing party, who must answer them in writing under oath.

<u>Legalese</u>: Lingo, jargon, confusing to lawyers and non-lawyers alike. (Just kidding with this one, but I'm glad you took the time to read all this.)

<u>Lien</u>: A legally recognized claim on the property or funds of another person. A lien can be statutory or contractual.

Medical Examination Request: A discovery method requiring a party, usually a plaintiff claiming to be injured, to submit to a medical or mental examination by a medical professional chosen by the requesting party.

Motion: A request that the court make an order or judgment; can be *brief filed* with the court or an oral request in some circumstances.

Notice: Initiating litigation activity typically requires "notice" given in writing. It can be used as a verb but mostly it is a noun. A litigator would provide notice that discovery is *propounded*, a *deposition* is scheduled, or a *motion* hearing is set. Typical phrasing would be "Notice is hereby provided that…" or "Please take notice that…"

Oath: A promise to tell the truth or statement of a truth, a violation of which may be the crime of *perjury*.

Objection: An interjection by a lawyer conveying a legal ground to oppose the *admission* of *evidence* or a reason for refusing to do something.

Opinion: (1) A court's written explanation of a decision or ruling; (2) a statement or testimony containing a personal belief, view, or judgment. (Subject to rules as to whether or not *admissible* as *evidence*.)

Party(ies): The participants in a lawsuit or to a transaction, usually a plaintiff and/or defendant.

Peremptory Challenge: Lawyers in a jury trial are allowed to prevent, or veto, an unsuitable prospective juror. A peremptory challenge is exercised without need to provide a reason, though there are rules against such things such as excusing a juror solely because of race. The court grants each lawyer, or side, a limited number of such challenges. (See, *Challenge for Cause*.)

Plaintiff: The *party* initiating a lawsuit making a claim of wrongdoing and harm or seeking other orders against a *defendant*.

Pleading(s): A formal statement, usually written, setting forth the *cause of action* or defense theory(ies) of a case.

Propound: The big verb for "send" or "sent." The plaintiff "propounded" interrogatories on the defendant. Sounds heavy, doesn't it? It just means that the interrogatories have been sent, or *served* which then requires a response from the party to whom they were propounded.

Record: A written account of all the acts and proceedings in a lawsuit. (This is the derivation of the common idiom, "I am saying it for the record."

Request for Admission: A discovery procedure requesting a party to agree to a certain fact so that no further proof of it is needed at trial. Example, "Please admit that you entered into a valid contract with the plaintiff on X date to provide roof repair services."

Service (or Service of Process): To serve a document means to deliver, by hand, mail, or electronically, legal documents on someone, and will be accompanied by a statement under oath by the process server that service was accomplished, and when. Service usually begins a countdown on the time to respond to the document.

Statute: A law put into effect by the legislative branch of a government.

Statute of limitations: A law setting the maximum amount of time to file a lawsuit from when the problem arose, depending on the type of case or claim. With some exceptions, filing after the deadline forfeits the right to sue.

Subpoena: A document *served* by a party, though under the authority of the court, on a person or organization requiring them to give *testimony* (a *deposition*) or to produce documents or tangible objects.

Summons: A document issued by the court when a *complaint* is filed, it is *served* on a *defendant* with the *complaint* advising the *defendant is now sued* and contains instructions, including the 30-day deadline to respond.

Testimony: Evidence presented orally by *witnesses*.

Transcript: A verbatim record of a trial or other proceeding.

<u>Vicarious Liability</u>: One may be responsible for the acts of another. For example, under the law, an employer is legally responsible for the acts of its employees, automatically, unless the employee acts outside the scope of his/her duties. In this example, vicarious liability is also known as "respondeat superior, Latin for "let the master answer."

<u>Voir Dire</u>: Questioning of jurors before they are selected for a case to determine their suitability for the case.

<u>Witness</u>: A person called upon by either side in a lawsuit to give testimony before the court or jury.

About the Author

Michael J. Larin has been a practicing litigator in Los Angeles for more than forty-eight years. He specializes in cases involving all kinds of accidents, injuries, and property damage. He has served as an interim judge in the Los Angeles court system and is an active mediator. He has been married to his college sweetheart for fifty years, and they have two children. His dad gave him his motto: "Learn something new every day."